DATE DUE

More Praise for *Startup Asia*

"With the Pacific Century well underway, *Startup Asia* is required reading for anyone serious about the next wave of technology entrepreneurship. Rebecca Fannin elegantly weaves impressive facts, stunning anecdotes, and insightful visions of the future to paint a highly engaging portrait of this amazing region and its new class of leaders. She has written another gem!"
—David Lam, Managing Director, WestSummit Capital, and Board President, Asia America MultiTechnology Association

"Rebecca Fannin manages to take a still picture of a scenario that is almost too fast-moving to photograph. Dip into her book on entrepreneurial Asia, and adventure will grab you by the throat."
—Peter Rupert Lighte, banker and sinologist

"Once again, the author of *Silicon Dragon* has written a book based on original research and firsthand insight. *Startup Asia* offers a unique overview of promising startups from Asia's emerging entrepreneurs. Rebecca Fannin includes personal profiles of the individuals behind each venture, which makes the book an enjoyable read and gives it a girl-next-door perspective. Her detailed snapshot of Asian innovation amply demonstrates why the world's most dynamic continent will continue its ascent in the global economy."
—Dan Schwartz, Chairman Emeritus, AVCJ, and author of *The Future of Finance*

"Rebecca Fannin is quickly establishing herself as the ultimate expert on Asia and its countless budding entrepreneurs. Fannin profiles up-and-comers in China, India, and Vietnam; delves into the hottest market sectors; and details strategies for startup success. A must-read about Asia's burgeoning startups."
—William H. Draper III, General Partner, Draper Richards and Draper International, and author of *The Startup Game*

"While there are books galore about the innovation model in the West, rarely are books written on what's happening about innovation in Asia. Rebecca offers a fascinating view of how innovation is developing in the world's fastest-growing region. *Startup Asia* is highly recommended for business leaders, policy makers, students, and entrepreneurs alike."

—Stanley Kwong, Managing Director/Professor, Greater China Programs, School of Management, University of San Francisco

"This is a critical time for making the right decisions in a very complex and at times baffling Asian market. Rebecca's ability to get to the real players in the market and get them to talk about what they are really thinking and planning is fascinating. The stories and strategies are insightful and at times enlightening. *Startup Asia* should be on the reading list of everyone who wants to understand Asian thinking and investing. I believe this will be a classic in its time, too, like her previous book, *Silicon Dragon*."

—Egidio Zarrella, Clients and Innovation Partner in Charge, KPMG China

"There have been many attempts to replicate Silicon Valley's successes, and to date all other regions have failed to challenge the Valley's dominant position. *Startup Asia* makes a compelling case that for the first time in venture capital history, a region has the potential to challenge the Valley's dominance."

—Kevin Fong, Special Advisor, GSR Ventures

"Rebecca Fannin's newest book, *Startup Asia*, makes an important contribution to the discussion of China's rise and deepens our understanding of how and why. *Startup Asia* helps us formulate our own views of what the world will look like in the coming years. So, get ready: The probability that your son or daughter, or possibly you yourself, will be spending time in Asia, perhaps learning Chinese, is higher than ever before. Asia's rise, and China's with it, cannot be ignored. This book helps us understand and evaluate what it all means for us in the twenty-first century."

—Ken Wilcox, Chairman, Silicon Valley Bank

Startup Asia

Startup Asia

TOP STRATEGIES FOR CASHING IN
ON ASIA'S INNOVATION BOOM

Rebecca A. Fannin

WILEY

John Wiley & Sons (Asia) Pte. Ltd.

Published by John Wiley & Sons (Asia) Pte. Ltd.
1 Fusionopolis Walk, #07-01, Solaris South Tower, Singapore 138628

Other Wiley Editorial Offices
John Wiley & Sons, 111 River Street, Hoboken, NJ 07030, USA
John Wiley & Sons, The Atrium, Southern Gate, Chichester, West Sussex, P019
8SQ, United Kingdom
John Wiley & Sons (Canada) Ltd., 5353 Dundas Street West, Suite 400, Toronto,
Ontario, M9B 6HB, Canada
John Wiley & Sons Australia Ltd., 42 McDougall Street, Milton, Queensland 4064,
Australia
Wiley-VCH, Boschstrasse 12, D-69469 Weinheim, Germany

Library of Congress Cataloging-in-Publication Data

ISBN 978-0-470-82990-5 (Hardcover)
ISBN 978-0-478-82992-9 (ePDF)
ISBN 978-0-470-82991-2 (Mobi)
ISBN 978-0-470-82993-6 (ePub)

Typeset in 11/13pt, New Baskerville by MPS Limited, a Macmillan Company,
    Chennai, India

Printed in Singapore by Markono Print Media

To my family—
John, Mom, Deborah, Tom, Kyle, and Kelly—
for hanging in there with me
throughout the journey

Contents

communications boom. As the Internet moves from the personal computer to the mobile phone, these startups are poised to capture the burgeoning opportunity to emerge profitably and quickly from China and India. Mobile startups **inMobi** and **JustDial** are benefiting from a surge in mobile advertising and look likely to go public before the end of 2011.

early on this trend and invested millions into startups that became
publicly listed firms, such as **MindTree** in India and a host of Chinese
outsourcing firms including **Neusoft**, **VanceInfo**, and **iSoftStone**.
While India offers natural advantages, China's contenders are edging
in on the turf of this Asian neighbor.

costs, improve efficiency, or appeal to local tastes. Yet, advances are coming from spinouts of research from leading universities in Singapore, Bangalore, Beijing, and beyond and experienced teams who've left GE and other multinationals to do startups. From clean energy to mobile communications, Asian entrepreneurs are moving up the ladder of invention. Venture investors positioned to benefit include **Sonny Wu** of GSR Ventures and Helion's **Ashish Gupta**.

Foreword

There are amazing opportunities in the Chinese Internet space.

Powerful American companies such as AOL, MSN, eBay, Amazon, MySpace, Google, Yahoo!, YouTube, Facebook, and Twitter all had a hard time in China for various reasons, such as short-term profit focus, powerless local teams, and a lack of attention to tailoring products to the Chinese culture.

Their lack of traction has created an opportunity for Chinese companies in the Internet space to scale. The first wave of Chinese companies was largely content-oriented, such as Sina, Sohu, and Netease. The second wave of Chinese companies was mostly entertainment-oriented, such as Tencent, Shanda, Giant Interactive, and Perfect World. Of course, Baidu and Alibaba were two notable exceptions.

We believe that we are now witnessing an explosive third wave led by startups in the mobile Internet, e-commerce, social network, online gaming, and cloud computing.

This was why I left Google to found Innovation Works, an incubator and captive fund dedicated to opportunities in the Chinese Internet.

So I am pleased to see Rebecca Fannin's new book about this same topic.

Rebecca has reported on my career for several years, since she first interviewed me at Google China in Beijing in 2006, to when I set up Innovation Works in 2009, and still today as we enter our second year. Her book *Silicon Dragon* played a role in documenting the changes in the tech scene in China. She has followed several startups from zero to IPO, and many of the characters she has profiled later become tech celebrities and well-known names.

Her new book, *Startup Asia*, builds on *Silicon Dragon* and takes the technology innovation theme to new frontiers. It shows the parallels with China in mobile, gaming, e-commerce, and the Internet, and puts China in the lead, followed by India.

She deserves credit for being one of the few Western journalists to cover China's growing tech economy from a close-up perspective with regular firsthand interviews over the past decade. Now, she has taken the time to interview entrepreneurs and venture investors in Asia's emerging markets and document their own path. Rebecca has not stood on the sidelines but has been an active participant in and chronicler of the tech scene in Silicon Valley and China. With her outreach, she is helping to build an East-to-West bridge in the tech community.

Her ambitious and comprehensive book *Startup Asia* shows us through case studies and narratives that entrepreneurs in Asia are beginning to set the pace and the standards for innovation.

Kai-Fu Lee
Chairman and CEO of
Innovation Works, Beijing

Introduction

James Vuong first introduced the concept of VIC to me. We were eating Vietnamese pho beef noodle soup at an outdoor food court in Hanoi. When I wondered if it were another dish I hadn't sampled yet, he gave me a little triumphant grin and explained that VIC stands for Vietnam, India, and China. It takes some getting used to, after the all hype about BRIC—Brazil, Russia, India, China—as the next economic frontier.

But Vuong, a young venture capitalist in Vietnam, may be on to something. The firm that Vuong works for in Vietnam, Pat McGovern's Boston-based IDG Ventures, invests hundreds of millions of dollars in tech startups in Vietnam, India, and China and has made tons of money. China is the gold mine, India is the land

Peacesoft founder Nguyen Hoa Binh with IDG investor James Vuong in Hanoi

of promise, and Vietnam is the frontier. IDG is a pioneer with this strategy. This odd-seeming group of nations belongs together because of a growing number of overlapping trends. Of all the dragon and tiger emerging economies in the East, the VIC countries best represent the entrepreneurial spirit and venture capital rush of *Startup Asia*.

Multiple Silicon Valleys have sprung up in Beijing, Shanghai, and Bangalore, and even Hanoi and Ho Chi Minh City could get on the tech map soon. From John Doerr's Kleiner Perkins to Jim Breyer's Accel Partners, all the Sand Hill Road shops are parked in Asia's boomtowns. Entrepreneurs and college graduates have landed in Asia's tech hubs, too, and haven't looked back. Alice Wang grew up in San Diego, California, and left Yale University during the spring semester of her junior year to move to Beijing and take a job as a sales director at Groupon China. She knew it was risky and challenging, but the lure of this tantalizing opportunity to join China's tech race was irresistible. Wang spent her first few weeks working past midnight to meet incredible sales quotas and described it as chaotic but "very exhilarating." This self-assured dynamo still found time to host a dinner for me in Beijing with a dozen 30-and-under members of a global entrepreneur network, Sandbox, she spearheads in China. There's a good chance your daughter, too, and certainly hundreds of the followers and friends Wang has on Twitter and Facebook will land in Beijing and stay for a startup career. Who isn't studying Mandarin today to get ahead? Even Facebook founder Mark Zuckerberg, who has a Chinese American girlfriend, is learning the language and checking out China as his next move.

The chance to become rich and famous with a startup is no longer just an American dream. It's happening in Asia, in record numbers. Take a look at these compelling sums that highlight Asia's progression and also point to a reverse brain drain of talent, energy, and resources flowing from the United States to China and India:

- **Startups:** Since 2005, more than 6,000 startups in Asia—56 percent of them in India and China—have been financed by venture capital.[1]
- **Venture capital:** China and India accounted for 13 percent of $37.8 billion invested in startups globally in 2010.[2] That's up from 5 percent in 2005. China has emerged as the second-largest venture market in the world, followed by India.

- **Patents:** China ranks fourth in the world for new patent applications, up from tenth place in 2005.[3] Two giant Chinese companies—ZTE Corp. and Huawei Technologies—place among the top four businesses globally on the patent scales.
- **Returnees:** As many as 200,000 skilled workers from China and India will leave the United States by 2014 and return to their homelands to seek new horizons. Immigrants led one-quarter of U.S. tech startups in the boom and bust dotcom era.[4] Chinese or Indians ran 24 percent of Silicon Valley tech businesses started during the 1980s and 1990s software, Internet, and semiconductor rush.[5]
- **Asian IPOs:** China accounted for 22 of 61 venture-financed initial public offerings in the United States in 2010.[6] China's video-sharing site Youku chalked up the best first-day return in more than five years with its NYSE IPO in December 2010.[7] India's online travel site MakeMyTrip scored one of the top Asian IPOs in the United States in 2010.[8]
- **Exits:** Some 138 venture-backed companies in China netted $21.4 billion in IPOs in 2010 worldwide. That dwarfed 46 U.S. startups with venture capital that raised $3.4 billion in IPOs the same year.[9]
- **Research and Development:** China's spending on scientific research and tech advances has steadily increased for a decade to reach 1.5 percent of the nation's gross domestic product. The United States comparable is a heftier 2.7 percent of its GDP to research and development. But China's allocations for climbing the innovation ladder still far surpass most other developing countries.[10]
- **Digital Communications:** China has leaped ahead as tops in the world for web and cell connections, with 440 million Internet surfers and 840 million mobile service subscribers. India is not far behind with 673 million mobile callers. Vietnam weighs in with more than one-quarter of the population online and 78 million mobile service subscribers in a country of 89 million people![11]

Asia's innovation hotspots are fast emerging as first-choice destinations for bright young entrepreneurs. China and India have grabbed the brass ring and are attracting top talent, capital, and tomorrow's leading startups. Meanwhile, Vietnam emerges with mobile gaming and search, Singapore helps to seed budding entrepreneurs with government handouts and skillful coaching, and Taiwan lures startups to move beyond their base in churning out more than semiconductors and electronic goods.

The supercharged emerging markets of Asia promise to deliver the next Facebook—a turning point that will spark a creativity surge like the social network did during this decade's digital media boom. Startups create jobs and wealth, plus enthusiasm for future innovations.

Once, Sand Hill Road investors rarely scouted deals outside the San Francisco Bay area. Now, they can't get enough of Asia. Silicon Valley leader Dick Kramlich of New Enterprise Associates left his Nob Hill home and art collection and moved with his wife to Shanghai for more than a year to be in the thick of this happening city. Venture heavy Gary Rieschel of Qiming Venture Partners left behind a career and his wine collection in the Valley and relocated to Shanghai, working from the 39th floor of JinMao Tower overlooking the Bund. Former Sequoia Capital India head Sumir Chadha—now back at WestBridge Capital Partners—moved from his comfortable suburban residence in Burlingame to a sea-facing condo in Mumbai. IDG's McGovern has made 100 trips to China and is now exploring new terrain in Vietnam and India, while financing dozens of scrappy young entrepreneurial ventures.

"The opportunity is now. In a few years, it will be too late," says Kai-Fu Lee, the former president of Google China. Now chairman and CEO of Beijing-based startup accelerator Innovation Works, Lee advises young Chinese entrepreneurs in Silicon Valley to "Go East." With backing from YouTube founder Steve Chen, angel investor

Innovation Works founder Kai-Fu Lee in Silicon Valley

Ron Conway, and Facebook financier Yuri Milner, he's already invested in 12 tech startups from a $180 million fund and is incubating 34 startup projects in mobile, gaming, e-commerce, and social networking.

Naturally, the United States, the font of venture capital, still is the kingpen with 70 percent of startup investments and 64 percent of deals globally.[12] *But*, Asia venture capital investment had tripled from $5.4 billion in 2005 to $15.6 billion in 2010, while the United States had barely grown to $26.2 billion in 2010, from $25.2 billion five years ago.[13] Granted, the United States towers as the world's superpower innovator. *But*, the U.S. share of patent filings slipped to 28 percent in 2010 from 34 percent in 2005, while China leaped ahead to 7.6 percent of the world's total.

A World Economic Forum report in 2010 ranked 138 countries on technology development and competitiveness and spotlighted the rise of the Asian tigers and dragons. Singapore placed second for two years in a row, Taiwan moved into sixth spot, Korea climbed to tenth, and Hong Kong trailed as twelfth. Both China and Vietnam have raced forward, with China leapfrogging to thirty-sixth and Vietnam advancing swiftly to seventy-third on the charts. India checked in as forty-eighth, lagging due to poor quality infrastructure and red tape, but earning points for a sophisticated financial market, well-developed tech clusters, and fast-growing mobile telephony. Meanwhile, the United States dropped to fifth place.[14]

These trends underscore a shift in entrepreneurial and inventive muscle to *Startup Asia*. As the center of gravity for tech innovation moves across the Pacific Ocean to China and onward to the Indian Ocean, America's long-term competitiveness and leadership are increasingly at stake. Consider just how much venture capital can fuel economic growth: Startups in the United States contributed 21 percent of the U.S. gross domestic product and 12 million jobs in 2009, as one example.[15]

Powerful tides are shifting, and swiftly. Chinese and Indian immigrants are returning home because of improved economic opportunities and family ties. Young professionals and the best and brightest college graduates are packing their bags and settling into a comfortable lifestyle and community of like-minded dynamos in Asia's top-tier cities. It's not a roundtrip ticket either, but a several-years' journey or a lifetime commitment. This mass exodus of Silicon Valley expats and Ivy League graduates is enriching Asia and laying a foundation for expansion and innovation in China,

India, and Vietnam and other Asian upstarts. Think of some of the great companies created by Chinese and Indian immigrants to the Valley: Sun Microsystems, Hotmail, Yahoo!, and YouTube.

"Silicon Valley will not forfeit its leadership, but China and India will compete heavily," says Ajit Nazre, a partner at top-tier venture firm Kleiner Perkins. "We will see hundreds of companies coming out from these markets with huge growth and lots of potential."

As the finest grads from Yale, Harvard, Princeton, Stanford, MIT, and Berkeley and the elite of Sand Hill Road—who jump-started Cisco, Google, and Facebook—go to Asia, the startup game is increasingly playing out in the world's fastest-growing region and its next superpower. PayPal alum Dave McClure organizes "Geeks on a Plane" tours for Silicon Valley techies to meet with star entrepreneurs in Asia, and not just for a joy ride but for inspiration and enlightenment.

This new dawn began in China early in the twenty-first century. I documented the rise in my first book, *Silicon Dragon*, which profiled several leaders of China's emerging tech economy, among them Robin Li of Baidu and Jack Ma of Alibaba. Since then, several of those startup founders I wrote about have become high profile, namely, Joe Chen, who runs Renren, and Peggy YuYu, who leads Dangdang.

The tech innovation trends I described in *Silicon Dragon* are evolving. Sure, China still copies some of the best Internet sites. Have you heard there are more than 1,000 Groupon clones in China, not to mention two close replicas of LinkedIn? But microinnovations are coming. Sina's microblog layered in photo and video sharing before Twitter did. Web sites are not just blankly copied but tweaked for the local culture. The ecosystem for the mobile Internet is building out more rapidly in Asia's tech hotspots than in the United States because of high volume and no legacies.

And here's the really interesting phenomenon: Just as China copied the U.S. success models Facebook, Google, and Amazon, India has copied China's best, and so has Vietnam. In Ho Chi Minh City, social networking and gaming startup VNG wraps in both of China's leading tech companies, Tencent and Shanda.

The digital communications boom is happening at an unprecedented pace. "There is nothing in India or China that can compare to the size or value of Facebook—and in the short time it was created," says Bill Tai, a partner at Charles River Ventures. "There are only a handful of companies that are pioneers in their category, such as Tencent, which has Facebook-like characteristics." But startup innovations are speeding up, he says, due to always-on Internet and mobile communications. "Far greater market values are being created in shorter periods than ever before thanks to data that is coming from cloud computing that is connected to data devices," he explains.

Each market has different origins and progressed at its own pace. China's base is in manufacturing, while India built up a service economy around outsourcing. China leaped ahead of India with startups that have excelled with big IPOs on Wall Street and hefty investment returns for Sand Hill Road. China, too, is moving to the next level by developing an indigenous venture capital community, local currency funds, and its own stock exchanges. China's Silicon Dragon is becoming more distant from Silicon Valley and ultimately could pass the United States in transforming research and development into commercially viable enterprises.[16] India, meanwhile, is charting a separate course and still is years away from closing the tech gap with its large neighbor to the north. But India's startups have the chance of going global more readily than do China's emerging businesses, owing to the commonality of the English language and Westernized concepts that filter in uncensored. One landmark alone—online travel site MakeMyTrip—could be a door opener for more Indian startups to get on the stage.

A good chunk of the content in *Startup Asia* belongs naturally to the two giants of the region—China and India. But looking to the future, this book paints a portrait of Vietnam and the country's wired entrepreneurs, who most remind me of those I saw in the first generation of China's technopreneurs. Singapore takes nearly a chapter because it is arguably the Asian tiger with the most advanced government-supported ecosystem for tech entrepreneurship. Taiwan and Hong Kong are getting dwarfed by Mainland China's rapid ascent but are leveraging their strengths as high-end tech production centers and financial trading hubs.

I take you on a journey to the best practices of these nations' entrepreneurs in the fastest-growing market sectors—mobile, cleantech, consumer commerce. Then, this book delves into top strategies for winning market leadership, from taking a startup from zero to IPO, to disrupting the standard, to going global. The entrepreneurs I profile in these following chapters have distinct paths and experiences but share an ability to, as Steve Jobs said, "think different." All have the hallmarks of successful entrepreneurship: creativity, imagination, perseverance, and passion. *Startup Asia* is upbeat, and meant to be, just like the entrepreneurs I've met during this long journey of reporting and researching—a lively, successful group who just say no to naysayers.

Yes, several of the tiger and dragon economies lack the many benefits of democracy, a free press, a built-out infrastructure, a tech superhighway, a fair and just legal system, and top-rated educational systems—all the deep-rooted cultural foundations that have given the United States its universal stature and dominance. These pillars that have allowed U.S. tech stars like Mark Zuckerberg and Larry Page to shine are hard to duplicate through government dictate or budgetary spending. Perhaps this is one reason why no Chinese-born scientist has been awarded a Nobel Prize for research done in Mainland China, but several have won Nobels for work conducted in the West.[17] It will take years before we will see a grassroots entrepreneur in China or India who could shake up the establishment as much as Steve Jobs has.

Several of the cast of characters you will read about in *Startup Asia* are people you've probably never heard of from distant locales in China, India, Vietnam, Singapore, and Taiwan. But I predict you will be hearing more about this select group of up-and-coming entrepreneurs I've identified as the next generation, loudly and clearly, and soon.

PART I

Asia's Hotspots of Innovation

This section is a close-up look at the key growth trends that shape emerging entrepreneurship in China and India plus the frontier market of Vietnam.

China, the world's largest mobile and Internet market, is in the lead with an unmatched number of rising stars in search, gaming, mobile communications, e-commerce, and social networks. China also ranks tops for startups that have made it to the big time by going public on NASDAQ or the NYSE. Already, the Chinese market is going to the next stage and becoming more localized, as founders and venture investors take fewer cues from Silicon Valley.

India is closing the gap with gains among tech-centric startups from cleantech to mobile to the Web. Indian startups have the chance of going global more readily, too, though comparatively few have scored an initial public offering yet.

Vietnam has looked to China as the model for its own brand of tech entrepreneurship and scrappy startups.

Many of the same venture investors who funded young businesses in Silicon Valley moved into China, then India, and are now finding their way to Vietnam, Taiwan, Singapore, and other emerging markets. These investors are taking lessons learned in one country and applying it to the next.

Local entrepreneurs and returnees alike are becoming more sophisticated and savvy as they scale made-in-Asia startups.

Throughout Asia, tech hubs are forming that are the rival of the original Silicon Valley.

Additional material related to *Startup Asia* and to its predecessor, *Silicon Dragon,* can be found at www.siliconasiainvest.com. The site contains news, events info, video interviews with entrepreneurs and venture capital investors, articles, research, and updates on speaking appearances.

China's Next Generation Tech Stars

Inspired by the first wave of Chinese entrepreneurial winners such as Robin Li, gutsy next-generation stars are poised to profit from startups tuned to the local culture and cranked up with big money and dreams. The next **Jack Ma** of **Alibaba** fame is coming up but hasn't arrived quite yet. Count on that taking maybe another two or three years, in China's lightning-fast time zone. **Kai-Fu Lee**'s incubator lab Innovation Works is a spark, and so are angel investor **William Bao Bean** and networking groups MobileMonday and Great Wall Club. Savvy venture investors, including **Neil Shen** of **Sequoia Capital**, **Gary Rieschel** of **Qiming Venture**, **Sonny Wu** of **GSR Ventures**, ex-Kleiner pro **Joe Zhou** of **Keytone Ventures**, and **Ruby Lu** of **DCM**, are front and center with sizzling deals and public market trophies from NASDAQ and the NYSE. But how long will the boom last?

Not too many young Chinese women could land $4 million from a big-time venture capital firm for their first startup—and on their own terms. But then, Si Shen, 29, is far from average. At age 16, she entered the MIT of China—Beijing's Tsinghua University—to study computer science and then went on to ace two master's degrees at Stanford University within three years. Next stop: Google. Shen moved to Beijing in 2007 to run Google's Northeast Asia mobile business, expanded the team to 40 staffers, and a year later, started Papaya Mobile. This tech superstar, who looks fashionably cool and dresses in an artistic style, describes her brand in geeky terms as the "mobile Facebook on Android."

Founder Si Shen of Papaya Mobile in Beijing

By 2009, 3.5 million users downloaded apps for Papaya Farm, where as Papayans they could raise virtual animals and grow virtual crops, send instant messages and photos, and buy avatars with an online currency. Revenues poured in, and so did profits. That progress put quick-study venture capitalist David Chao on alert. In mid-2010, his U.S.-based firm DCM invested $4 million in the startup Shen had founded with former classmate and chief technology officer Wenjie Qian. Chao made sure the business named after the tasty fruit was set up offshore in the Cayman Islands, a prelude to going public on Wall Street, following the lead of DCM-backed online bookseller Dangdang and social network Renren. With the top-tier venture firm on board, Shen got coaching from DCM's entrepreneur-turned-venture maven Hurst Lin, the chief operating officer who had guided China's largest portal SINA to a ground-breaking NASDAQ IPO during the dotcom era.

Fast-forward one year, and Payapa Mobile has nearly tripled to 10 million users, thanks to loads of popular games and its iPhone killer, Android software for smart phones. In May 2011, Keytone Ventures' Joe Zhou, best known for his winning investment in leading Chinese gaming company Shanda, put $18 million in Papaya Mobile, and DCM joined in again. Strong-willed Shen says she set the deal terms in the contract negotiations.

Every day, her fast-track experience in China is being repeated by Web 3.0 upstarts in Shanghai and Beijing. Inspired and motivated by the hero status of Robin Li of search engine Baidu and Jack Ma of online marketplace Alibaba, thousands of bright, ambitious talents are jumping into the entrepreneurial pool and creating a big splash.

Quick pivots, shrewd tactics, first-mover jumps, flawless timing, venture capital checks, mini-innovations—it's all a part of their playbook to get ahead of the pack. Assertive and confident, these upstarts are claiming their stake in China's vast entrepreneurial revolution.

Over the past decade, China has bolted ahead with its own Silicon Valley. China has become the world's second-largest startup investor[1] and the world's second-largest market for venture funds.[2] Plus, China has developed its own local currency funds that, since 2008, outnumber U.S. dollar funds for startup investing in China. Search engine Baidu and instant-messaging service Tencent are now among the 10 most highly market-valued Internet companies in the world. (See Table 1.1.) Back in 2005, there were no Chinese companies in the ranks.[3]

Papaya Mobile investor Joe Zhou of Keytone Ventures in Beijing

A Silicon Dragon tech economy began in 2002 with Chinese returnees—so-called sea turtles who came home to lay their eggs—cloned Google, YouTube, and Amazon, grabbed Sand Hill Road money, and scored on NASDAQ and the NYSE. A lot has changed over the last decade as China has progressed from this first stage of startups to a bolder, more distinct Chinese-centric style of entrepreneurship. Today, homegrown Chinese entrepreneurs are snapping up venture capital from Chinese currency funds for even more clones—Beijing techie Wang Xing alone has cloned Facebook, Twitter, and a Chinese Groupon—and taking their startups public on NASDAQ-like local stock exchanges in China. But as GSR Ventures' Kevin Fong observes, "Going public in the U.S. has that Gucci status."

The needle is gradually moving from "made in China" to "invented in China." Microinnovations tweaked for the local

Table 1.1   Most Valuable Internet Companies

December 31, 2005		
Rank	Company	Market Capitalization
1	Google	$122.50
2	eBay	$60.24
3	Yahoo! Japan	$60.09
4	Yahoo!	$55.59
5	Amazon	$19.54
6	Rakuten	$16.51
7	Apollo (UOP)	$10.67
8	IAC	$9.04
9	E*Trade	$8.55
10	Expedia	$8.22

December 31, 2010		
Rank	Company	Market Capitalization
1	Google	$191.50
2	Amazon	$82.02
3	Tencent	$40.55
4	eBay	$36.67
5	Baidu	$34.59
6	Yahoo!	$21.85
7	Yahoo! Japan	$20.35
8	Priceline	$19.85
9	Salesforce	$17.38
10	Activision Blizzard	$15.16

*U.S.$ billions.
Source: Bloomberg.

culture are cropping up more often. Sina's Weibo, a hybrid Twitter-Facebook, layered in video and photo sharing before Twitter did. The long-awaited promise of disruptive technology from China is coming, too, symbolized by China's climb to fourth place worldwide for new patent applications.[4] GSR Ventures–funded LatticePower in Nanchang counts more than 150 patents for making low-cost, efficient LED lightbulbs for households and businesses.

Venturing in China has transitioned from its roots along Sand Hill Road to hubs such as Tsinghua Science Park in Beijing. Over the past five years, Sequoia Capital and Kleiner Perkins have set up shops in Beijing and Shanghai with Mandarin-speaking partners to scout for deals in mobile communications, the Internet, health care, cleantech, e-commerce, and retail—an area that's exploding judging by lines at Ikea furniture outlet and at Apple's store for the iPad 2.[5] Angel investors such as William Bao Bean of the L.L. Bean family in Maine and Baidu co-founder Eric Xu are the Ron Conways of Valley angel investor fame. Ex-Google China honcho Kai-Fu Lee has powered up Innovation Works thanks to funds from YouTube co-founder Steve Chen and other elite investors to coach smart young Chinese coders and jump-start projects from serial entrepreneurs—an echo of IdeaLab during the Internet boom and Y Combinator and TechStars for the Web 2.0 generation.

The Zhongguancun district of Beijing, where Innovation Works is based, is home to 10,000 high-tech startups, 150 incubators, more than 1,000 research and development centers, three leading universities—Tsinghua, Beida, and Beihang—and China's 10-year-old university and science center known as TusPark.[6] That's according to Chris Evdemon, general manager of incubation projects at Innovation Works and principal of its fund. A native of Greece who once did corporate promotion for the Summer Olympic Games in Athens, Evdemon kick-started his Asian trek in Singapore as a tech exec and angel investor and joined this exciting new launch pad in Zhongguancun in November 2009.

China's sprawling Silicon Valleys are spreading from Shanghai's Zhangjiang Science Park and Beijing's Haidian district to the less-expensive hinterlands. Second-tier cities with business specializations such as automotive for Chongqing, software for Chengdu, outsourcing for Dalian, and digital media for Hangzhou are a reminder of how Boston, Austin, Raleigh, and Seattle developed as tech off-shoots of the San Francisco Bay area's software and semiconductor strongholds. China Internet leaders Tencent and Alibaba are spreading their wings to Japan, France, the United States, India, Vietnam, and elsewhere through acquisitions and multilingual web sites.

The backdrop is China's booming economy, its world-leading mobile and Internet markets, government incentives to foster tech growth, and the rise of a shop-till-you-drop consumer class eager to travel, buy cosmetics, dress in brand-name fashions, diet, exercise, and buy the latest mobile gadgets.

From around the world, Jack Ma wannabes are streaming into China to earn career stripes and make names for themselves. Yu Minhong, the superrich CEO of NYSE-listed New Oriental Education & Technology Group, is sponsoring trips for bright Ivy League grads to get their China initiation. From preppy college campuses to Park Avenue corporate offices to Wall Street to the Bay Area to anyone with a passport, visa, and suitcase, the action is China, China! Let's go!

It's the modern-day equivalent of the 1850s Gold Rush to California—"Go West, Young Man," or, in the case of China, "Go East, Young Entrepreneur." Even Facebook's Mark Zuckerberg now wants to scale the great China wall and may partner with Baidu to do it.

To be sure, China's emerging tech economy has some cracks in the wall. What's missing? For starters, China lacks the creative thinking, open communications, and advanced educational system that can foster full-scale, disruptive innovation like the kind that made Silicon Valley the home to world-famous brands such as Oracle, Cisco, and Apple. Potential political and regulatory changes, social unrest, poverty, fallout from troubled bank loans, inadequate financial controls, accounting irregularities, and an overheated real estate market are looming as big issues. Doing business in China also means dealing with corruption, fraud, lack of the rule of law, inflation, censorship of Web content, and China's notorious counterfeiters, who have popularized a whole industry of cheap knockoff or *shanzhai* cell phones.

That's a long list of ills, but the tides are shifting and swiftly. As China's Silicon Dragon evolves as a startup frontier with multiple undercurrents, it could even one-up the original Silicon Valley and become a technology superpower. That may be only a decade or two from now.

Already, China has become the world's top place to dream big and strike it rich for young Chinese and non-Chinese alike. A friend of Groupon China recruit Alice Wang, Yuan Zhou, also has transitioned from the Yale campus to China. Zhou moved to China in March 2011 for a career after graduating with a master's in East Asian studies. Born in the small town of Liyang in Jiangsu province near Shanghai and with an undergrad degree from Tsinghua University, his smarts, enthusiasm, and dedication helped him land a job within a few weeks as a marketing director of cloud computing startup Dao-Gene in Beijing. Then there's Andy Chairisi, who has a head start on getting initiated, since his older brother happens to be

Ashton Lee, the chief technology officer of Shanghai-based online travel startup Travelzen. Chairisi, who was raised by Chinese grandparents in Thailand, graduated in May 2011 from the University of Virginia with a major in East Asian studies and studio art. He moved to Beijing not long after he picked up his diploma, found a host family to live with, and enrolled in the Beijing Language and Culture University to refresh his Mandarin before starting a career. "China really is an exciting place to be, it's got the feeling of 'This Time, This Place' that will go down in the history books. I can't think of a more exciting place to live and work in," says Chairisi, who is 24.

Mid-career U.S. and European professionals in their 30s and 40s are making it in China and can't get enough of the place. Fritz Demopoulos, 43, a Southern Californian and MBA grad from UCLA's Anderson School of Management, hasn't mastered Mandarin but has scored two Chinese Internet successes over the past decade. In June 2011, Baidu invested $306 million in the travel search engine Qunar he formed in 2005, and he stepped down as CEO, turning management over to Chinese staff. Demopoulos, who was born in the United States to a Greek dad and Austrian mother, got his start in China as business development manager for Rupert Murdoch's News Corp., working alongside Wendi Deng in the late 1990s in Hong Kong and mainland China, and running information technology portal Chinabyte.com. He next joined NASDAQ-listed Chinese portal and gaming company Netease and worked closely with the CEO on a two-year turnaround. In 2001, his first China startup, sports portal Shawei, was bought by Hong Kong–based Tom Group for $15 million. With his credentials, Demopoulos could write his own ticket. He's exploring opportunities to start another business or become an active investor, and he plans to continue working in either Hong Kong or Beijing. "I don't think I will be based at the debtor to China, i.e., the U.S.," he says.

Richard Robinson, 43, hails from Boston and still drops the *r* with his accent, though he's long ago broken through the language and cultural barriers on a whirlwind tech startup career in China. Robinson arrived in Hong Kong in 1996 after bumming around Europe and getting an MBA from Rotterdam's RSM Erasmus University, just in time to catch the dotcom boom. Within five short years, he was at the helm of three startups that went public, including the original Renren Chinese community site that raised $31 million from Rupert Murdoch and almost was delisted after its IPO.[7]

In 2003, seeking more job security when his wife was pregnant with their first child, Robinson signed on as a vice president of international at wireless entertainment player Linktone, one year before it went public on NASDAQ. He soon got the entrepreneurial itch, frustrated as the last *laiwai* or old outsider left as the company went from startup mode to the big leagues.[8]

And so he charged in again, spearheading seven startups in wireless technologies and even running his *Beijinger* wife's venture, Kooky Panda, a mini-Zynga mobile social gaming business, on a minuscule $40,000 budget before Infinity Ventures funded it.[9] "In China, you can live on a penny and a big dream," notes Robinson, who points out that burn rates or monthly costs to ramp up a business in China are about one-tenth of those in Silicon Valley. The latest gig for the hyperkinetic Robinson is heading up international for Beijing startup Youlu, a mobile phone address book that leverages social network connections. Youlu's CEO is rock star Zany Zeng, the former chief technology officer at China's Facebook-plus site, Oak Pacific Interactive.[10] "I really feel we have lightning in a bottle with this one," he says. Certainly, it helps that Robinson is proficient in Mandarin. "I use Chinese all day with my staff and Chinese family and have been a perpetual student for 15 years," says Robinson, who also produces live standup comedy shows, ChopShticks, for the expat community.

Spurred on by seeing his friends and colleagues venture over to China and succeed, Silicon Valley tech executive Elliott Ng found he could not resist the lure to go eastward. In early 2011, the over-achiever—Harvard MBA grad, ex-Microsoft product manager, McKinsey associate, co-founder or director of four tech startups, and angel investor—joined Google to lead product management for Greater China. He'd lived in the Bay area for 14 years, his wife had a full-time job as a pediatrician, and their three young boys were pretty happy where they were. But in July, he and his family relocated to Beijing. "Silicon Valley is still the best, most open startup/tech eco-system in the world," says Ng. "Beijing is the center of Chinese culture, government, and information technology." The one drawback? Polluted Beijing air. "In the end," says Ng, "we felt it was a good decision for the entire family."

Family reasons have kept social media goddess and Taiwanese native Christine Lu from making the break herself. The 35-year-old single mother has her support network in Los Angeles for her five-year-old son, and she's managing to stay very involved as an entrepreneur at the intersection connecting China and the United States. Her latest adventure is Affinity China, a private network that provides members access to unique luxury, lifestyle, and travel experiences, an area that matches her interests well as a shareholder in two swanky Shanghai cocktail bars, CVRVE and M1NT. Well known in the China–Silicon Valley business community, Lu has organized Rethink retreats in Hawaii and Shanghai and two initiation tours in Asia for PayPal alum Dave McClure's Geeks on a Plane. She's had some grassroots experience in China as well, designing and launching two clothing lines for her family's apparel business on the Mainland, launching an e-commerce site for women during the dotcom days, and working in Shanghai for five years from 1999 to 2004 as head of marketing for TV Shopping Network. Her conversational Mandarin is a plus, and quarterly trips to Shanghai keep her plugged into what's happening. "If it wasn't for my parents forcing me to visit China for the first time in 1995 as a freshman in college, I would be late to the China game today, playing catch-up. That trip changed everything. The entire city was under construction. There was no skyline in Pudong. There was no expressway to the airport," recalls Lu. "But there was an energy, a feeling that in 10 years, things were going to be much different . . . and I wanted to be part of it."

Since moving to China in 1997 to study Chinese at Shanghai's East China Normal University and marrying a Chinese woman he'd met on campus, suave Parisian native Bruno Bensaid, 39, has not looked in the rearview mirror. After working in finance for Cisco Systems from Singapore, he moved back to Shanghai and managed a tech accelerator that launched several venture-backed mobile startups from France in China, then joined French venture firm Ventech to do China deals, and in 2008, started his financial advisory group ShanghaiVest in 2008. Though his travel schedule is intense, since he advises both Chinese and European clients on expansion strategies in China, Bensaid says he has no intention of moving back to France. He's well rooted in the tech community as a founder of the Shanghai chapter of industry networking group MobileMonday and an angel investor with Shanghai's tuned-in AngelVest. "I'm very involved in business development with the startups I invest in," says Bensaid, who's recently backed a luxury travel network, a mobile apps engine for kids, and a social marketing company with an all-star team. He adds that the experience can be "a good ego boost."

Robert Strawbridge, 42, grew up on Long Island's North Shore and spent summers in Newport, Rhode Island, and Maine, later moving to San Francisco in time to ride the dotcom boom as IPOs were soaring. In 2008, he left behind his Cape Cod–style home overlooking the bay and rented an apartment in Beijing to catch the next big trend. A Hambrecht & Quist alum from the mid-1990s who later co-founded a sportswear manufacturer and worked as a VP at a Zurich investment bank, Strawbridge launched Beijing-anchored Sea Cliff Capital International in 2008. The boutique merchant banking firm specializes in cross-border transactions with a focus on helping cleantech and energy-related companies expand into China and raise capital. Strawbridge, who served in the U.S. Marine Corps for five years and was a combat diver, likens his China experience to "deployment" and says he's in Beijing for the long haul.

China: The New Assertiveness

Building a career in China is not for the timid. But it can be rewarding if the hurdles can be overcome, especially in a rapidly advancing superpower nation with newfound confidence. A new "we own the world" mentality can be spotted in the can-do, pushy attitude of China's new generation of street-smart whiz kids who think nothing about butting into a taxi line, blowing smoke in your face, or barging into conferences that they were not invited to attend. The upfront exchanges on China microblogs are a microcosm of this new in-your-face Chinese society. Take the fired-up insults and curses between Dangdang CEO Li Guoqing and a mysterious banker over Morgan Stanley's handling of the company's initial public offering on Wall Street. Their battering would make a shouting match by taxi drivers in a midtown Manhattan crash seem tame.

China's young entrepreneurs today are not as risk averse as the prior generation—not as prone to opt for a secure corporate job out of peer or family pressure. Grassroots entrepreneurship is at a higher level of sophistication and maturity than with the Web 1.0 generation. Networking groups like Mobile Monday and the Great Wall Club hold well-attended events in Beijing and Shanghai and have fostered a spirit of we're all in this together, let's make it happen! Like Silicon Valley in the 1990s, it's all very buzzy.

But China technopreneurs are still in those awkward years of adolescence. The next Jack Ma of Alibaba fame has yet to emerge. What are the gaps? Operational experience, imaginative thinking, and the financial smarts and finesse of, say, a Goldman Sachs hire. Typically, the startup executive has the polish and the skills but often can't assemble an experienced C-suite team or middle management staff.

While mindful of China's rise, Sand Hill Road investors acknowledge the fissures in the wall. Don't blink though. A new dawn is coming in China. "It's just a matter of time and maturity" before China has a full-fledged entrepreneurial ecosystem and innovations breakthrough, says veteran early-stage investor Fong of GSR Ventures.[11]

From Drought to Flood

It was a hot May day in Beijing, and a bunch of techies and dealmakers were crowded into the atrium at Tsinghua Science Park, where our Silicon Dragon Beijing 2011 program was being held. There, the panelists did not try to disguise the frothy market. "It's great to have a bubble," said Sonny Wu, managing director of GSR Ventures, which took wireless security startup NetQin Mobile public on the NYSE in early May 2011 and had six more initial public offerings lined up. He was grinning widely. "Bubbles are great," agreed Richard Hsu, managing director, Intel Capital China, which put 9 percent of its $327 million venture investment in 2010 into China deals. Intel Capital scored three China IPOs in 2010 and two more by the first half of 2011.

These seasoned investors have survived dotcom meltdowns and market crashes on both sides of the Pacific. They can spot the signals: megavaluations for deals, giant funds, out-of-whack IPOs and share prices for companies only marginally profitable. Most planned to keep the pace and score before the best opportunities evaporated.

While cautious about investing in deals at inflated market valuations, they figured a crash could never reach U.S. dotcom proportions. Unlike the U.S. Web startups that flamed out in the late 1990s onward, China Internet startups today have substantial site traffic, real revenues, and in many cases, profits, too, they pointed out. This is light years away from U.S. startups that famously got funding after scribbling a business plan on a napkin and went public before profitability.

Panelist Jenny Lee, a Shanghai-based partner at GGV Capital, has financed several successful Chinese startups, including NASDAQ scorer HiSoft Technology, as well as a few losers, such as China's first blogging site, Bokee, which shut down in 2008 after burning through $10 million in venture money. Observing that startup valuations had risen fivefold over the past half year, she raised a red flag over doing deals at such inflated values.

Ruby Lu is a Beijing-based partner of DCM who sourced and led China deals with e-retailer Dangdang and auto service BitAuto, both of which timed NYSE debuts in late 2010. Lu said she was recently pitched a deal by a stellar team seeking a valuation in the triple digits. She passed. "We're in the midst of a bubble but a good bubble," which will lead to a much-needed market correction and "a flight to quality," she said. "The bad companies will lose momentum or die. The market will shrink to a small base of companies."

These experienced investors were ready to ride the roller-coaster highs and lows of this cyclical venture business. They ticked off the tactics to avoid those steep dips. Invest smaller sums in startups. Take on the extra risks of backing a green-field company at its very beginning. Make bets only on proven market leaders and entrepreneurs. Coinvest with other dealmakers. Hans Tung, managing director at Qiming Ventures, said he was looking to finance serial entrepreneurs who earned their career stripes at China's leading tech titans, Baidu, Alibaba, and Tencent. It was a reminder of how PayPal and Google alumni have spawned Web 3.0 startups in the Valley.

The China venture chase kicked in during the second half of 2010 and was going at full throttle with megafunds, giant deals, and stellar IPOs by midyear 2011, a big change from the slowdown of the financial crash in 2008 and 2009. In 2010, the number of China venture funds nearly doubled

Dangdang venture investor Ruby Lu of DCM in Beijing

to 158, the number of China investment deals nearly doubled to 817, and investment totals also increased nearly twofold to $5.7 billion (Table 1.2).[12]

Seemingly every top Silicon Valley fund inked a Groupon clone deal in China, as more than 1,500 copycats sprang up, several with giant-size financing. (See Table 1.3.) Lashou raised the most of all, some $166 million from lead backer GSR Ventures and several premier investors after turning down a buyout offer from Groupon in early 2011. Meanwhile, Groupon launched in China with partner Tencent as Gaopeng. But hiring too many foreigners as local bosses and expanding too rapidly led to a retreat, signaling a shakeout.

It takes only one deal out of 10 to give a venture firm the home run return needed to raise the next fund. Who wants to be left out?

Several leading China venture firms raised their third or fourth fund (Table 1.4), many larger than the preceding one. Their backers were large pension fund CalPERS, fund of funds investors including Horsley Bridge Partners, and university endowments from Stanford, Princeton, and Yale looking to China to boost dismal returns globally. Venture funds in the local yuan currency

Table 1.2   China Venture Investment in Startups Climbs

	# of Deals	Amount Invested
2010	817	$5.4 billion
2009	477	$2.7 billion
2008	607	$4.2 billion
2006	440	$3.2 billion
2005	324	$1.8 billion

Source: Zero2IPO, April 2011.

Table 1.3   Groupon-Like Startups in China

Brand	Venture Capital Investors, Backers
Meituan	Sequoia Capital
Manzuo	Kleiner Perkins
Dianping	Qiming Ventures, Lightspeed Venture Partners, Sequoia Capital
Lashou	GSR Ventures, Norwest Venture Partners, Milestone Capital, Tenaya Capital
Tuan.qq	Tencent

Source: Silicon Asia.

Table 1.4   New China Funds in 2011

Venture Firm	Amount Invested
Accel-IDG	$1.3 billion
Matrix Partners	$350 million
Qiming Venture Partners	$450 million
GSR Ventures	$350 million
Lightspeed Ventures	$200 million
Innovation Works	$180 million

Source: Silicon Asia.

Table 1.5   U.S. and Chinese Venture Firms Active in China

Sequoia Capital	Innovation Works	Redpoint Ventures
Matrix Partners China	Lightspeed Ventures	Draper Fisher Jurvetson
DCM	Charles River Ventures	Mitsui Ventures
Qiming Venture Partners	Norwest Venture Partners	Softbank
GSR Ventures	ePlanet Ventures	Greylock Partners
Focus Ventures	Morningside	Walden International
NEA	Steamboat Ventures	DT Capital
Gobi Ventures	ID Tech Partners	SIG Capital
Keytone Ventures	Infotech Pacific Ventures	BlueRun Ventures
KPCG China	Legend Capital	Ceyuan Ventures
Softbank China VC	Intel Capital	IDG Capital
WI Harper	Vickers Capital Group	

Source: Silicon Dragon, Silicon Asia.

caught on and became dominant in 2008[13]—though the Sand Hill Road elite looked down on these first-timer China fund managers for lack of experience (Table 1.5).

Kai-Fu Lee's Innovation Works wrapped up a $180 million fund in August 2011, far larger than the initial goal. The money was lured in from several tech hotshots and private investors: Russian billionaire Yuri Milner of Digital Sky Technologies (think Facebook, Groupon, and Zynga), legendary angel Ron Conway, and Salesforce.com CEO and founder Marc Benioff.

Meanwhile, entrepreneurs and investors were going crazy with China startup IPOs. Neil Shen, the leader of Sequoia Capital China, racked up nine IPOs in 2010 among the firm's large China portfolio. (See Table 1.6.) On December 8, 2010, two high-profile Internet deals, video-sharing site Youku and online retailer Dangdang, both landed large market caps on their opening day of trading.

Talk swirled, too, of hyped valuations for Facebook, Twitter, and Groupon, not to mention Microsoft's stunning $8 billion acquisition of Skype. How long would it last? Echoes of the late-1990s dotcom boom and bust could be heard as 2011 flew by. As the tulips bloomed along Park Avenue (a reminder of the Dutch tulip bulb mania of the 1630s?), the month of May set a four-year high of IPOs on U.S. exchanges, many of them China-seeded startups, including China's Facebook Renren.

By the second half of 2011, both Qiming and GSR had six Chinese portfolio companies each getting ready to go public soon in the United States. GGV Capital was poised to take video-sharing site Tudou public after a delay the previous year and did, in August

Table 1.6   A Sampling of Venture-Backed China IPOs in the United States: 2010 and First Half 2011

Venture Firm	Company
Sequoia Capital China	Noah Holdings, Country Style Cooking Restaurant Chain, Sky-Mobi, Bona Film Group, Mecox Lane, Le Gaga
2011	Qihoo, NetQin Mobile
DCM	BitAuto, Dangdang
2011	Renren
AsiaVest Partners	iSoftStone
Sutter Hill Ventures	Youku
2011	ChinaCache
Qiming Venture Partners	
2011	Taomee, Jiayuan
GGV Capital	HiSoft Technology
GSR Ventures	NetQin Mobile
WI Harper	21Vianet

Source: Silicon Asia.

2011. Plus, GGV had two more IPOs in the wings. Sequoia Capital China had at least nine more in the queue for 2011.

Yep, the ever-growing China bubble was threatening to pop.

A more sobered outlook set in on Wall Street in late spring 2011, as regulators were on the alert for fraud and accounting irregularities among Chinese tech stocks. The Securities and Exchange Commission (SEC) launched an investigation into Chinese small-cap companies that gain listings in the United States through controversial reverse mergers, where a privately held business obtains a stock registration by acquiring a U.S. public shell company and avoids the scrutiny and costs of the traditional listing process. An SEC task force to examine accounting at overseas companies listed in the United States disclosed auditor resignations or accounting problems at more than two dozen companies based in China, from March through May 2011, while trading was halted on 17 NASDAQ stocks. An accounting scandal at NYSE-listed Chinese company Longtop Financial arose and sent more shock waves. (See Chapter 11.) Meanwhile, Carson Block, the founder of investment firm Muddy Waters Research, was a thorn in the side of several Chinese companies as he uncovered alleged accounting frauds, issued research reports, and shorted the firms' shares in a practice where short sellers profit when shares decline. One report on Chinese forestry company Sino Forest prompted its stock to fall more than 70 percent, leading to a multimillion-dollar loss by hedge fund billionaire John Paulson.[14]

The resulting sag in share prices for several China IPO newcomers had less to do with the value of the dollar, the real estate market, or world trade conflicts. It was a reflection of fears over small Chinese stocks and the true worth of these still-young companies vying to be center stage. Several Chinese tech companies canceled or postponed IPOs, citing market conditions. By September 1, 2011, share prices had dropped an average 23 percent for 12 U.S.-listed China IPOs that year. Some Chinese firms looked to go private.

Sea Turtle or Pancake Turtle?

As the timeline moved on a developing China tech venture ecosystem, telling cultural changes could be seen in a remarkable clash of the first generation of overseas-educated, experienced entrepreneurs with the next wave of China-trained locals turbocharging enterprises.

Renren founder and CEO Joe Chen labels this new generation "pancake turtles," a Chinese delicacy known also to be ferocious fighters in the sea. The pancakes are fiercely competitive, spirited, and nimble—and startup by startup, are one-upping the returnees. It used to be that Silicon Valley know-how and money were essential for a trump card in China. Not any longer. Stanford graduate Chen, who raised nearly $500 million from Valley players and modeled his Chinese startup on clones of Western Internet brands, today looks to what's hot on the China Internet for clues on games, social media, and e-commerce sites that can boost his now publicly traded company Renren. He's rarely in the Bay area anymore.

Savvy returnee Chen got first-hand experience battling with a novice local rival, Cheng Binghao, founder of a competing Facebook-like site, Kaixin001. If it's the creator who really matters more than the money or the model behind a startup's success

Renren investor David Chao of DCM with founder Joe Chen in Silicon Valley

or failure, then the clashing personalities, managerial styles, and backgrounds of these two founders was bound to become even more riveting. Kaixin001 was gearing up for a U.S. IPO following Renren's NYSE debut on May 4, 2011. (See Chapter 11.)

As the unpolished Cheng prepared to take Kaixin001 public in the United States, I was reserving a front-row seat to see how the street would buy into his purely made-in-China startup and his character.

These two rivals had already been at it in one catfight in China. The clawing began in late 2008, when Chen, spotting a sudden surge in popularity for the addictive Kaixin001 site, nabbed the Kaixin URL, purchasing it for a few thousand bucks from another source. He then cloned the Kaixin001 site with a matching color scheme and layout, and branded his site Kaixin.

"We take business seriously at our company," Renren's CEO told me. "We registered the URL."

An outraged Cheng sued in 2009. Cheng told me that his challenger's lawyers were trying to postpone the case by arguing that the suit was filed in the wrong district and against an incorrect entity. Meanwhile, confused users were logging on to the Renren-owned site rather his original, and Renren was growing like mad. Cheng hit the ceiling when his competitor folded the Kaixin interface into the Renren site and absorbed the new users. "It's not nice," complained Cheng, when I interviewed him at his Beijing office in May 2010.

This match ended in October 2010, when a Beijing court ruled that while Renren was the legitimate owner of the Kaixin.com URL, Renren had to cease use of the name and pay damages of $60,000 to Kaixin001. The ruling was upheld in April 2011.

Dynamic and crafty Chen has used his wits and gotten ahead by taking cues from financial and strategic wizards Warren Buffett and Jack Welch. Chen grew up in Wuhan as the son of civil engineers sent to work in the countryside during the Cultural Revolution. When his family migrated to rural Delaware in his teenage years, he learned English quickly and got a job flipping burgers at Wendy's. Chen went on to earn a master's in engineering at the Massachusetts Institute of Technology, then an MBA at Stanford, and sold his first startup—student social networking site ChinaRen—to Sohu for $33 million in 2000, right before the dotcom crash.

After a few false starts at some new ventures, Chen moved to Beijing in 2002 and soon began ramping up his Chinese social network. Through quick pivots from one business model to another and ample financing of $500 million from a who's who of investors, including Masayoshi Son of Japan's Softbank, Chen built his social powerhouse by acquiring and developing in-house sites.[15] Renren (which means people) weighed in with 124 million registered users by midyear 2011, and a few months later aligned with MSN China to pick up more users with a unified account log-in. Like many fast-expanding Chinese sites, Renren was bulking up but losing money. Net revenues grew to $76.5 million with a net loss of $64 million in 2010. Renren turned the corner on losses with a net profit of $.8 million in the second quarter of 2011.

As Chen rang the opening bell in a suspense-filled IPO, Wall Street was keen on China tech stocks, and investors were eager to buy into the first social network to go public. (LinkedIn had a stellar debut just a few weeks later.) Renren raised $743 million in a sizeable IPO, and Chen cashed out $50 million in stock. (See Chapter 11.)

The contrast couldn't be much greater between this web builder and quiet, unassuming Cheng Binghao, a geeky web site developer who is guided by a Confucian social philosophy. Cheng grew up in Beijing as the son of a farmer and a factory worker, studied nuclear chemistry at the China Institute of Atomic Energy, and learned software coding at a school computer lab. His talent landed him a job and promotion to chief technology officer at leading Chinese portal SINA, where he worked for 10 years under the mentorship of his boss, SINA co-founder and now DCM venture capitalist Hurst Lin.

When continual 10-hour workdays on a computer developing a search engine caused his vision to blur and he could no longer read small characters on the screen, and SINA abandoned the search project, he took a break. Reflecting on life values, he concluded that friends were more important than money or career. At the age of 36, he got back into the race by designing a Web game that became the basis for this face-off. Cheng called the site Kaixin ("Be Happy") and tacked on 001 to the name because the URL was already taken.

Kaixin001 launched in 2008, and its extremely popular Chinese version of Facebook's Farmville—where players grow virtual fruits and vegetables, steal from one another's gardens, and then exchange funny comments about their exploits—helped it reach 60 million users within two years. The game was especially popular among China's young office workers as a stress buster. Cheng told me the psychology behind the game:[18] "Open your heart to your

Kaixin001 founder Cheng Binghao in Beijing

friends, open your heart to the world." Speaking through a transla-
tor, he said, "Chinese are more conservative, more inward, not very
open in this world. If two very close people see each other, they
don't hug or kiss but say hello with eyes only. On this site, if I steal
some vegetables, I am showing my affection, like a hug."

The little web site that could—Kaixin001—climbed to 90 million registered users and $30 million in revenues for 2010, accord-
ing to market research firm RedTech Advisors. While not the
market leader, Kaixin001 had the upper hand for demographics,
attracting a higher percentage of white-collar workers, contrasted
with Renren's base of college students. That's a plus in drawing
advertisers but Kaixin001 was losing its appeal next to new social
games. The pressure was on to beef up and join the IPO gang.

Not propped up financially as well as its chief competitor,
Kaixin001 still managed to pull in a respectable $23 million from
China startup investors Qiming Venture and Northern Light
Venture Capital in 2009. "We didn't go out to find venture capital-
ists. They came to find us," Cheng, who looks a little like the *Star
Wars* movie character E.T., once told me during a rare flash of brag-
gadocio at an interview in Beijing.

How the duel between these contrasting figures plays out on Wall
Street will point to prospects for a new generation of homegrown
techies against the slicker Chinese returnees of the earlier era.

The Giants of China's Web

The Chinese Web is slightly more than a decade old but is already transitioning into a third cycle of growth: from the Web portals of the late 1990s—Sina, Sohu, and Netease—to the search, gaming, mobile, and e-commerce companies—Baidu, Shanda, Tencent, and Alibaba—that rose from the dotcom bust to today's social networking powerhouses. (See Table 1.7.) "We are seeing another shift in the evolution of the Net, from content portals to search to social networking. It's a brand new category of net history," says veteran Asian-Silicon Valley investor Chao of DCM.

Competition is heating up rapidly among key contenders in China's Web that dominate social commerce, networking, gaming, and messaging, chiefly these now well-known players Baidu, Alibaba, and Tencent. That makes it tough for a startup to squeeze in, but hasn't stopped the China engines. Renren's CEO Chen once remarked that continually aiming to outsmart these super-sized, hypercompetitive brands was his biggest challenge. Only half-jokingly, Chen said he does "battle with the BAT, the evil BAT," his shorthand for the three Chinese Internet titans.

It's no secret that big American Web brands have been unable to gain traction in the Chinese marketplace. To blame: failure to tailor services to the local market, slowness in reacting to customer needs, and unempowered local management to decide and act on tactics. A fourth important factor is that thorny issue of censorship that experts such as free speech advocate Rebecca MacKinnon claim has led to blatant protectionism of local brands.

The U.S.-to-China dotcom street is littered with failures: eBay ended up selling to domestic Chinese player Tom Online in 2006 after buying local site Eachnet in 2003 for $180 million, while Amazon-acquired Chinese online bookseller Joyo[19] is unprofitable

Table 1.7   China's Leading Technology Markets

	2007	2008	2009	2010
Internet # of users	210 million	298 million	384 million	457 million
Mobile # of users	539 million	641 million	747 million	859 million
Semiconductor market size	$77 billion	$83 billion	$80 billion	$99 billion

Source: China Internet Network Information Center, Ministry of Industry and Information Technology, IC Insight.

and ranks second in the market behind newly publicly traded Dangdang. Meanwhile, the fact that the big-name American brands YouTube, Facebook, Google, and Twitter are blocked in China puts them on the sidelines.

Acting and being local in China is the only way to go as the Chinese Internet takes on its own identity. Startups that can swim with the China currents and figure out what niches remain to be fished will get ahead.

Twenty and 30-year-olds, who make up most of the traffic on the Chinese Web, typically surf for entertainment content but also for online news blended in with blog posts. Music, gaming, videos, and blogs are the popular pastimes for most Chinese users. In the United States, search, e-mail, and e-commerce features keep individuals glued to their screens.[20] Internet cafes in China, from sleek joints to hole-in-the-wall shops, are filled with youngsters playing games, videos, and music or jumping on the Net to write a microblog and be heard. Having a voice for personal expression is still quite new in China—and can be risky and daring, at least judging by how a Middle East–style Jasmine Revolution here from social media activists was quickly snipped.

E-commerce is booming in China,[21] led by fast-moving business-to-consumer web sites such as Redbaby (see Chapter 6) and Alibaba's Chinese auction portal Taobao.[22] The development of e-commerce had been slowed in China due to logistics problems and distrust of credit cards. But now payment has been solved by escrow accounts and cash, and Chinese youngsters are becoming avid online shoppers.

Another burgeoning opportunity is the mobile Internet. The arrival of 3G service is building out China's ecosystem for mobile startups but is still too expensive. College students and white-collar workers alike want to save up enough to afford expensive smart phones, priced in the range of $600 to $1,000, though the launch of Android phones for $150 will boost usage. "The ecosystem needs devices, bandwidth, applications to create a virtuous cycle," says Innovation Works' Evdemon. He notes that 83 percent of mobile Internet users are younger than 30 and want apps that focus on entertainment or killing time, not productivity or saving time. He cited music, games, and text messaging as examples of popular apps. Evdemon predicts that the Chinese mobile Internet will evolve the same way as the Chinese Internet: from basics such as browsing and photo sharing to entertainment with music, games, video, and social networking to advanced uses like e-commerce, advertising, location-based services, search, and e-mail.

Larger Sand Castles

As this ecosystem evolves, Internet leaders are racing to assemble all-in-one popular Web services in one sandbox. Google, Facebook, Apple, and Amazon—the Gang of Four that Google Chairman Eric Schmidt described as the dominant consumer technology companies—have ventured into each others' turf in the United States and internationally. Likewise, the giants in China are making larger and larger sand castles in the Chinese Web. They are crowding out startups without original ideas and solid management teams.

The point is to build large, horizontally integrated social networks or be left behind, noted then *Forbes* Beijing bureau chief Gady Epstein.[23] He pointed out that the Chinese Web is becoming an oligarchy of conglomerates that combine social networking, online video, microblogs, group buying, search, and portals under one roof, and cited Tencent, Sina, Sohu, Netease, Renren, and Alibaba as examples (see Tables 1.8 and 1.9). Stand-alone companies like video sharing site Youku, he argued, are in a scary environment and could be snapped up if and when the price is right. It's a sign that the market is fast maturing.

Table 1.8   Valuation of Listed Chinese Companies in Major Tech Sectors

Company	Valuation	Sector
Tencent	$50.1B*	Instant messaging, games
Baidu	$42.6B	Search
Netease	$5.87B	Web portal
SINA	$5.63B	Web portal
Sohu	$3.18B	Web portal
Shanda	$1.98B	Games
Giant	$1.17B	Games
Perfect World	$1.12B	Games

Valuation current as of March 16, 2011.
*In U.S.$ billions.
Source: NYSE, NASDAQ, HKSE.

Table 1.9   Top-Ranked Chinese Companies by Market Capitalization

IPO Year	Market	Company	Sector	Market Cap, 2010*
2004	HKSE	Tencent Holdings	Internet	$39,891.3
2005	NASDAQ	Baidu.com	Internet/media	$34,000.7
2007	SZSE	Xinjiang Goldwind Sci & Tech	Green Tech	$9,101.3
2007	HKSE	Alibaba	Internet/media	$9,046.3
2009	HKSE	China Longyuan Power	Green Tech	$6,828.1
2003	NASDAQ	Ctrip.com International	Internet/media	$5,980.9
2003	SHSE	NARI Technology Dev.	Tech	$5,732.0
2007	SZSE	Shenzhen Laibao Hi-Tech	Tech	$4,303.3
2003	SHSE	Aisino Co.	Tech	$3,847.6
2010	SHSE	Zhejiang Chint Electrics	Tech	$3,645.7
2010	NYSE	Youku.com	Internet/media	$3,588.3
2010	SZSE	Shenzhen Aisidi Co.	Tech	$3,339.5
2010	SZSE	Navinfo Co.	Software	$3,301.3
2005	HKSE	AAC Acoustic Technologies	Semiconductor	$3,278.4
2005	HKSE	Focus Media Holding	Internet/media	$3,139.9

*As of December 31, 2010, in millions.
Source: Bloomberg, WIND.

The competition is intense. For example, Renren vies with social networking services Kaixin001 and 51.com for players' attention, but also with niche sites and deep-pocketed players, points out RedTech Advisors. Narrower sites designed for specific interest groups started popping up in 2008: Taomee for children, Douban.com and Neocha.com for young trendy users, iPartment for women, Jiayuan and Zhenai for dating, and Tianji and Ushi.cn for business.

As social networking sites have become popularized, the nation's leading portals have jumped in with their own specialized versions. China's largest Internet company, Tencent, launched Qzone to engage young teens and rural dwellers online. Baidu rolled into the social networking space during 2006 and was trailed by Sina in 2008. Sohu.com joined the race with a 2009 launch of Bai Shehui ("White Society"), targeting the white-collar demographic.

Alibaba developed its own social network geared for business professionals, Ren Mai Tong.

Microblogs or Twitter-plus knockoffs have emerged as the newest new thing in this fast-multiplying Chinese Web loaded with all-in-one social networks. Large Chinese news and information portal Sina dove into this sector in August 2009 after Chinese Twitter clone Fanfou was shut down over political sensitivities. Sina's hybrid Twitter-Facebook Weibo reached 140 million users by April 2011,[24] zooming past Twitter's 20 million U.S. users[25] and 200 million globally. Tencent launched its own twittering site in April 2010. Within a year, Tencent counted 160 million users.[26]

To gauge the speed at which these microblogs are taking off, consider that it took Sina Weibo only 177 days to reach its first 10 million users by late April 2010 and one year to get to 100 million.

Going international is the next step for China's growing tech footprint. Leading China instant-messaging service Tencent launched English, Japanese, and French versions of its popular QQ chat, video, and news portal in 2010. The same year, online marketplace Alibaba launched an English-language site AliExpress and acquired U.S. e-commerce company Vendio—its first overseas acquisition—as part of a strategy to enter the U.S. market.

It takes guts and will power to play in this jungle as social networking maverick Chen knows all too well. Back in 2007, his then-named Oak Pacific Interactive combined Chinese versions of MySpace, YouTube, Facebook, and Craigslist. Today, Renren runs three major sites with social networking as the centerpiece: Renren social network, Renren Games, and the business social network Jingwei, launched in 2011. The company has moved into the Groupon clone territory, too, with its own group-buying e-commerce web site Nuomi, which rolled out in June 2010. Nuomi's first social commerce deal offered a big discount on tickets to a new Jackie Chan Movie Theatre in Beijing. More than 150,000 pairs of tickets were sold.

Despite new web advances, online advertising and games remain the primary moneymakers for Renren. Some 42 percent of 2010 revenues came from sales of display ads and campaigns by 248 advertisers, including Coca-Cola, Nike, and leading Chinese companies. The remainder is chiefly from games, traditionally one of the most lucrative channels on the Chinese Internet.

One role-playing game popular with women, Tianshu Qitan (roughly translated as "Tales about the Heavenly Book"), is based on a Chinese animated feature film[27] and accounted for nearly a third of Renren's online game revenues and, amazingly, 14 percent of overall revenues in 2010. Other cash cows are VIP memberships and sales of virtual goods, such as accessories and pets, to players.

A key advantage of the Renren business model is its integration. Sites are leveraged to drive traffic to each company brand. The social network channels users to the gaming and buying sites, for instance. More than 60 percent of the Nuomi social commerce users also log on to Renren, while many of the game players gain access from the social network.

Post-IPO, Renren is flush with cash to fire up its marketing power to lure more users and advertisers. If and when Facebook enters China, Renren will face possibly its biggest threat. At 124 million users, Renren has a low penetration rate of China's huge Internet market compared with Facebook's dominance in the United States. That means opportunity!

Harvard-educated Facebook founder Zuckerberg has a goal of connecting the whole world, and that's not possible without figuring out how to enter China—that in spite of Google's struggles in China over censorship and service blockages and its withdrawal from the Chinese market in early 2010 after a prolonged effort. Since the pullout, Google's market share in China has shrunk to 19 percent while local search rival Baidu has widened its lead with a 76 percent share.[28]

Facebook's Zuckerberg is learning Mandarin and visited China in December 2010 to meet with the heads of Baidu, Sina, and Alibaba. In turn, Baidu execs visited the Palo Alto offices of Facebook as the search site seeks to gain traction in social networking. Zuckerberg was planning a second visit later in 2011. The rumor is that Facebook may partner with Baidu to penetrate the market and get over hurdles that have tripped U.S. Internet brands in China. But Facebook still would face censorship, as all Chinese web sites do. Facebook has been blocked in China since 2009. A different name would be a good start if Facebook does enter China. The unlucky Chinese transliteration of Facebook in China, *Fei Si Bu Ke*, means "doomed to die," points out Michael Clendenin, founder and managing director of Shanghai-based RedTech Advisors.

Destined to Innovation Fame

Not too much is plug-and-play in China, as a peek into the front lines of China's emerging tech culture at Innovation Works shows. On its launch in September 2009, just months before Google withdrew its servers from the Mainland to Hong Kong, founder Kai-Fu Lee was mobbed with more than 7,000 resumes, compared with 3,000 for Google China back in 2006, when Lee was at the helm. Some 1,000 applications for startups poured in. Lee culled the pile to 34 projects. The vast majority of these seedlings are in product development, and many have pulled in initial financing from Innovation Works and venture partners, while nine have picked up sizeable follow-up venture sums.

Visiting Innovation Works' bustling new headquarters at Beijing's Haidian high-tech zone in May 2011, I saw how fast it's grown since my prior look around a year earlier. I spotted product teams writing code on PCs spaced side by side and no doubt spurred by peer pressure. I got a sampling of the startups in progress: Zhihu, a Quora-like Q&A online service for China; Ascending Cloud, a social gaming platform like the popular social network game developer Zynga; Tapas Mobile, a mobile operating system developed by top directors Lei Zhang from Baidu and Mily You from Tencent; and Diandian, a Tumblr-like blog-hosting platform meant for China's heavy mobile use. Diandian was started by high-profile Internet entrepreneur Jack Xu, notably the former CIO at student social networking site XiaoNei (which Renren's Chen acquired in 2006 as a base for his social network).

Two among this elite group attracted follow-on financing from top-tier venture firms, a validation of Lee's vision for Innovation Works. Diandian was funded by Sequoia Capital and Ceyuan Ventures (spearheaded by former head of Morgan Stanley Asia and honorary chairman Jack Wadsworth). Tapas took in $4 million from GSR Ventures in a coinvestment deal in early 2011.

Evdemon, who heads the incubator teams, points to Tapas Mobile as an example of the leading-edge work generated by the lab. Capitalizing on Google's exit from the market, Tapas is replacing Google mobile applications with enhanced features customized to the Chinese market. It's geared for Gen Y users with apps for text messaging, social networking, synching lyrics with music, reading books, playing games, and photo editing. Kai-Fu Lee's favorite Chinese phone is powered by Tapas, so it's bound to catch on, just like his microblog draws millions of readers every day.

To run these startups, Innovation Works recruits CEOs and founders with prior entrepreneurial experience in China. Programming champions at Baidu or other top Chinese Internet sites are also in demand.

Reaching out to budding entrepreneurs in China, the launch accelerator runs a JumpStart program that incubates 10 to 15 teams for three months. Additionally, the labs have three entrepreneurs in residence working on projects under the Innovation Works roof. Zhou Limin, an ex-chief architect at Baidu, is charging up Wandoujia ("Wonder Pod"), a software tool to manage video, music, and e-book downloads. Experienced tech entrepreneur Ryan Xu is gearing up Buding, a location-based service for mobile phones. Ma Jie, a former R&D director at China's large software security company Rising, is working on a cloud security startup.

What's hot at this new launch pad? Android smart phone applications, a market stimulated by DCM's $100 million 2011 A-Fund, a takeoff of Kleiner Perkins' iFund.[29] And yes, more clones of Western Internet models. Examples are Yingyonghui, a Chinese version of mobile phone app store GetJar; Wandoujia, an iTunes for China smart phones; and Buding, which is modeled on Yelp.

Ebbs and Flows

Just as economic reforms have transformed China over the past three decades, so has the venture market undergone sweeping changes. It has become increasingly localized. Chinese American venture leaders began investing in the mainland in the mid-1990s, namely, Lip-Bu Tan of Walden International and Ta-lin Hsu of H&Q Asia Pacific. Then, the California VC heavies Mike Moritz of Sequoia Capital and John Doerr of Kleiner Perkins got excited about China. So did Accel partner and Facebook investor Jim Breyer. Early on, in 2004, Accel backed online dating site UUMe.com, which Joe Chen's Oak Pacific Interactive acquired a year later. In 2007, Accel teamed up with IDG to raise a $700 million China fund, and IDG-Accel since raised several larger funds and inked dozens of

Facebook investor Jim Breyer of Accel Partners

deals in China. Breyer says he sees China as a priority market. No doubt he has urged Zuckerberg to figure out how to tap into the market.

Today, the third-generation venture capitalists have arrived. Most speak Mandarin, know how to get from Beijing's central business district to Tsinghua in the northwest, are funding local entrepreneurs in China's renminbi currency, and are taking Chinese startups public in Shanghai and Shenzhen.

Several of the Sand Hill Road elite have parked themselves in China. Venture capitalist Gary Rieschel left the San Francisco area in 2006 for the happening scene in Shanghai, with vast software parks and trendy art galleries alike, to form Qiming Venture Partners. Raising a family in Shanghai, he plans to be there for a victory lap. Silicon Valley Bank chairman Ken Wilcox resigned as chairman and moved with his wife to Shanghai in mid-2011 to spearhead local banking for the innovative financing group.

Meanwhile, the same Sand Hill Road dealmakers who had made big bets and done well funding nascent technologies in the Valley—the guys in a garage of Silicon Valley legend—were doing things differently on the mainland. A who's who of Sand Hill Road—Kleiner Perkins, GGV Capital, Accel Partners, Sequoia Capital, and New Enterprise Associates—all opted to spend more time and money cultivating a broad array of emerging companies in China rather than just startups. They looked to these so-called growth capital deals to reduce risk and generate solid, quick returns as the portfolio companies scaled rapidly and profitably with China's low costs and booming economy.

In the United States, Sequoia Capital made its name and fortune with Google, YouTube, Yahoo!, and Oracle. Sequoia entered China in 2005 with a $200 million fund to seed Chinese champions. But by 2007, the firm was investing from two funds: $250 million for venture and $500 million for growth-stage businesses.

And guess what? Sequoia's first three exits among its 50 deals in China were all from the growth fund: Hong Kong IPOs of sporting apparel retailer Peak Sport Products in September 2009 and underground shopping mall developer Renhe in October 2008, plus a NASDAQ listing in December 2007 of outsourcing vendor VanceInfo Technologies.

A look at the growth deals in Sequoia's China portfolio— including China LiNong International, a highly profitable and rapidly expanding supplier of freshly packaged and premium-priced vegetables—shows just how far this legendary tech investor strayed from its Sand Hill Road roots.

Neil Shen, Sequoia's founding managing partner in China, told me in Hong Kong that he hadn't given up on scoring a big hit with early-stage tech investing, and indeed, the fund's track record of IPOs from venture investing in 2010 and 2011 has proven him to be correct. His heart is in venture investing, given his own entrepreneurial background as a co-founder of two NASDAQ-listed Chinese companies, travel booking service Ctrip and economy hotel chain Home Inns.

Some diehard venture firms such as GSR, Northern Light Venture Capital, Qiming, and DCM remain committed to funding Chinese startups and the possibility of home run returns. The challenges of investing in startups in China are pronounced. Successful deal making requires good connections with government officials, hand-holding with entrepreneurs who lack managerial experience in a capitalistic-like economy, expert lawyers to navigate regulations and gobs of intellectual property issues, and most of all, patience to realize a payback for all the hard work and time. Perseverance could pay off, however, assuming no catastrophic meltdown.

Riding the RMB Wave

As the venture chase increasingly happens within China's borders, the supercharged deal-making game can no longer be played from the U.S. sidelines. The new norm is investing local funds in the local Chinese currency renminbi. Since 2008, RMB funds have outgrown U.S. dollar funds investing in China startups, and the trend keeps growing as local exchanges such as ChiNext, launched in October 2009, take off. In 2010, 146 renminbi funds from such local firms as Hony Capital and CDH Investments raised $6.9 billion, compared with 12 U.S. dollar funds at $4.3 billion.[30] (See Table 1.10.) It's not just the local Chinese shops that have RMB funds. So do several leading U.S.-anchored venture firms, such as IDG Capital, Sequoia, Qiming, and Draper Fisher Jurvetson, which manage these local Chinese funds alongside their U.S. dollar funds.

Chinese yuan deal making is in vogue because it opens up avenues for investors: fewer restrictions on industries, less regulatory oversight, and access to listing a portfolio company in China. Moreover, municipal governments in Shanghai, Beijing, and beyond are green-lighting foreign capital investment in these Chinese venture funds as a stimulus for the domestic economy.

Even so, seasoned China investors scoff at these newcomer funds. Andy Yan, managing partner at SAIF Partners, says he's doubtful the majority of new Chinese currency funds will make it. He cites inexperience among "first-timers." "I bet you can't find

Table 1.10   RMB Funds Catch On

	# of Funds	Amount Raised
	RMB/U.S.	RMB Funds* Compared with U.S. Funds
2010	146/12	$6.9 billion/$4.3 billion
2009	84/10	$3.6 billion/$2.3 billion
2008	88/28	$4.9 billion/$2.3 billion
2007	20/29	$1.1 billion/$4.4 billion
2006	12/27	$774 million/$3.2 billion
2005	7/22	$219 million/$3.8 billion

*RMB fund amounts converted to U.S.$.
Source: Zero2IPO, April 2011.

one with more than five years' experience," he says. "It takes time to get over the learning curve."

General partner Jim Boettcher of Focus Ventures recounts how his firm coinvested with Kleiner Perkins China in a water company. During the negotiations, the investors discovered that two locally run venture shops offered the entrepreneurs an opportunity that could not be beat on financial terms alone—the investment term sheet was left blank, allowing the entrepreneur to fill in the valuation figure.

Let's Go Chongqing!

In China today, it's hard to ignore eager tech entrepreneurs. They turn up everywhere as multiple Silicon Valleys sprout up in the mainland, beyond the hubs of Beijing and Shanghai. In Nanjing, a former capital of China, I was invited to attend an opening ceremony and celebratory dinner marking the launch of a new biotech center in a modern software park on the outskirts of the city. The mayor showed up and so did the provincial leader. It was a sign that Nanjing officials are taking very seriously the goal of becoming a "life science valley," as it was being promoted to overseas investors and high-level business executives, including those from Goldman Sachs who were part of the delegation. And, yes, we all did have our obligatory shot of the Chinese liquor *baijiu* to show our appreciation.

One U.S. pharmaceutical executive who has taken the bait of tax incentives and funding being offered in Nanjing is Chinese American Chuck Zhu. After years of working in the United States at a large New Jersey pharmaceutical company, he started up a drug-testing facility in an office called NJ Pharma Tech Corp. The Mandarin-speaking Chinese returnee Zhu jokes that the NJ stands either for Nanjing, where he recently moved, or New Jersey, his home state.

Nanjing is seen by trendsetters such as Zhu as a good location because of its abundant universities and colleges, some 48 in all. This historic city is home to the well-regarded Nanjing University and its school of medicine, where Qian Gao is now the dean, after an assistant professor post at Yale's medical school. The Nanjing life science corridor also sports a Chinese herbal medicine operation that is seeking to standardize the process of treating conditions with herbs. Another contract research outfit here is GenScript, which is a miniature Chinese version of the publicly listed highflier Genentech in Boston and is financed by well-known venture firm Kleiner Perkins. GenScript set up in Nanjing in 2004 and already employs 1,000 full-time scientists in China, CEO Frank Zhang told me during a visit at his office in spring 2010.

One more company that has set its own course from Nanjing is an online trading service that connects Chinese suppliers with global importers and exporters. Founder and CEO Shen Jinhu, 43, who grew up in a rural area of Jiangsu province and attended university in Shanghai and Nanjing, set up the aptly named company Made in China in 1998. In 2009, the startup had grown to $34 million in revenues and a profit of $14 million! It went public, not on NASDAQ or the NYSE, but on the Chinese local exchange in Shenzhen. During an interview in the lobby of a hotel in downtown Nanjing, Jinhu told me that he thought it made sense to list in China rather than the United States because the company's customers are in China and the startup's investors are locals.

Chongqing, where I traveled in summer 2010, is another of the rising hotspots of Chinese entrepreneurial activity. The city's developers—with the help of the central government—are focused on positioning it for megagrowth.

This western frontier city seems still somewhat out of the loop, with a rougher edge than Beijing or Shanghai. But give it a few more years, and this hilly and often fogged-in river town could become one of China's next big tech and commercial centers. Three of my adventures revealed why and gave a taste of China's entrepreneurial passion and positioning.

It was on the late-night minibus from the Chongqing airport to my hotel that I met Hong Wei. I had barely noticed her huddled in the backseat when I got in, but once we began to talk, she made a lasting impression.

Over the 45-minute ride, she told me she had traveled to China's western frontier city for an automotive parts trade fair that had been billed as a blockbuster event. I also learned that she was going to be one of the exhibitors, demonstrating a new breakthrough rust-proof technology for car exteriors that she claimed she and her husband had developed in their hometown of Nanjing. She was here to get distributor deals, and she urged me to stop by her booth.

The next morning, I strolled through the maze of exhibits at the automotive bazaar, thinking I might spot this determined lady entrepreneur again. No luck. The auto industry is one of China's fast-growing industries, and seemingly every entrepreneur as enterprising and motivated as this woman had set up an exhibit here. What was the center of attention were the glamorous models posing in front of shiny new Chinese-made vehicles. Chinese automakers had surely gone to school on Detroit's old sales tricks, though I didn't see many deals getting done. It will take a few more years before car ownership in China becomes a rite of passage like it is in the United States.

After I left the auto bazaar, I headed for the outskirts of the city and across the Yangtze River from the central business district, toward what's called the New North Zone: a manufacturing, science, and research hub that has already attracted automakers Ford and Fiat, as well as electronics and information technology giants Microsoft, Ericsson, and Cisco.

I have been to other software parks in China—in Nanjing, Dalian, Pudong, and Shenyang—but none turned on the promotional juice like Chongqing. On a steamy day in the city, which has furnacelike temperatures, I got a tour of the new infrastructure that is in place. The numerous corporate headquarters here could fit in well in Silicon Valley, and newly built schools, hospitals, shopping outlets, and hotels abound along tree-lined streets. Indeed, fast-growing China's tech infrastructure makes U.S. corporate parks look outdated.

This is all made possible by the deliberate efforts of the region to make the city attractive for business investment. After my tour of the New North Zone, I soaked up more Chongqing facts over a luncheon of hot pot, a peppery variety that is a regional specialty. This dish is a favorite of my host, Wang Yi, who runs the zone and comes to this fancy hillside restaurant at least once a week, often with foreign business executives he wants to impress.

As Wang regaled me with facts about Chongqing, his college-age daughter helped to translate, with impeccable English. Chongqing, they taught me, is the largest city in western China, a transportation hub linked by the Yangtze to Shanghai, and a low-cost labor center that also offers favorable investment policies, such as reduced income tax of 15 percent for high-tech businesses.

The pitch appears to be working in drawing investment. For instance, the software business here is growing faster than in any other area of the country, by more than 200 percent annually.

Developing Chongqing is key to a long-range plan to urbanize central areas and draw people and jobs to this inland port from the congested coastal cities.

China's visionary agenda to rely on innovative young businesses to build its economy and transform it from a "made in China" to an "invented in China" base is only beginning to take hold in the outlying cities. But as thousands of young businesses get started by eager entrepreneurs, attract venture funding, and rely on supportive governmental policies and modernized infrastructure, you can count on inland cities such as Chongqing to claim their place in China's tech economy.

Venture investing in China may be only slightly more than a decade old, and, yes, it does still harbor risks, challenges, and surprises for the uninitiated deal maker and entrepreneur. But it is getting through those growing-pain years very quickly. Those financiers and startup whizzes who ignore its potential will surely regret missing out on the vast opportunities unfolding in China's new golden era.

CHAPTER 2

India Emerges to Narrow the Gap

The only other tech market in Asia that is halfway as exciting as China is India. It has the promise to close the gap with China but is no match yet. India's mobile market is large, venture spending is vibrant, and high-profile IPOs such as MakeMyTrip are happening. Plus, India has proven it is rich in R&D and a lot more than outsourcing. Even so, red tape and poor infrastructure hold back the entrepreneurial spirit here. Investors **Bill Draper**, **Lip-Bu Tan**, and **Sumir Chadha** did the trailblazing in India. Today venture honchos such as **Vinod Khosla**, **Ashish Gupta**, and **Sudhir Sethi** are looking for the next new thing in mesmerizing India. The country's democracy and freedom of speech could prove the ultimate boost for imagination that underscores all the best creations.

My passage to India begins with a 1:35 A.M. arrival on a new, direct Dragon Air flight from Hong Kong to Bangalore, in the southern part of India, where its air-conditioned climate and abundance of techie engineers have earned the city a reputation as the Silicon Valley of India.

Passport checked, customs cleared, luggage in tow, I take in the nighttime balmy air. I'm here throughout February 2010 to assess and discover if India really has the jewels to fully develop a tech entrepreneurship culture that can compare with Sand Hill Road or Beijing's Zhongguancun high-tech zone.

The new airport opened in May 2008, but there's no high-speed train here to whisk me into the city like I've grown used to

47

Mumbai scene: where SMS meets tradition

in Shanghai. No six-lane wide boulevards as in Beijing, either. Thankfully, my hotel has booked a taxi for me.

Bumping along dusty roads, we eventually arrive at the Ista Hotel Bangalore, in a good location not far from Mahatma Gandhi Road, but unfortunately also overlooking a massive construction project to erect an elevated railway. As we pull up to this contemporary business hotel, a uniformed guard swings open the gate and, in a vestige of the Mumbai terrorist attack in 2008, inspects the car interior and trunk, before we're ushered in by a turbaned doorman. My room is modern, spacious, and clean. The electric power stays on—unlike one of my earlier stays a few years ago at a luxury hotel in Mumbai. A quick check of e-mail on the hotel's broadband Internet connection—working fine—and I hit the pillow before dawn. I've been warned about sanitary conditions in India: Don't drink the water, eat only hot foods, and get your shots. I've never gotten sick—maybe luck?

Waking up to the sound of jackhammers—a sign of India's slow but steady progress toward updating its faulty infrastructure— I have breakfast at the hotel's surprisingly tranquil garden patio, then taxi over on streets crowded with rickshaws, mopeds, and buses to the offices of IDG Ventures India, a leading investor in startups here.

Along the way, I'm bracing for the beggars to come running out, thin arms outreached as they lean into the car windows, as I've seen on prior visits to India's cities and palaces. I do see an occasional cow ambling by, ignoring the blare of honking horns. One of the world's poorer countries and the second most populous nation after China, India has made strides in reducing poverty and improving literacy rates as economic reforms have taken hold since the early 1990s. As India's economy has boomed, urban areas have been transformed, and a middle class has developed, but still some 455 million Indian citizens live on less than $1.25 per day, below the poverty line. The notoriously ancient infrastructure, bureaucracy, and corruption scandals—as highlighted by the hedge fund insider trading case involving Indian business icon, former McKinsey head, and Goldman Sachs Director Rajat Gupta[1]—also have damaged Brand India, the world's second-fastest-growing economy and Asia's third-largest economy.

As I travel in Bangalore, Delhi, and Mumbai, I see vast slums but spot signs of India's rise: the Starbucks-like Café Coffee Day; the upscale luxury hotel brands Oberoi, Taj, and Leela that are on par with Hyatt, Four Seasons, and Shangri-La; the Infosys and Wipro outsourcing campuses that are more sprawling and modern than Oracle in Redwood Shores; and the multistory shopping malls with designer fashions. There's even a spiffy Indian fast-food chain, KaatiZone, started by one of India's pioneering venture investors, Kiran Nadkarni.

Here, at IDG Ventures in Bangalore, I'm meeting with Sudhir Sethi, who is chairman and managing director and runs the tech media company's $150 million India fund. It's one of five funds in the IDG Ventures network established by Pat McGovern, the visionary founder and chairman of International Data Group in Boston. If a strategy works in one locale, then IDG works to bring the formula to startups in other places. China has proven to be a gold mine for IDG, where it's made multimillion-dollar returns from early investments and successful IPOs of instant-messaging service Tencent and search engine Baidu. India could be next. As I go to see Sethi, I recall McGovern telling me, "We look at the extraordinary returns in China and realize maybe we could have started earlier in India."

Venture champion Sudhir Sethi of IDG
Ventures India

Sethi is one of the more experienced venture investors and technologists in India, having held leadership posts at top tech firms Wipro and HCL before joining Walden International in 1998 and later, in 2006, setting up IDG Ventures India. He's an ardent advocate of India's progress in developing innovative technology products and moving beyond the world's outsourcing services hub. "It's a myth that India's venture investors and entrepreneurs don't have the patience or risk appetite to build product companies," says Sethi.

Over the next several weeks—timed during the midst of Chinese New Year so not to miss much in China and to avoid monsoon season in India— I travel throughout this most amazing, exotic, and mysterious country on a self-guided tech tour, interviewing venture investors, technologists, and entrepreneurs. At meetings with India's leading capitalists and during casual conversations with locals, I discover a deep philosophical thread that underpins the society, as questions are pondered before answers are given. It's something I've noticed on prior trips to India, dating back to 2004, when I interviewed the billionaire founders of India's booming outsourcing business,[2] Narayana Murthy of Infosys and Azim Premji of Wipro.

Nothing seems plain black or white, as it strikes me in China when questions are replied to in a split second. What else is there to be expected from the world's largest democracy, a place with hundreds of media outlets and free-flowing communication that leads to reflections and debates over major issues. India is perplexing and complex, a country where Hindi and English are the official languages but individual states have adopted Punjabi, Tamil,

Urdu, and several others as their own mother tongue. More taxi drivers can speak English in Shanghai than in Mumbai.

During early 2010, I meet with startups in India with advances for everything from detecting lung cancer at an earlier stage to recycling electronic waste in a cost-effective way, to bringing solar power to villagers, to offering superfast mobile searches, to three-dimensional online games, to robotic-powered vacuum cleaners. India's also become a mecca for low-cost and sometimes jerry-rigged inventions—in Hindi, *jugaad*. Tata Motors' tiny Nano car at an itty-bitty price tag of $2,500 and the Indian government-backed tablet computer selling for $35 are some examples. So is my favorite find: a Nokia cell phone with a built-in flashlight. India may not have a Google, Apple, Baidu, or Tencent yet, but it is moving into more technical work than writing software and answering phones.

But all things considered, India's entrepreneurial journey is at least five years behind China's path. There's no Jack Ma or Robin Li in sight or a big-time IPO. India lacks the entrepreneurial buzz and fast pace of China tech clusters. Indian entrepreneurship has been led by grassroots efforts, and the government hasn't always been venture friendly. If India is ever to break through, it needs to ditch an image as just for outsourcing or low-cost engineering and business services—a major challenge for the world leader of the booming $500 billion global outsourcing market.[3] But India could eventually become a tech minipower and grab some of the limelight from China. Contemporary corporate centers such as Whitefield on the outskirts of Bangalore and the Gurgaon satellite city in Delhi showcase that India is on an uphill climb. For sure, India needs a lot more deals with the stature of online travel site MakeMyTrip, a deal that barely gets noticed next to China's high-profile Internet home runs. After all, MakeMyTrip listed on NASDAQ in August 2010, nearly seven years after Ctrip, China's leading travel site, had its own debut.

The gap hasn't stopped leading Indian venture capitalist Ashish Gupta from betting his career on the rise of tech stars in his home country. "One good reason to set up a venture fund is that you really don't know where the white spaces are going to be in India whereas in the U.S. there are already established players," says Gupta, a technologist who joined Helion Advisors in 2005 as senior managing director. He's already funded three winning Indian startups: MakeMyTrip, job site Naukri, and now IBM-owned Daksh eServices. "In tech, we're out another four to five years. It's already happening in enough bulk in India not to be called an accident," adds Gupta, who has a computer science degree from the elite Indian Institute of Technology and a PhD from Stanford.

What's in the pipeline to speed up the pace of innovation? Startups powered by India's pool of talented engineers[4] and MBAs in leading-edge fields such as social networking, mobile communications, cleantech, biotech, the Internet, and e-commerce, and all funded by experienced investors. "The companies we are backing are less than five years old, and are run by founding teams who are under 40 years of age. Already, they are well-funded, generating revenues, have a global customer footprint and patents to their credit—all originated from India," IDG's Sethi points out.

India's fast-growing digital communications markets are a catalyst for the subcontinent country's emerging tech economy (Table 2.1). The Internet is not nearly as widespread as in China,[5] but just about everyone has a cell phone. Only 74 million of India's 1.2 billion people had Internet access in 2010,[6] but more cyber cafes are popping up.[7] Mobile communications are where the action is in India. Thanks to new low-cost networks from Airtel and Reliance, the number of mobile phones in India surpassed 752 million in 2010, second worldwide only to China's 842 million users.[8]

India's always-on mobile communications, global customer outreach, engineering talent, and thirst for education all spell promise and hardly conjure up India's rich cultural history of snake charmers, yogis, fortune-tellers, and those wonderfully colorful silk saris.

Table 2.1   Growth in India's Online Population

Internet Users*							
2007	2008	2009	2010	2011	2012	2013	2014
42.4	53.1	63.0	74.3	93.8	117.2	144.7	163.5

Mobile Services Subscribers*						
2008	2009	2010	2011	2012	2013	2014
331	506	673	805	926	1.037	1.115

*In millions.
Source: IDC Asia/Pacific.

(I couldn't resist having a red sari custom made to wear for my debut as a keynote speaker at the Bombay Ad Club.) The NASDAQ listing of travel portal MakeMyTrip in 2010 was a landmark deal for India, in the same stratosphere with newly listed Chinese tech companies Dangdang and Youku. Look for more to follow. Mobile advertising service inMobi, which is backed by Kleiner Perkins, is set to go public on NASDAQ before the close of 2011. Meanwhile, mobile search player JustDial is primed to go public in Bombay by the end of the year.

Finally, another catalyst is not to be overlooked: As the Indian economy has bounced back from the recession and grown by nearly 10 percent in 2010, India has emerged as a land of opportunity for returnees. Highly educated and skilled immigrant entrepreneurs and professionals who made their career in the United States are returning to their home country for job opportunities and enrichment. It's not just those who are stuck with temporary, nonimmigrant work visas like the H-1B who've had to move back to India, but it's those who believe the grass is greener at home.

Indian immigrant Raj Gilda, 43, is one of the new breed. In early 2011, Gilda quit his vice president post at Citigroup in New York after working the night shift on India time for eight years. He returned to India to work with his wife, Sunanda Mane, on an exciting new social enterprise venture, Lend-A-Hand India. Founded by the couple in 2003, Lend-A-Hand India provides vocational training to high school students in remote Indian villages. With contributed funds and government resources, Lend-A-Hand trains young students in trade skills. The three-year program with weekly classes is taught by local carpenters, plumbers, electricians, and agriculturists. The program has expanded to 61 villages and 10,000 youth in three states, Maharashtra, Karnataka, and Goa. "Our core focus is on scaling up grass-roots innovations," says Gilda, who now lives in Pune. "The impact of this model has been outstanding. Over one-third of our students are now getting admission to much sought after higher technical schools, absenteeism and drop-out rates have decreased significantly, and students are learning skills required in rural India." There are thousands more like Gilda who are returning to India as the country leaps ahead.

What's fueling the startup engines is India's large venture capital pool. India is the world's third-largest venture capital investment market,[9] after the United States and China. Venture capital in India has closely trailed China levels, except for one year, 2007, when India surpassed China for investment in startups. India's angel investor community is also huge, numbering 1,000, including the Mumbai Angel Network and Indian Angel Network.

India venture is on a time lag with China. India deal making kicked into high gear in 2005—about two years behind China. By 2007, the pace was fast and furious, and the peak was 2008. Several of the same Sand Hill Road firms that took off to fund startups in China during the past decade looked to India as their next destination. They included all the big names: Sequoia Capital, Kleiner Perkins, Draper Fisher Jurvetson, Accel Partners, Lightspeed Ventures, Norwest Venture Partners, New Enterprise Associates, Bessemer Venture Partners, Greylock Partners, Matrix Partners, and Charles River Ventures (Table 2.2). Only two venture firms dropped out during the bleak 2009 recession: Battery Ventures in India and Bessemer Ventures in China.

The venture passage to India dates back to 1996 and a few early adventurers. At the lead were San Francisco–based venture statesman Bill Draper of Draper International in 1996 and Asian investor Lip-Bu Tan of Walden International in 1998. Sumir Chadha, a young whip-smart Goldman Sachs banker and McKinsey consultant, put India venture in fast-forward in 2001 by setting up WestBridge Capital Partners at a time when his former colleagues thought he was crazy to try venture investing in a virgin

Table 2.2   Venture Investors in India

Helion Venture Partners	Lightspeed Venture Partners
Draper Fisher Jurvetson	Inventus Capital Partners
Norwest Venture Partners	Accel Partners
Kleiner Perkins Caufield & Byers	Bessemer Venture Partners
IDG Ventures India	Sequoia Capital India
NEA-IndoUS	Walden International
Clearstone Venture Partners	Greylock Partners
Nexus Venture Partners	Matrix Partners
SAIF Partners	Charles River Ventures
Sierra Ventures	Mayfield Fund

Source: Silicon Asia.

territory. Chadha proved them wrong. He struck it rich with an inaugural $140 million fund, a merger with Sequoia Capital in 2006 to form Sequoia's first outpost in India, subsequent larger funds of $400 million in 2006 and $725 million in 2008, plus investments in 90 companies—not to mention numerous IPOs and M&A deals, many of them in outsourcing niches. Only a few deals met the Grim Reaper. "It's very hard to make money in venture capital," admits Chadha. "Late stage is relatively easier. We proved that you could make money on venture in India, though it is not easy. The deals are overvalued and there is too much capital" ready to invest in young businesses, he says, in a precursor of his later groundbreaking move.

Sand Hill Road firms on the hunt for high-impact startups in India followed the pattern of China. They set up offices locally with partners at home with the culture and put out the welcoming

Venture pioneer Bill Draper of Draper International in San Francisco

mat. And they stopped sending in jet-lagged partners from the West Coast for quick deal sourcing and check-ins with the portfolio companies. The movers and shakers relocated to Mumbai, Delhi, and Bangalore. Chadha relocated from the Bay area to Mumbai in 2009. Mohanjit Jolly left Silicon Valley to establish Draper Fisher Jurvetson's office in Bangalore in 2007.

These venture investors got to work funding the same types of business models that worked in the United States and China. Take a look at online travel. There's Expedia in the United States, Ctrip in China, and four clones in India: MakeMyTrip, Cleartrip, Yatra, and Travelguru. Promod Haque, managing partner of Norwest Venture Partners and an investor in Yatra, says, "We looked at Ctrip and were interested in the travel market because it works with multiple channels for selling—online and storefront sales. One of the reasons we invested in Yatra is because the business model was like Ctrip and had been proven in the U.S. and China."

Look-alike Indian startups also got funded for all kinds of Internet and mobile plays. For job portals, there's Monster.com in the United States, 51.com in China, and Naukri in India. Yahoo has SINA in China and Rediff.com in India. In digital mapping, there's MapQuest in the United States, AutoNavi in Beijing, and MapMyIndia in Delhi. For online payment, there's PayPal, 99Bill in China, and PayMate in India. The highly popular online gaming sector sparked multiple copies, too: in India, three up-and-coming players are Kreeda, Nazara, and Games2Win, India's first online games site.

India caught on as a garden for startups, with several natural advantages. Due to its British colonialist days before independence in 1947, India's judicial system is based on English common law, and English is a second language. India's emerging companies with English-language sites and services have a quicker runway to going global and scaling up. Personal computer help service iYogi, Pearson-owned online tutoring system TutorVista, and mobile advertising firm inMobi already have gone global. (See Chapter 12.) "Our view is that India companies must be global; we attempt to do that with our startup companies in the first few years of a life cycle," adds Sethi.

Another factor and a double-edged sword is democracy. While slow-moving democratic decision making has been blamed for

India's lag, the political system does not suppress communications. There's no online censorship in India like in China. America's favorite content-rich online brands, Google, Twitter, and Facebook, have become popular in India. That's a 180-degree turn from China, where local social networking and search startups have grabbed the lead over restricted U.S. sites.[10] The drawback is that the American brands' dominance in India's Internet hasn't left much room for Indian replicas to fill. But homegrown startups tailored to the culture have emerged, including Twitter-like mobile service SMS GupShup, Facebook-like education networking site Minglebox, online book seller Flipkart, social commerce brands ShopSocial.ly and SnapDeal, and even online matrimonial site Shaadi, a Sanskrit word for "wedding."

Taking a lead again from the United States and China, cleantech is happening in India. Delhi startup Attero operates a recycling facility for transforming electronics waste from throwaway cell phones, PCs, and TV sets into gold, platinum, silver, and other precious metals. ConnectM monitors energy for cell phone towers and utilities; d.Light Design makes solar-powered LED lanterns, Reva produces electric cars, and Kotak Solar makes solar equipment and water purification pumps. These made-in-India green startups are scaling in size. They are funded by the same cleantech investing firms looking for deals in the United States and China: Kleiner Perkins and Draper Fisher Jurvetson, to name two. (See Chapter 5.)

The search for breakthrough technology is on in India, too, but trails China. So far, much of what has been found in India is small scale. Tellingly, India is not even among the top 15 countries in international patents. Indian applications for new patents rose 15 percent to number 1,109 during 2010. India's overall performance over the past five years is stagnant, while China has ascended rapidly to emerge as the fourth-ranked patent power in the world.[11]

Some made-in-India innovations are cropping up, notably Biocon, founded in 1978 by entrepreneurial scientist Kiran Mazumdar-Shaw as India's first biotechnology company. Her Bangalore-based public company is credited with starting an Indian biorevolution. It's among the top three ranked Indian company patent filers and has been granted more than 223 patents, several of those in the United States. Biocon is in phase three trials to develop the world's first oral insulin and, capitalizing on India's competitive cost base and exceptional scientific talent, is doing cutting-edge research for diabetes and oncology. While no comparison with Biocon's heft, venture-backed Indian startup Perfint, a developer of an image-guided, minimally invasive robotic device for cancer biopsies, is promising. On the lighter side, other startups with patented technology I met with are Robhatah Robotics Solutions, a designer of reasonably priced robotics-powered vacuum cleaners, and 3DSoc, a maker of three-dimensional, interactive smart phone applications. (See Chapter 10.)

India's venture capital market would never have flourished without strong ties and roots in Silicon Valley. Credit for cultivating these seeds goes to TiE (the Indus Entrepreneurs), the Indian technologist networking organization that software maven Naren Bakshi co-founded in 1992. TiE now has 57 chapters around the world and 13,000 members, and it fosters the next generation of entrepreneurs through mentoring, workshops, and seminars.

There's no shortage of Indian venture and tech superstars in Silicon Valley. Vinod Khosla, co-founder of Sun Microsystems and cleantech investing maverick at Kleiner Perkins, formed Khosla Ventures to do more deals. Vinod Dham, "Father of the Pentium chip" at Intel and former CEO of Broadcom Corp., founded Indian tech investment firm NEA Indo-US Ventures. Kanwal Rekhi, CEO of three venture-backed tech companies and the first Indo-American to take a venture-funded company public on NASDAQ (Excelan, later merged with Novell), turned venture capitalist as a co-founder of Inventus Capital Partners.

It's well known that the Indian community in the Valley has made its mark at running tech startups, too. Research by AnnaLee Saxenian, a professor at the University of California at Berkeley, showed that 7 percent of Silicon Valley tech businesses started from 1980 to 1988 had an Indian founder. A follow-up report by Duke University research director Vivek Wadhwa discovered that Indian-born founders were at the helm of 15.5 percent of the Valley's tech companies in 2005.[12] "These are pretty astonishing numbers, considering that in 2000, less than 0.7 percent of the U.S. population and only 6 percent of the Silicon Valley high-tech workforce was born in India," notes Wadhwa.[13]

Technology entrepreneurship in India has evolved to look a lot more like California's tech valley. While outsourcing and software gave India its base, today the action has shifted to a broad range of products, from medical devices to cleantech to cyberspace security. "Venture is turning to product companies, with strong intellectual property and patents, led by serial entrepreneurs who have a product background and know how to build global companies from India," Sethi notes. As an example, he cites Manthan Systems, an IDG-funded software product in business intelligence and analytics for the retail sector.

To prove his point, Sethi points out that his IDG Ventures analyzed 400 tech business plans during 2009 through 2010. The majority of those 400 were in software products, 60 were in medical devices, 30 in business intelligence, and 70 in security. "If you look at our definition of tech, it is not just Internet. India is about a much more diverse set of technologies," he says, listing aerospace, nanotech, biotech, health care, and cleantech as fertile areas. "The emergence of the new age venture investor with deep operating experience in India and a global company in the product space is a catalytic factor in increased technology investments and interest in India," he contends.

Historically, the reality is that India deals haven't measured up to the high valuations or international profile of China startups. The tiger economy is no match for the dragon in startup IPO trophies. Of the 61 IPOs of venture-backed companies on NASDAQ and the New York Stock Exchange in 2010, China counted 22, several of them with multibillion-dollar market caps on opening day. India had one: MakeMyTrip. China's streak in 2010 wasn't an anomaly and dates back to 2003, with only a dip during the recessionary years of 2008 and 2009.

Why do so few successful Indian startups get on the global radar? First, the number of IPOs and M&A deals among venture-funded tech startups is fairly small: only 15 in 2010 (67 percent of all Indian IPOs and M&A transactions in 2010), up from 8 in 2009—though several have scored large investment returns. (See Tables 2.3 and 2.4.)[14] A second factor is that Indian businesses are required to go public first on domestic exchanges. The exception is if they're set up with an offshore holding structure, for instance, in the Indian Ocean island of Mauritius. Only that way can they list directly on NASDAQ or the NYSE, like many China startups have,

Table 2.3   2010 Tech Venture Exits in India

Company	Sector	Exit
MakeMyTrip	Internet	IPO
Meru Networks	Software	IPO
Infinite Computer Solutions	IT Services	IPO
Adventity	BPO	Strategic sale
i-Mint	Other	Strategic sale
7Strata	Software	Strategic sale
BA Systems	Software	Strategic sale
Lifeblob	Internet	Strategic sale
Mango Technologies	Software	Strategic sale
Skelta Software	Software	Strategic sale
CarWale	Internet	Strategic sale
NetMagic	Software	Secondary sale
Pangea3	BPO	Strategic sale
Rupeetalk	Internet	Strategic sale
Ticktvala	Internet	Strategic sale

Source: Venture Intelligence, Zephyr, Thomson One Banker.

Table 2.4   Top 10 Technology Exits by Value in India, 2004–2010

Company	Sector	Amount
Educomp	Education	$970M
Firstsource	BPO	$605M
Progeon	BPO	$490M
NIIT Ltd.	Education	$484M
MakeMyTrip	Internet	$478M
OnMobile	Mobile VAS	$450M
MindTree Consulting	IT Services	$360M
Naukri	Internet	$311M
Nipuna Services	BPO	$184M
Daksh eServices	BPO	$170M

Source: IDG Ventures India research based on Venture Intelligence data.

Table 2.5   Tech VC Exits in India, 2004–2010

Exit Type	# of Exits
M&A	63
IPO	14
Buyback	13
Secondary sale	10
Total	100

Source: IDG Ventures India research based on Venture Intelligence data.

using the Cayman Islands as their base. A third contributor is that strategic sales are far more common than IPOs among venture-funded tech companies in India, unlike China. (See Table 2.5.)

Proud India Displays Its Gems

At IDG Ventures, dealmaker Sudhir Sethi can't wait for me to meet the founder of one of his star portfolio companies. He brings me down the hallway to an office, where I find a bulky, industrial-looking contraption bigger than an office desk. What in the world? I soon find out its purpose.

Turns out it's a robotics-operated medical device developed by a team that used to work with GE Healthcare in India and launched Perfint Healthcare in Chennai in 2005. The CEO, S. Nandakumar, turns on a switch and, pointing to a computer screen display, demonstrates how the device, called Piga, can precisely guide a needle to biopsy a tumor with a safe and simpler procedure meant to diagnose early-stage cancer. Perfint has filed a patent for this invention in the United States and India.

After the brief but loud demo is done, Nandakumar tells me about the business plan. Perfint raised $3.5 million from IDG Ventures and Accel India in 2007 and $7.2 million in 2010 from Norwest Venture Partners plus the prior investors. Its scientific advisory board includes such noted surgeons and researchers as Dr. Mahmood Razavi from Stanford University Hospital in California and Dr. Yuman Fong from Memorial Sloan-Kettering Center in New York.

Founder S. Nandakumar of Perfint Healthcare in Chennai

The co-founders are going after a $1 billion-plus market, aiming for Perfint to reach $15 million revenues and profitability in 2011 before climbing to $50 million revenues by 2015. With product development costs less than half that of the United States, Piga sells for $30,000, compared with similar applications in the United States for $120,000.

By early 2011, Piga had just crossed the 100-customer mark in India and had contracts signed in Malaysia, Bangladesh, South Africa, and Middle East. Regulatory approvals were needed before a U.S. launch planned for 2012—good timing as health care costs soar and cancer diagnoses continue to rise. The next milestone is to bring to market another device the team has been laboring over: medical equipment to remove tumors safely without surgery.

At IDG's Bangalore office, I next interview M. Srinivas Rao, a short, wiry fellow who paces nervously around the room as he tells me about Aujus, India's first home-grown information technology security startup. It's an interesting example of the kind of market intelligence and entrepreneurs-in-residence programs that have helped IDG profit from startup investments in China first, India second, and next Vietnam. (See Chapter 3.) Sethi had identified digital security as a promising sector and had been searching for an experienced entrepreneur to launch an Indian startup in the space when he connected with Rao on LinkedIn in late 2007. A former senior VP at Cisco and co-founder of now IBM-owned Network Solutions, Rao was looking for a new entrepreneurial project. A match was made, based on entrepreneurial experience, business background, and domain knowledge.

After some tough negotiations over contract terms, investment stakes, and organizational structure, in February 2008, IDG Ventures India invested $3 million while a team led by Rao forked over $1 million. Aujus was started, the name coming from the Sanskrit word that means "strength and energy of a warrior." Within three months, Aujus landed its first customer and, by December 2010, was handling 200 projects in 15 countries from offices in the United States, the Middle East, and Europe, with international markets bringing in more than 25 percent of revenues. By 2013, Rao projects revenues will top $40 million, and thanks to a new big order from the government of India to provide unique identification for every Indian resident, Aujus may be close to reaching that goal.

Another innovative cyberspace security startup I encountered at IDG's Bangalore office is iViz, a spinout in 2006 by Bikash Barai from his alma mater Indian Institute of Technology in Calcutta. It is backed with $250,000 in angel finance and $2.5 million from IDG in 2007. Barai gives me a demo of a mock cyber-security attack on his computer and how his software uses artificial intelligence to automatically simulate next-generation hacking techniques, detect security threats, and prevent identity theft. "Our vision is to stay ahead of the hacker," says CEO Barai, who bootstrapped the startup as a grad student and aims to scale the product globally. "It works like a cat and mouse game."

Lunchtime! Office manager Raghu Rao has ordered in box lunches of spicy Indian curries, chicken tandoori, saag paneer, basmati rice, and nan from the upscale Taj West End hotel for us. We sit around the conference room table, and Sethi gives me a brief history of the evolution of India tech entrepreneurship. Between bites, I type as fast as I can on my netbook computer and—something I couldn't have done in China—tweet some of his more relevant points.

To sum it up, the southern city of Bangalore, protected by seas and away from political strife in the northern mountains region close to Pakistan and China, became an engineering hub post-democracy, thanks to its abundance of defense-related business and science and tech colleges, including the 100-year-old Indian Institute of Science established by J. N. Tata, the legendary founder of India's large family-owned conglomerate, Tata Group.

The turning point was 1977, when the Indian government asked large American multinationals IBM, Pepsi, and Coca-Cola to leave the country and India's engineers began developing proprietary hardware and software systems. With the reopening of India markets in 1991, Indian companies started integrating their technology into global systems and began offering tech development services at a fourth the cost of work done in the United States. Bangalore was at the forefront, and with the rush of software development to handle Y2K, it emerged as a leader in software outsourcing, giving rise to such titans as Wipro and Infosys. The city's pool of entrepreneurial talent deepened with training at these multinational outsourcing corporations.

Those beginnings of a software hub in Bangalore coincided with the inflow of venture capital in the mid- to late 1990s. Bangalore, commonly referred to as a garden city for its tree-lined streets, became a venture hub, Sethi tells me. Today, Bangalore-based start-ups account for 40 percent of Indian tech venture investment.

Delhi Delights and Mumbai Moves

Leaving Bangalore, the city with arguably the best lifestyle in India, I fly to Delhi on India's new privately-owned Jet Airways, an improvement over my past flights on AirIndia. The hustle and bustle in Delhi and the vast distances to travel from one startup to another are kind of a turnoff—but not the founders of some novel startups I'm meeting, including cleantech upstarts d.Light Design and Attero Recycling (see Chapter 5), mapping portal MapMyIndia, and PC help service iYogi (see Chapter 12).

With no time this trip to visit Agra and the Taj Mahal, as on a more relaxed itinerary a few years earlier, I skip to India's financial and commercial center, Mumbai. Here, I catch up with Sequoia investor Chadha at his skyscraper office in southern Mumbai's lower Parel business district, easier to get to now, thanks to the recently completed Sea Link bridge.

It was February 2010 and Chadha had recently moved to this booming metropolis from the comfy suburban area of Burlingame near San Francisco to be closer to the Indian deal-making scene. He seemed relaxed and secure—and why not? Over the past decade, as I've covered his career, his investment strategy has become bolder and his returns higher. Chadha has shown that money can be made on investing in companies with a strong Indian DNA.

Chadha started out doing outsourcing deals from 2001 to 2005 and, gaining confidence, ventured into software (AppLabs), Internet (Travelguru, TutorVista, and Shaadi), mobile gaming and social networking (Mauj), financial services (SKS Microfinance), retail (Café Coffee Day), luxury brands (Genesis Colors), and health care (MarketRX).

He can tick off the investment returns from most of his deals, particularly the home runs. Sequoia made $35 million on a $7 million investment in 2007 in legal outsourcing service Pangea3 when it was sold to Thomson Reuters for $100 million in 2010. The firm raked in a three to four times return on the sale of portfolio company MarketRX for $150 million in 2007 to Cognizant Healthcare Solutions. The biggest home run was with Hyderabad-based SKS Microfinance, which went IPO on the Bombay Stock Exchange in July 2010 and reached a $1.6 billion market capitalization.[15] The SKS deal brought the Sequoia Capital India partners a $250 million gain in three years' time from a $25 million investment in India's largest microfinance organization. India's best-known venture investor, Vinod Khosla, made out, too, on a $2.5 million bet he had made in the microfinance outfit back in March 2006.

Chadha has been on a winning streak for a while. Of his firm's 18 investments from an inaugural India fund in 2001, he tells me there were only three write-downs or losses. That's not a bad track record for venture investing, especially on new turf.

"Venture capital is not easy, and many firms don't have the skill set or risk appetite for it," says Chadha, who has McKinsey & Co. credentials and is the son of a foreign diplomat.

In 2007, Chadha moved from investing only in young companies to doing deals with emerging and fast-growing businesses; interestingly, Sequoia Capital China made the same shift. Then, in a real shocker, in early 2011, he abruptly split from Sequoia to take his core WestBridge team and form a new group to do private investments in publicly traded companies. But we're getting a little ahead of our story here.

Back in the Valley

Venture capitalist Bill Draper, distinguished-looking at 83 years of age, was the first investor from Sand Hill Road to get comfortable enough with India to start doing deals there. Like Chadha, he's made money from venture investing in India. Starting in 1994, Draper took his insights from a long and illustrious career at big-time posts at the United Nations and the Export-Import Bank and headed to Asia on an exploratory deal-making mission. "That's where the rising tide was," explains Draper. He traveled to China, India, Vietnam, Hong Kong, and Indonesia and, by the end of his third trip, had decided on India over China.

Seated in his San Francisco office next to a wall of framed photos from India of temples, turbans, and palaces, he confidently ticks off the reasons he chose the mysterious and exotic India for his international venture foray. First, India has an English-speaking business community. Second, it's a democracy. Third, India has a rule of law to deal with contracts and intellectual property protection. Then, too, India's economy has opened up to free enterprise, and trade barriers have been taken down. Plus, there is India's dynamic entrepreneurial population—one proof being the success of Indian engineers in the Valley. And finally, he says with a broad grin, he prefers Indian food to greasy Chinese cuisine.

His instincts were right. Within six years, his $70 million Draper International fund made small investments in 25 companies and, catching the Internet and tech boom of the late 1990s, returned 16 times its limited partners' money. Among the successes were a $2 million bet on enterprise software maker Selectica that realized $20 million for Draper after a listing on NASDAQ in 2000. There also was Torrent Networking Technologies, a Cisco-like router sold to Ericsson in 1999 for a $20 million return on Draper's $2 million investment.

Another company he cashed out of with a big gain was Internet security startup, Ramp Networks, sold to Nokia in 2001 following a NASDAQ IPO for a $5.6 million return on capital. He also hit it right with Yantra, a supply management software spin-off from

Infosys that was merged in 2004 into an AT&T division for a triple return to the Draper fund.

Only one company remains in the Draper International portfolio: Rediff.com, an Indian news, entertainment, and shopping portal that listed on NASDAQ in 1997. It's still there, explains Draper, because his fund invested rupees in Rediff.com and can't sell the stock until the company lists on the Mumbai stock exchange, only permitted under India rules after a company reaches a threshold of three years of profitability. Overall, though, Draper is pleased with his India track record. "We had a surprisingly large number of successes, without home runs in the sense of multibillion companies," he says.

While I'm in California, I stop by the Sand Hill Road office of venture leader Kleiner Perkins Caufield & Byers to interview partner Ajit Nazre. A PhD with dual master's degrees who worked alongside the CEO of business software leader SAP for several years, Nazre today heads up the firm's India investment initiative. He's funded seven startups in India: mobile ad network inMobi, solar equipment maker Kotak Urja, shopping site FutureBazaar.com, digital navigation service MapMyIndia, job portal Naukri, online payment system PayMate, and travel site Cleartrip. This is a major pivot from just six years ago, when Kleiner Perkins was reluctant to invest beyond the East Bay, he points out, implying not much farther than Oakland.

Today, Nazre is in India five or six times

Kleiner Perkins' India dealmaker Ajit Nazre in Menlo Park

each year. He's pushing his entrepreneurs to capitalize on India's fast growth markets and take advantage of English as a global business language to scale to supersize in international markets. "In my view, which is obviously biased, all of these companies could be as large as Baidu or Alibaba," says the cool and confident investor.

Lip-Bu Tan has done a slew of deals in Asia and the United States at the firm he founded, Walden International, in 1989. He's seen plenty of up-and-down cycles of venture investing, yet remains an optimist. (In 2009, he also became president and CEO of San Jose–based semiconductor maker Cadence Design Systems while continuing at Walden.) Walden was the first Silicon Valley venture firm to open an office in India, dating back to 1998, when Tan recruited Sethi to build Walden's presence in India. Sethi invested $33 million in 11 startups in four years before the dotcom crash led Walden to close its India office in 2002 and focus more on China. By 2007, Walden was back to this emerging market, hiring Rajesh Subramaniam, the former CFO at outsourcing firm Firstsource Solutions, as managing director to reopen an Indian office.

Tan had good reason to see the upside. In 2007, outsourcing business MindTree Consulting, started by former Wipro exec Ashok Soota, went public in India and reached a market capitalization of $520 million. Walden had invested in MindTree at its start in 1999 and again in 2001 and was MindTree's largest outside investor, with 16 percent of its shares. "We enjoyed a home run return as an early investor," Tan says, in his characteristic understated tone.

Today, he's still convinced that India entrepreneurship will ultimately shine in a broad range of tech sectors. From his corner office at Walden on Market Street, where the tall and slender Tan has a spectacular view of the bay, he tells me, "I am very bullish about India. It is about five to ten years behind China, and over the next two to three years, it is catching up."

As president of India for the innovative financial provider SVB Financial Group and an investment committee member for its China funds and deals, Ash Lilani has a front-row seat on tech trends in India and China. Indeed, the group helped to jump-start Silicon Valley–style funding in both these Asian markets.

I catch up with the heavyset Lilani at his office in Palo Alto, shortly after he has returned from one of his frenetic trips to India, where he spends half his time. In 2003, a team from the bank led a group of venture investors from Silicon Valley on an exploratory trip to tech hotspots in China and India, laying the foundation for cross-border connections and then offering the Silicon Valley group space to set up shop at the bank's offices in Bangalore and Shanghai. Several leading venture partners went on that trip and soon had desks and phones in spare space at the bank's locations.

SVB also invested in some early Indian venture funds, including WestBridge Capital Partners, JumpStartUp, and Infinity Venture. The tech financial group made money on two of those funds—"not bad in the venture world," Lilani notes. He points out that the ecosystem for venture investing in Silicon Valley that took two decades to evolve was "compressed to four years in India."

When I ask why India does not have the string of entrepreneur success stories that China does, Lilani takes a deep breath and then five minutes from his tight schedule to explain why he believes tech entrepreneurship in India will catch up to China within 10 years.

The Indian brand of entrepreneurship has developed from a "service mentality," he says, noting that most of the early outsourcing startups—for example, MindTree Consulting and Firstsource Solutions—are in niches of the industry popularized by India's giant firms Infosys and Wipro. The followers relied on business models that were really just twists on outsourcing: for example, online tutoring service TutorVista and PC fix-it service iYogi (see Chapter 12). It hasn't been until the past few years, he says, that Indian engineers have broken out of that outsourcing mold and become more experimental.

"Venture investing started off slow and steady in India. China in the short term will deliver greater returns, but we are long-term optimistic on India," says Lilani. "You have a vibrant, stable market in India. While India may seem bureaucratic, you have fewer of the regulatory and restructuring issues that you have in China due to currency issues." He adds, "India has the most dynamic entrepreneurs, and the good news is that there are so many of them."

Made It in India

The venture chase in India was well under way by 2007. For a brief 12 months, India venture capital investment in startups even exceeded China's, though by 2008, China edged ahead with $9.1 billion compared with $8.3 billion for India. (See Tables 2.6 and 2.7.) The peak for Indian venture fund-raising was 2008 at $1.4 billion, more than double the year before.[16]

Table 2.6   Venture Capital Investments in China and India

	2005	2006	2007	2008	2009	2010
India	$1,116.7	3,590.5	10,341.7	8,300.4	2,500.0	5,835.7
China	$2,161.8	4,005.9	8,718.1	9,084.6	3,070.1	7,620.0

Note: In millions of dollars.

Table 2.7   Number of Startups with Venture Financing

	2005	2006	2007	2008	2009	2010
India	93	216	290	294	170	211
China	204	344	574	475	250	303

Source: AVCJ.

In 2008, Helion Venture Partners launched a second venture fund of $210 million, just two years after the firm's initial $140 million Indian fund. So did Nexus Venture Partners, with $220 million for investment in young startups, after its first $100 million venture fund in 2007. "Innovation in India is going to come from many different sectors. We are bullish on India. If you play the game the right way and work closely with entrepreneurs on operations and team building, the opportunities are huge," partner Naren Gupta told me shortly after his team began investing the new fund.

His positive outlook was echoed by partner Sandeep Singhal: "After the first wave of investing in companies based on cost arbitrage, India is finally ready for venture capital in companies driven by innovation. Some of the best employees at companies in India such as Google, Microsoft, and Intel are thinking about starting their own companies. Moreover, professionals in large Indian corporations and in companies around the world are stepping into Indian entrepreneurial ventures targeting the burgeoning domestic economy. They need risk capital. The time to back them is now."

During those boom years, I attended meetings of the India Venture Capital Association at Sand Hill Road's Quadrus Conference Center. At the first one, in 2007, a panel of leading India investors complained about greedy entrepreneurs putting priority on high valuations for their startups over top venture partners. There was simply too much money chasing too few high-quality deals, said Navin

Chaddha, managing director at the Mayfield Fund, who oversees the firm's India fund of $150 million.

In October 2008, I attended a second India venture program at the same place. This time, the industry talk was about an end to the euphoria of inflated expectations and a welcoming reset in expectations. "There has been a bit of hubris and arrogance in India that has not fully come down," said Gupta of Nexus Venture. "There has been an expectation that a company could go public in four years and everyone would live happily ever after, whereas in the 1980s, the average company took eight years to reach an exit. Entrepreneurs need to understand that creating great companies takes great courage," he pointed out.

Ravi Viswanathan, a partner at New Enterprise Associates, added that with the market downturn, he was seeing a welcome return to normalcy. "More and more entrepreneurs in India are focused on long-term value and are selecting venture capital firms to work with them for added-value factors rather than high valuations," he said, adding that more world-class managerial teams were originating from India than just a few years ago.

It was the sort of talk I was hearing in China at about the same time. As the global financial crisis hit in fall 2008, India venture fund-raising plummeted to $321 million in 2009 while new funds from China also sank. (See Table 2.8.) By 2010, fund-raising picked up to $553 million but was still less than half the amount just two years earlier.

The optimistic spirit of venture capital finally resurfaced in August 2010 with the IPO of MakeMyTrip, India's long-awaited trophy deal. The 10-year-old startup from Delhi scored a market valuation of $903 million[17] on its NASDAQ IPO. Not only was MakeMyTrip one of the top IPOs from Asia that year but also it was the first Indian firm to go public in the United States since 2007. (See Chapter 11.)

Table 2.8   India Fund-Raising

	2005	2006	2007	2008	2009	2010
India	$487.3	$687.7	$620.4	$1,414.7	$321.0	$552.9
China	$1,358.7	$1,757.8	$3,803.3	$4,044.8	$1,509.6	$1,707.5

Note: In millions.
Source: AVCJ.

MakeMyTrip founder and CEO Deep Kalra and his co-founders Keyur Joshi and Sachin Bhatia had funding of $39 million from lead investor SAIF, Helion Venture Partners, the Tiger Fund, and Sierra Ventures and rewarded them with an ample, double-digit return—just the spark more young Indian founders need to cultivate their own startups.

Bob McCooey, a senior VP with NASDAQ, told me he had three Indian startups getting ready to list on the exchange by the end of 2011. One could be mobile advertising service inMobi in Bangalore, formed by Harvard MBA and ex-McKinsey consultant Naveen Tewari. It has three major positives: The startup is capitalizing on a surge in mobile communications in India, it's gone global, and marquee investors Kleiner Perkins and Sherpalo Ventures are the backers. (See Chapter 4.) Second in the queue could be Tejas Networks, a Bangalore-based telecommunications networking equipment maker started by famed serial entrepreneur "Desh" Deshpande of NASDAQ-listed Sycamore Networks. Tejas is funded with $73 million from Mayfield Fund, Battery Ventures, Intel Capital, and Goldman Sachs and is geared up, having postponed an IPO during the market doldrums of 2008.

Pearson Swoops In

The big moneymakers for venture investors in India tech are not IPOs, however, but mergers and acquisitions. In one notably rich example, London-based media company Pearson took a controlling 76 percent stake for $127 million in Bangalore startup TutorVista in January 2011, after a minority investment in June 2009 for $12 million. One of its three backers, Sequoia Capital India, made $30 million on a $5 million investment in TutorVista, according to Chadha. Such a high return from an acquisition hasn't been out of the ordinary in India. Sequoia made a four to five times return on an $11 million investment in pharmaceutical software sales developer MatrixRX, Inc., in a $140 million, all-cash acquisition in November 2007 by NASDAQ-listed Cognizant Technology Solutions Corp.

Tracking China again, India venture is no longer just venture. It is also growth-stage or pre-IPO investing. Putting capital into companies that need to get to their next stage of growth to come out of the gate is a way that venture capitalists can ride the economic

boom with more mature companies and avoid the risks of backing an unproven loser. In India, quite a few firms broadened their
portfolios to include more developed companies, Accel Partners,
Norwest Venture Partner, and Sequoia included. At the same time,
at least a dozen firms have remained committed to funding only
startups. Nexus showed its colors by launching a fund in 2010 to
seed as many as 50 young startups with $50,000 to $500,000 over
the next five years.

Some venture firms quit India altogether, as the financial crisis took its toll and they struck out with deals. Internationally oriented Battery Ventures, which invests in Israel and Europe, packed
up shop. Partner Mark Sherman, who had been heading up the
India initiative, left the firm in late 2009. The firm's general partners were planning to visit India the fall of 2009 but put on the
brakes and froze further capital investments in India. Battery's
partner in India, Gautam Patel, also left, while a third partner,
Ramneek Gupta, returned to the firm's Silicon Valley base. Battery
had made four investments in India. While Tejas, one of the four
deals, could be a winner for Battery, two India deals didn't work
out. Travelguru, in which Battery had coinvested $15 million
with Sequoia Capital India in 2006, was sold for $12 million to
Travelocity in 2009. Another deal, High Mark Credit, which Battery
backed with $1 million during 2009, is no longer in the venture
firm's portfolio.

Battery's departure is nothing compared with the upheaval
at Sequoia Capital India. Former Sequoia investor Chadha got
tempted by the big returns from investing in public deals and
couldn't resist. His team put more than $200 million in 14 publicly
traded Indian companies before the end of the decade. Then, in
early 2011, he pulled a fast one, catching the industry by surprise
by splitting from Sequoia with his three core partners and making
plans to relaunch WestBridge, not for venture, but with a $500 mil-
lion fund for PIPE (private investment in public equity) deals.

I remember back to 2006, when Chadha told me that he
had made his best business decision, merging his young firm
WestBridge Capital Partners with the well-known tech investor
Sequoia Capital. The move certainly did jump-start his career.

In an interview shortly after his team departed from their
Sequoia perch in early 2011, Chadha made it clear why he turned
to PIPE deals. Why do venture when you can invest $10 million

Sumir Chadha, ex-Sequoia Capital India in Mumbai

like Sequoia did in late 2008 in publicly traded Nagarjuna Construction Co. and get $23 million in six months? Or when you can invest $14 million, like the partners did in listed financial service firm Manappuram Finance in 2007, and make $70 million within three years? Or when you can score again by investing $20 million in outsourcing firm eClerx, like Chadha did in 2009, and realize a three times return in 18 months? He explained that with public companies, the team can take a large ownership stake at a "wonderful valuation" and work closely with the boards to build value in the companies before exiting within a few years. "We want to have the courage of our convictions, and we believe public investing offers high-quality deals and long-term success," he said. "We're young guys, and we want try a new direction with something we have fun doing," said Chadha, who just turned 40 in mid-2011.

In the interim, Chadha and his three partners are remaining on 20 boards among Sequoia's portfolio in India. But their sudden shift reverberated throughout the industry. Could the odds for India startups be slimmer now that one of the most experienced venture teams in India was gone? Maybe.

As five remaining managing directors take over at Sequoia Capital India, it can hardly be business as usual, although Silicon Valley–based partner Mike Moritz reassured investors and entrepreneurs that the firm's approach will continue strong. India's leading venture firm has a giant portfolio of 94 tech, consumer, financial, health care, energy, and outsourcing deals. The new team is younger and less experienced, though two have been partners since 2008 and a third since 2010. Most were handpicked and trained by Chadha. What seems likely is that the current Sequoia team in India will invest from a smaller fund than during Chadha's time and stick to investing in a mix of startup and fast-growing deals. The month after the split, Sequoia Capital India invested $4.4 million in the Victoria's Secret of India, Lovable Lingerie, and has inked several more of its traditional tech deals since then. How Moritz handles the transition and charts the journey will signal prospects for the continued health and buoyancy of this key venture market in Asia, the largest after China.

Determined and dedicated venture trailblazers and energized entrepreneurs in India are beginning to reap results for all their hard work. But India is no China. India has moved up the tech ladder. No Alibaba is in sight yet. Returns pale next to Baidu or Tencent. The promise of unearthing the kind of disruptive tech companies that venture is known for in Silicon Valley—and increasingly in China—seems remote in India.

China seduces with its fast-forward economic, technologic advances and bold startups. India is moving on its own time clock, five years behind China. Democracy, a free press, and a comfort level with doing business in India are leading to a groundswell of entrepreneurship and a spark of creativity. These strong undercurrents could put India's strengths in the spotlight.

CHAPTER

3

Vietnam: The Next Frontier

Scrappy is an understatement for the Vietnamese brand of entrepreneur. Vietnam is just like China, only about 20 years behind. Yet the echoes of China's boom reverberate here. If and when Vietnam does break through on the tech surface, it will be because of the strong-willed young business leaders; their finely tuned startup clones of **Tencent**, **Shanda**, **Facebook**, **Google**, and **Amazon**; and their drive to get ahead from practically nowhere. Their venture backers get credit, too, like IDG's **Pat McGovern** and Softbank's **Masayoshi Son**. No wonder **Google** and **eBay** are also scouting Vietnam on the Asian trail.

In the capital city of Hanoi, I'm climbing a darkened stairway to the third floor to meet with Nguyen Xuan Tai, the founder of a search engine he dreams of making Vietnam's equal to Baidu in China.

His six-year-old startup isn't profitable yet, and its spartan space in this building still under construction hardly spells success. Like Baidu's Robin Li used a home field advantage to score against Google in the mainland, Nguyen is betting his search engine Socbay—which means "squirrel" or "a smart, lovely, fast animal"— can win in Vietnam.

Nguyen, 28, is one gutsy entrepreneur. He's a programming ace who grew up poor and developed search technology optimized for the Vietnamese language as a Hanoi tech school undergrad. Nguyen turned down an offer by Google's Eric Schmidt in 2006 to acquire his

Socbay founder Nguyen Xuan Tai at his Hanoi office

one-year-old search startup at a time when funds were so tight that he had to keep the servers in the office bathroom. The fact that Google's offer was low made the decision easier.

Fast-forward five years, and today, Socbay leads Vietnam's booming mobile search market. A popular iMedia mobile application for chat, games, video clips, and MP3 music hit more than 8 million downloads within a year of its mid-2010 launch on several handset models. His startup has capital from Pat McGovern's IDG Ventures Vietnam and Japan's tech titan Softbank Corp. It even has nifty office space for the servers.

Nguyen represents the type of scrappy, ambitious entrepreneurs I'm meeting during a tech tour of Hanoi and Ho Chi Minh City in late 2009. Youngsters born after the Vietnamese war ended and the north and south were united as the Socialist Republic of Vietnam in 1976 are creating a revolution of their own. Homegrown techies are launching replicas of winners like instant-messaging service Tencent and gaming site Shanda from China, e-commerce player Rakuten from Japan, Cyworld social networking from Korea, and eBay and Google from the United States. Groupon clones are multiplying, too.

Big-name multinational tech leaders have begun investing in well-positioned Vietnamese startups in these fast-growing digital media and entertainment sites. Tencent purchased a stake in social networking and gaming startup VNG, eBay bought into Vietnamese auction portal Peacesoft, and Berlin-based Groupon cloner Rebate Networks formed a local social commerce site with NhomMua.vn.

Venture capital is on the upswing, thanks largely to IDG Group Chairman McGovern's foresight in cutting the ribbon to open Saigon and Hanoi offices early on. He gets a first read on emerging technologies in Asia from his company's publishing and research groups, then invests capital from venture shops in China, India, and Vietnam. Since 2004, his firm has backed more than 40 Vietnamese startups, including Socbay, Peacesoft, and VNG, plus clones of MTV, Amazon, MapQuest, PayPal, and Facebook. The son-in-law of the Communist country's Prime Minister Nguyen Tan Dung, Henry Nguyen, runs IDG Ventures Vietnam and its $100 million tech venture fund—the largest and first in Vietnam.

IDG struck it rich by betting on startups in China's emerging tech market. The fledgling market in Vietnam holds promise as a miniature China. In 2010, IDG sold a 10 percent interest in Vietnam's top social networking and gaming startup, VNG, for a 75 times return on capital, a figure that compares favorably with the firm's China deals. VNG is being primed to go public, as early as 2012. "Venture capital in Vietnam is heating up," McGovern told me during a luncheon at the swanky Aquavit restaurant in midtown Manhattan in August 2010. "The conditions are right for Vietnam to be the 'next China' for technology venture capital investors."

No wonder IDG Ventures Vietnam is raising a second and larger fund, this time at $150 million. "The Vietnamese market is where China was ten years ago," says IDG chief Nguyen, whom I interviewed at the firm's Ho Chi Minh City skyscraper office in November 2009. "We want to replicate what we did in China, and we are trying the tech media and telecom companies we have seen in China, Japan, and Korea. We are very bullish on Vietnam and believe it's a place with significant potential. It has all the right agents. It's a matter of using our collective experience."

The action in Vietnam parallels China's development more than a decade ago. Chinese tech brands Baidu, Alibaba, and Tencent caught on, thanks to local smarts and leverage, soon overpowering foreign-brand newcomers such as eBay, Yahoo!, and Google, which faced struggles with managing operations in faraway China and issues with censorship. In Vietnam, localized social networking and online news and information sites are gaining an upper hand because of better adaptation to the culture and censorship of popular global brands. Facebook is intermittently blocked in Vietnam, giving the local rivals an edge.

The rising tech stars in Vietnam are charged-up native techies like Socbay's Nguyen—just like in China, where today's up-and-comers are hardscrabble locally trained and educated geeks. As with China, expats are thriving in Vietnam and staying. Over lunch at the French bistro Refinery, tucked in a courtyard in central Ho Chi Minh City, Jonah Levey told me he was not looking back after establishing a successful career in Vietnam. He left behind an executive search career in New York and moved to Ho Chi Minh City in 2002. Today, he runs local recruitment service leader Navigos Group and a related job search and career center, Vietnamworks. He's also a director at private equity firm Mekong Capital.

With a population of 89 million, this former French colony is dwarfed by its close neighbors China and India for size and lags behind other Asian countries for digital advances. But the modern conveniences of technology are increasingly woven into the local culture of this up-and-coming nation since the World Wide Web became available here in 1997 and digital media content took off.

A relatively high percentage of Vietnam's population uses the Internet—32 million[1]—and online access is projected to reach 41 million people by 2014.[2] (See Table 3.1.) Like in China and India, mobile is where it's happening. Subscribers to mobile services topped 78 million in 2010, more than twice the number just two years prior.[3] (See Table 3.2.) High-speed 3G telecom service arrived in Vietnam in 2009, and within a year, 11 percent of mobile subscribers signed on to stream videos, share photos, play games, and browse the Web over their smart phones.[4] Just about every youngster in Hanoi and Ho Chi Minh City hangs out in cyber cafés to play games and chat, and seemingly everyone is glued to a mobile phone. In fact, Vietnam's online gaming industry exceeds that of India, with 8.6 million online gamers in 2010, compared with 5.6 million for India. (See Table 3.3.) Moreover, the number of social network subscribers in Vietnam is nearly equal to India's, despite the huge difference in population. (See Table 3.4.)

Table 3.1   Internet Users in Vietnam

2007	2008	2009	2010	2011	2012	2013	2014
9.1*	12.4	16.3	25.5	32.0	34.7	37.5	40.6

*In millions.
Source: IDC Asia/Pacific.

Table 3.2   Mobile Service Subscribers in Vietnam

2008	2009	2010	2011	2012	2013	2014
38.1*	57.2	78.3	78.6	83.6	86.4	87.4

*In millions.
Source: IDC Asia/Pacific.

Table 3.3   Online Gamers in Vietnam

2008	2009	2010	2011	2012	2013	2014
3.7*	6.1	8.6	8.3	8.7	9.6	10.6

*In millions.
Source: IDC Asia/Pacific.

Table 3.4   Social Network Subscribers in Vietnam

2007	2008	2009	2010	2011	2012	2013	2014
0.7*	1.1	1.9	3.2	4.3	4.9	5.3	5.6

*In millions.
Source: IDC Asia/Pacific.

Digital technology has seeped into the Vietnamese culture, and broadband Internet and mobile phones are in the lingo. PricewaterhouseCoopers is even predicting that the digital boom[5] will lead Hanoi and Ho Chi Minh City to rank as the world's fastest-growing cities economically (outdistancing southern China's Guangzhou), with average GDP gains of 7 percent annually over the 2008–2025 time period.[6]

Whether investing in Vietnam's still-developing tech ecosystem will pay off big time is still a big question mark. But you can't blame McGovern and a small group of venture pioneers for trying.

The field is limited to a small but astute group, including Softbank China & India Holdings, a $100 million emerging markets fund for Asia backed by Japan's Softbank Corp. and Cisco Systems, run and fully invested by Shanghai-based angel investor William Bao Bean and former Deutsche Bank director Kabir Misra. Silicon Valley venture leader Tim Draper has DFJ VinaCapital Technology, a $32 million fund launched with CEO Don Lam of Vietnam's VinaCapital family of funds in 2006 as part of his far-reaching global network, Draper Fisher Jurvetson. (See Table 3.5.)

IDG's VP of technology and investment James Vuong is promoting the acronym VIC—shorthand for Vietnam, India, and China—as a new twist on the BRIC countries of Brazil, Russia, India and China to sum up the Southeast Tiger's promise. But as he's observed since moving to Vietnam from Silicon Valley three years ago, the pace is a lot slower than the Bay area. "People in Vietnam move at about half the speed," he notes. E-mails take a few days to be returned, for instance, and it's common for workers who come from the countryside to Hanoi or Ho Chi Minh City jobs to curl up for an afternoon nap on the office floor—something I've never seen in a Shanghai or Beijing office.

Table 3.5   Venture Investments in Vietnam

	2007	2008	2009	2010
Venture amount*	$525.4	$205.6	$42.7	$110.2
Number of Deals	46	39	9	14

*In millions.
Source: AVCJ.

Henry Nguyen and James Vuong at IDG Ventures Vietnam

Now that a few venture investors have discovered Vietnam, you can bet they would like to keep it an insiders' secret. There's greed at work here. The longer it takes for word to get out that Vietnam has potential as an Asian tech hub, the longer these gold diggers can strike deals at bargain-rate terms. Valuations to invest in Vietnamese startups are a fraction of those from China vintage 2005, judging by eBay investments in China's e-commerce site Eachnet then and Vietnam's Peacesoft six years later. The investment landscape could be crowded within a decade. Now is the time to reap the financial rewards of first-mover advantage.

Not a lot of risks are being taken on gambling with investments in disruptive technology startups here. Safe bets, like clones of sites that worked in China and India, are instead the craze. Auction portals, job sites, online payment services, e-book retailers, and gaming and social networks—based on original ideas from the United States, China, and other Asian tech hubs such as Korea and Japan—are getting funded and then scaled as market leaders. (See Table 3.6.) Vietnam really doesn't have the leading-edge research that is becoming a driver of tech entrepreneurship in China and, to a lesser extent, India.

Table 3.6   Sampling of Venture-Backed Startups in Vietnam

Startup	Sector
iSphere Software	Software development, social networking platform modeled on Korea's Cyworld
Peacesoft Solution	e-Shopping and auction site ChoDienTu
Socbay	Local search engine primarily for mobile phones
Tamtay	Social networking site with instant messaging, content sharing of blogs, videos, photos
VinaPay	Electronic payment service for mobile phones
Vatgia	e-Commerce web site for B2C and C2C transactions
VietnamWorks	Job recruitment web site
VinaBook	Online bookseller and retailer of movies, software, music
VNG	Online games and social networking services modeled on China's Tencent
Yan TV	Music site like MTV

Source: Silicon Asia.

Tamtay founder and social media entrepreneur Tran Thanh Son in Hanoi

Coffee Bean Community

Vietnam's fledgling tech entrepreneur market is close-knit, and the kind of networking that helped Silicon Valley take off in the 1990s is just starting to happen here. The centrally located Coffee Bean shop in central Saigon is a popular hangout. Launch, a Facebook group made up of 760 Vietnamese techies, fosters info exchange and a sense of community. Formed in 2010 by IDG's venture investor Vuong, it's a playground for local founders to collaborate and move the needle on Vietnam's tech frontier. A former Bay area chip designer and Berkeley MBA, Vuong came to Vietnam in 2006 as one of 30 elite Kauffman fellows in a two-year postgraduate apprenticeship in venture investing. His mentor was IDG's Nguyen, and today Vuong is always on his iPhone hustling for deals. His wife moved back with Vuong in early 2008. Today, she runs a Vietnamese startup modeled after the Gilt Groupe that sells U.S. premium brands at bargain-hunter prices through an online store, fashion events, catalogs, and mobile channels.

The venture capital model is so new to Vietnam that when IDG launched its fund in 2004, it had to start from scratch. IDG developed a list of 10 sectors that were ripe for new business concepts. Nguyen and his small team went out and met with would-be entrepreneurs. He offered resources and capital to test and incubate projects in-house, get funding from IDG for the most workable ideas, and hatch them as commercial enterprises. "One of our challenges was how to define and introduce the concept of venture capital," tells Nguyen. "The Silicon Valley–like model we were bringing to entrepreneurs was novel."

Today, he has this hand-holding approach down to a science. He relies on entrepreneurs in residence to work with native entrepreneurs at IDG-funded companies. For instance, he handpicked serial startup maven Bryan Pelz, a Los Angeles expat in Ho Chi Minh City, to coach the local founder of VNG, Le Hong Minh, on strategy.

From Rice to Chips

Entrepreneurship and innovation bring economic progress to emerging nations, and Vietnam is no exception. Vietnam's economy is based on agricultural products such as coffee, rice, and cashews; tourism of everything from beach resorts to battlegrounds; and low-cost manufacturing of textiles and toys. But more of those rice paddies could be corporate hubs in the future, as slow but steady progress is being made. The Vietnamese government aims to have 500 high-tech firms in such fields as software and biotechnology housed at industrial parks by 2020, contributing about 45 percent of the nation's gross domestic product, up from about 10 percent in 2011. Moving the Southeast Asian nation closer to its goal of bringing in foreign investment in factories and research hubs, German-based Bosch Group opened a software and engineering center in Ho Chi Minh City during 2011. The emerging tech ecosystem here extends to the IBM Center for Innovation established in 2009 in Ho Chi Minh City—one of dozens worldwide that IBM Managing Director Claudia Fan Munce oversees to salt startups with software resources.

The formerly war-torn nation began economic and political reforms in 1986 to alleviate corruption and inefficiency at state-owned enterprises, following the postwar collectivization of farms and factories, a period when millions of impoverished people left the Communist regime for brighter shores. When President Bill Clinton lifted the trade embargo to Vietnam in 1994, investors poured in, and the hype was about the country becoming the next Asian tiger well before the infrastructure—industrial parks and water and power supplies—were in place. Now, luxury hotels such as the Park Hyatt and the carefully named Hilton Hanoi Opera Hotel, the Sofitel beach resorts in Nha Trang, and well-stocked supermarkets are plentiful, as private ownership has been encouraged in a new Socialist market economy. It's a big difference from the limited options I had on an earlier tourist visit to Vietnam in 1998, when I cruised the Mekong River in a motorboat, crunched into the Cu Chi tunnels used by Vietnamese soldiers as escapes and supply lines in the war with the United States, and checked out the famous rooftop Saigon Bar, once a hangout for war correspondents. Aside from the swarm of mopeds on city streets and some landmarks like the French colonial-style Metropole Hotel in Hanoi, I don't spot many familiar sights in Hanoi or Saigon today.

Squirrel Climbs the Tree

As Socbay and others ramp up, Vietnam is getting on the tourist *and* tech map globally. How the local search market is playing out represents a telling case study in the contrasts and differences between Vietnam and China.

Unseasoned but determined Chinese entrepreneur Robin Li grew up in a coal-mining town, rejected an offer from Google in 2005, then ran past the search giant to claim first prize and a NASDAQ listing for his startup Baidu. Vietnamese entrepreneur Nguyen turned down a Google offer in 2006 and went on perfecting his search engine locally. Both grew up in poor regions, Li in inland China and Nguyen in the central Nghe An province. Both are software coding addicts. Socbay has a cute squirrel for his logo; Baidu has a bear paw. The similarities trail after this point.

Baidu won the search market in China by developing a superior search engine in Mandarin and leveraging local market know-how, while Google struggled with miscues, censorship, and blockages for four years—and eventually withdrew its servers from the Mainland to Hong Kong in 2010.[7]

Socbay has fine-tuned search for the Vietnamese language but is a tiny player in the local search market and doesn't stand a chance of going public any time soon. Google entered Vietnam in 2008 and claims 81 percent of the market's online search.[8] That compares with 2 percent for Socbay online.[9] But Nguyen hasn't given up. He claims his search engine leads Vietnam's fast-growing mobile search market with two-thirds of the local market—and mobile is what increasingly matters. Keep in mind that Google is the undisputed champion of mobile search worldwide.[10]

Vietnam's little search engine that could is earning bonus points. The World Bank agency-sponsored InfoDev selected the startup as one of the top innovative small and medium-size enterprises in South Asia in 2011.

Meanwhile, Socbay is piling on more goodies besides precise search results to its bag of tricks, such as so-called value-added services that subscribers pay for, like ringtones, another concept that worked in China.

A turning point came in mid-2010, when Socbay launched an application designed for mobile phones offering search results for daily news and information queries, plus search-directed downloads of digital entertainment such as MP3 music, video clips, and games. Within 12 months, this Socbay iMedia application made for Samsung, Nokia, and HTC phones topped 8 million downloads— 2 million more than the search service on its own in 2010.[11] A version of the app designed for Nokia's Ovi Store, rolled out in June 2010, logged nearly 7,000 downloads per day in the first four months of 2011, and 1 million downloads in total. Nguyen claims his handiwork is one of the top 50 leading applications on Nokia worldwide. "One million downloads is so meaningful to us. This is a special event for an application's development, especially for one in a foreign application store," says Nguyen. "We are very surprised at this news because after the release campaign in June 2010, we hadn't conducted any other advertising."

Nguyen grew up as the son of a former government worker in a very poor hilltop town in central Vietnamese countryside. He fell in love with computers at age 13, when he first touched a keyboard, and he has never let go. His common upbringing is what Nguyen says "really gave me the desire for a great career."

As an early teen, he began borrowing computer books from his older brother so he could learn and practice programming languages and commands. By 15, he was writing software programs, and by the time he graduated from high school, this young champion was winning provincial prizes. Encouraged, he applied and got into Vietnam's largest technical university, the Hanoi University of Technology. "I was addicted to the PC," says Nguyen, who looks no more than 20 years of age. "I wanted to get into that university so I could work with PCs all day. I wanted to work on something incredible."

On campus, Nguyen convinced two computer science professors to mentor him and guide his research into search, a project outside of classroom studies frowned upon by administrators. By his third year of university, he and four classmates began studying automatic Web page monitoring programs, known as spiders. They came up with their own program to crawl local servers and compile all Vietnamese Internet content into a single database. That search technology won third prize in a ministry-level competition for science and technology advancements and became a basis for Socbay.

Next, Nguyen interned at a local software and telecom business, Elcom Corp., which invested $200,000 into development of the search engine and provided office space, personal computers, and an Internet connection. He was given a tight deadline to come up with a search prototype within a year, but Nguyen got fed up with his impatient supporters, gave up his ownership stake, and left to venture out on his own. Recalls Nyugen, "I think I can't rely on those sponsors anymore. Their patience is limited. I want to start my own company, not under the Elcom name. I said to them, 'My company's name is my company's name, not yours.' You can take my percentage, and I will let you invest in my company."

The enterprising young man began fine-tuning the search demos with support from IDG's team in 2005. When IDG founder McGovern visited Vietnam in 2006 on one of his regular exploratory trips in Asia to scout for local deals, do research, and check on operations, Nguyen got his lucky break.

The programming whiz landed a meeting with McGovern and did a demo of his search engine. He told the corporate venture leader his dream was to create Vietnam's leading search engine, like Baidu in China. "He [McGovern] told me he was very impressed. He said you have a long way to go and many challenges, just like Google and Yahoo! did. He encouraged me to go ahead and try my best."

In 2006, IDG Ventures became the first investor in Nguyen's startup formed with two computer science classmates, Naiscorp Information Technology Service. Enter Eric Schmidt of Google. Schmidt had been overseeing a troublesome and complex rollout of Google's search engine in China. Vietnam was another emerging market on the Google horizon, though on a much smaller scale than China.

Within months of IDG's investment, Schmidt approached Naiscorp on a visit to Vietnam and invited Nguyen, his investor, and two classmates to come to Mountain View in the heart of Silicon Valley for a meeting. Schmidt proceeded to ask questions about the Vietnamese environment and the young programmer's background, how he learned English, and how he started the company. "He wanted to know how someone with a low education in Vietnam can do incredible research work like I have done," recalls Nguyen, in a sincere tone, as we're meeting in Hanoi in November 2009. In turn, Nguyen says he asked about Google's culture and its intentions for his startup.

That hour-long talk with Schmidt back in December 2006 ended with an offer. Google would buy the startup and relocate its team to the United States to work with the American search leader for one year. Recalls Nguyen, "He told me developing a search engine independently will be very difficult, but here's a chance to join the Google family."

But the stubborn Nguyen could not be budged so easily—his small frame can be deceiving! "I don't want it. I refuse it. I fear the U.S. environment where in the movies they can shoot and kick any time," he explains to me, relaying what he told Schmidt. He adds that Schmidt tried to change his mind by reminding him of the living standards in the United States and the "attractive, beautiful country." But Nguyen was not persuaded, telling Schmidt, "I think Vietnam is a better place to live." Nguyen offered a counterproposal. Google could invest in—but not acquire—his startup, and his team would work from Vietnam after a six-month initiation, not a full year, in Mountain View. Neither was bending. Once IDG's Nguyen weighed in that Google's valuation of Socbay "could be higher," the deal looked like a no go.

After a brief huddle with his two classmates in a hotel room in the Valley, Nguyen made up his mind. Consulting with IDG's savvy chief Nguyen, who was with him on the trip, the founder turned down the offer. "We said, 'Let's go our way and let Google wait a little bit and come back for a larger deal,'" remembers the young entrepreneur. "We don't think about selling the company now. Let the Google story go away and I develop my own company." They presumed the booming economy would help Socbay grow—this was pre-2008 financial crisis—and another bid at least double the valuation offer would come along. It hasn't.

IDG's Nguyen has a wistful look as he describes to me over lunch at the Refinery bistro in Saigon how this potential Google acquisition derailed four years ago. But he says he can't help but be proud for how the Vietnamese startup stood up to Google.

Naiscorp has continued to pass milestones from that very early stage. In early 2009, Naiscorp pulled in additional financing from Softbank China & India to supplement money from IDG. Revenue surged by more than 300 percent in 2010 and might have jumped higher except that a project to develop a travel portal with Vietnam's government failed to take off in the aftermath of the economic crisis. In 2011, the startup broke even with a 200 percent increase in revenues, relying on paid search and payments to download MP3 search, ringtones, and wallpapers.

Looking to the horizon, Nguyen is studying and learning from Google's experience in China, Russia, and Korea and getting a handle on why the search leader is not dominant in those markets. "What we find is that local, specific content and community is the key, that search is about culture," he says, speaking in fluent English. "Mobile is more personal, much smaller, and more entertaining than PCs and laptops, where Google succeeds. It's in mobile that vertical searches can grow and survive against Google."

Regardless of whether Socbay can continue to tough it out as an independent brand in this small but dynamic market without a potential suitor in sight, it's clear the founder has a lot going for him: gumption, creativity, and proprietary technology he's fine-tuned for Vietnam. Before I leave his office in Hanoi, Nguyen poses for a photograph with me and gently puts his arm around my back as the camera snaps. Later, he sends me an invitation to his wedding party in early 2011, and I wish I could have been there for the celebration. He continues to send me regular e-mails with significant updates about his startup's progress—outreach that is rare among Asia startups I've profiled.

eBay Bites into Local e-Commerce Site

As part of my initiation to Hanoi, I have lunch Vietnamese style at an open-air food court of stalls peddling everything from sticky rice wrapped in banana leaves to steaming pho to lemongrass chili chicken.

I'm dining with Nguyen Hoa Binh, 30, CEO of the eBay of Vietnam, a local consumer e-commerce site branded Peacesoft—a play on Binh's name, which means "peace" in Vietnamese. Peacesoft is not only the eBay of Vietnam, but it's the only one now partly owned by eBay, following an initial partnership in 2008. And it's the only one with a partnership with eBay's online payment service PayPal so buyers and sellers can handle cross-border transactions in multiple currencies through its Vietnamese-branded payment system, NganLuong.vn.

The strategic investment by eBay—one of the first by a tech multinational—is one more indication of Vietnam's still fledgling but growing tech prowess. After misfiring in China with a poorly managed acquisition six years ago, eBay's Asia Pacific general manager Jay Lee is primed to capitalize on this Southeast Asian country's quickly developing e-commerce market.[12] E-commerce in China has proven to be one of the more active sectors for public listings in the United States, and Vietnam stands a chance of having at least one or two breakouts either through acquisition or IPO.

As we wrapped up our outdoor lunch in late 2009, Peacesoft's founder Nguyen (is everyone named Nguyen in Vietnam?) is confiding to me that he is traveling the next day to Shanghai for a meeting with eBay and his venture firms about a possible investment deal. That was 15 months before the signing ceremony with eBay's Lee in Hanoi took place March 2011. Back then, Nguyen seemed pretty cool about the prospects, probably because his mind was on more important issues, like the fact that he had just become a father. His wife had given birth the day before to a son.

The eBay investment makes me recall first interviewing Bo Shao, CEO and founder of the eBay of China, Eachnet, at his Shanghai office in 2003. In 2002, eBay had invested in Shao's e-commerce startup—at $30 million for a 33 percent stake—and soon snapped up the remaining shares in 2003 for what was then a whopping sum of $150 million. Within three years of taking over Eachnet, eBay lost the e-commerce race to swifter-moving Alibaba and its rival Taobao site[13] through a series of management missteps, such as running the Chinese site from Cupertino and not Shanghai. Eachnet was absorbed into Chinese portal Tom Online in late 2006, a big disappointment for founder Shao.[14] That valuation—and hopefully the outcome—is in a totally different league from the $2 million eBay paid in 2011 for a 20 percent equity stake in Vietnam's Peacesoft.

Learning from the China experience, eBay is taking baby steps into the Vietnamese market. Its first foray was a cobranding partnership in 2008, then the small equity stake three years later, and perhaps next, if all goes well, an acquisition, Softbank venture investor Kabir Misra tells me.

As we're waiting for our lunch plates to arrive, Nguyen gives me a shortened version of his life story. He's a programming ace, like Socbay's founder. Since the 11th grade, Nguyen has had a dream of developing a big company. He, too, came to Hanoi from the countryside to study and to get some practical experience in information technology.

As a high school student, this son of a military journalist used his breakfast stipend to ride his bike to Hanoi and buy books to learn how to start writing software programs. Hooked, he enrolled in the College of Technology at Vietnam National University in 1999 and started working part-time at Vietnam's leading information technology business, FPT Corp.

His talents in science and technology were soon recognized, as Nguyen won several prizes on campus and at the national level for his research. By his second year of undergraduate studies in 2001, Nguyen had the bones of what would later become Peacesoft. Graduating in 2003, he became an exchange student at Nanyang Technological University in Singapore, was awarded a scholarship by the Japanese government, and went on to earn his master's degree from Osaka City University in 2007. Tired of commuting monthly between Osaka and Hanoi, Nguyen decided against going for a doctoral degree and jump-started his business from Vietnam with an IDG Ventures investment in 2007.

A year later, in 2008, Softbank followed, acquiring a 35 percent share for $2 million, leaving Peacesoft founders and managers with about a one-third share after eBay's chunk was factored in. The equity stake reserved for the hardworking founder and his management staff doesn't seem much, compared with other startups I've run across in China, where the entrepreneurs are wise about keeping a majority ownership interest.

But Nguyen is not complaining, and the eBay link has been a boost. Peacesoft has grown to 250 employees, and its registered users have escalated from 100,000 in 2007 to more than 500,000 by 2009 and by early 2011, to 1 million—the goal the founder had in mind years ago when he was dreaming of doing this e-commerce site.

It's been a long uphill climb for Peacesoft, since the concept of a consumer-to-consumer online marketplace has been so new to Vietnam. When Peacesoft was commercialized in 2007, shopping over the Web was unfamiliar, and no online payment system existed. Credit cards and bank transfers weren't common, so Peacesoft set up its own PayPal-like system for online payments. More recently, Peacesoft has upgraded, expanding to an affiliate ad network of web sites and blogs and a local online marketplace to connect buyers and sellers through social shopping sites—the biggest phenomenon to hit the Internet since Twitter arrived.

Keeping pace in the local marketplace while the industry evolves to social commerce hasn't been easy. Swift up-and-comers such as Vatgia are a threat, with its site styled after Japan's leading business-to-consumer e-commerce company, Rakuten—a contrast with Peacesoft's consumer-to-consumer buying and selling.

I met with Vatgia's founder, Nguyen Diep Noc, 33, at his Hanoi office outfitted with sleek folding chairs and tables. Most of his staff is from the countryside and have little formal education but a thirst for digital gadgets and services. They were taking off their slippers and getting ready to lie down for an early afternoon nap when I visited.

Nguyen told me he launched Vatgia in 2007 after graduating with a master's in economics from Kyoto University and working

Vatgia founder Nguyen Diep Noc in Hanoi

as a consultant for a Japanese investor in the import-export trade. When his initial idea for online trading between Japanese and Vietnamese buyers and sellers didn't catch on, he shifted focus to the fast-growing domestic market and was able to raise $1 million in late 2007 from—you guessed it—IDG Ventures.

By the second year, he says, his startup reached profitability. Today, he claims Vatgia is the leading e-commerce web site in Vietnam and points out that his online venture is the first Vietnamese web site to be ranked by Google in the top 1,000 sites worldwide for traffic. Like Peacesoft, Vatgia recently got some extra validation when, in early 2011, an unnamed lead investor injected $10 million in Vatgia. That's a major sum by Vietnam standards.

Reluctantly leaving behind my colonial-era room at the recently renovated and upgraded Metropole Hotel, where I've had the good fortune of staying, I take a two-hour flight on Vietnam Airlines to Ho Chi Minh City and arrive on a Saturday evening. On the drive in from the airport, I see a dynamic city aglow with activity. Neon lights shine from storefronts, and the warm night air has young couples doubled up on mopeds heading to the riverside for a late-night date. The city pace is faster here, and I have a good view of the nonstop action from my corner room at the Renaissance Saigon.

Here, I'm particularly interested to meet with Nguyen Thanh Van An, 39, the founder of online bookseller Vinabook.com, an Internet bookstore that is a clone of China's online bookseller Dangdang.com,[15] itself a version of Amazon. The Chinese e-book retailer was selling my first book, *Silicon Dragon*, so why not its Vietnamese equivalent?

In five years, Vinabook has expanded to 200,000 customers and 30,000 catalog titles, including books about Mark Zuckerberg and Warren Buffett. Following the lead of Dangdang and Amazon by aiming to become the market's leading online retailer, Vinabook is selling not just books but also software, movies, music, and calendars.

Like Dangdang during its early growing-pain days, well before it became a NYSE-traded company in late 2010, Vinabook has dealt with logistics and deliveries headaches. As with Dangdang, Vinabook delivers purchases by moped, and most customers pay by cash. Toward an aim of becoming Vietnam's leading e-commerce platform, Vinabook also has strayed into Groupon territory and developed its own daily discount site. Which site in Vietnam doesn't have a Groupon-like add-on to spur sales?

Vietnam's Tencent + Shanda

My last visit in Vietnam is at the startup best positioned to make a splash globally. Perched on four floors above a Big C supermarket on a corner jammed with mopeds, the Ho Chi Minh City headquarters of VNG is easy to miss. But inside, amid funky warehouse decor and lots of young staff leaning into big computer screens, is Vietnam's leader in online gaming and social networking services. VNG aims to be one of the first homegrown Internet successes in this tiger economy, a Vietnamese counterpart to China's Shanda and Tencent.

As I chat with CEO and Chairman Le Hong Minh in his quiet conference room away from the buzzing atmosphere of the game developer studios just outside, I immediately sense from his strong bearing and quiet confidence that he is worlds apart from the younger, scrappy entrepreneurs I've been meeting on this journey.

Born in Saigon, Le is the only Vietnamese entrepreneur I've met who has international professional experience at major companies outside his home country. His background includes a degree in finance from Australia's Monash University and an investment banking post at Vina Capital Group, plus work at PricewaterhouseCoopers.

That finance background should come in handy as Le seeks to realize his dream of an international listing for VNG within a few years. "The toughest challenge is to have the company financials audited, and to match the Vietnamese accounting standards with international standards," Le says.

With estimated 2010 revenues of $65 million and a 30 percent growth rate in 2011, VNG is capitalizing on Vietnam's rapid rise of digital communications. Le, 34, was an avid gamer himself until he started up VNG in 2004 with a few fellow gamers, some three years after he had returned to his homeland. Since forming VNG, Le has cut his playing time to one hour a day from previously almost half a work day.

A large player in a relatively small pond compared with China or Korea, VNG has a commanding 60 percent share of Vietnam's

VinaGamer at VNG in Ho Chi Minh City

fast-growing $120 million online games market. Its titles attract 3.5 million to 4 million gamers a month and are ubiquitous at Internet cafes nationwide. The most popular is a localized version of Swordsman Online, a game developed by China's Kingsoft Corp. and licensed by VNG that focuses on martial arts and old Chinese culture.

Nearly all of VNG's games have been licensed and adapted for the local market from Chinese and Korean gaming companies. It's a strategy that has helped to keep its operating costs low. But the goal is to develop more in-house designed games.

By introducing more games created within its own studios, VNG could avoid some misjudgments, such as a mistake made in introducing hard-core, martial arts features to Vietnam's less advanced gaming market. After three years of development work, VNG rolled out in 2010 a better-suited game drawn from Vietnamese history and culture. "Gaming is a content business. It has to do with current tastes in the market," says Le.

Following the lead of Tencent, China's popular service, VNG has moved into chat, music, and social networking. In 2007, VNG launched Zing MP3 for music and Zing Chat for instant messaging. The next year, as Zing fever caught on, VNG introduced Zing News, an entertainment news portal that within seven months of its launch was ranked by Web research service Alexa.com as the top web site in Vietnam.[16] Meanwhile, its social networking service ZingMe was rolled out in August 2009 to offer music, entertainment, news, e-mail, and instant messaging. ZingMe has caught on with 7 million active users.

As the startup has moved beyond online games to the social networking sphere for Vietnamese youth, the company name was changed in 2010 from VinaGame to VNG to represent the business pivot. VinaGame was initially being groomed as the Vietnamese equivalent of online gaming Shanda, and now it's becoming Shanda plus Tencent—thanks to IDG's insights into how the China Internet market evolved. That's a good example of the China Internet trend spreading throughout the Asian tech frontier. "Our code name for VinaGame used to be mini-Shanda, but now it's mini-Shanda plus Tencent," says IDG's venture investor Nguyen at IDG.

Is it any surprise that VNG and Tencent share IDG Ventures as an early backer? IDG invested $500,000 in VNG in early 2006, when investor Nguyen was looking for projects for the new fund to invest in and met Le through a friend. With IDG's venture teams often comparing notes about deals and trends from one market to the next, it was a simple step for Nguyen to spot an opportunity to bring online games and instant-messaging business models from other Asian markets to Vietnam.

It was also a way to help VNG diversify and move away from juggling the highs and lows of the gaming business revenues by adding stabler lines of business in social media, online music, news, and entertainment. "The online game business is not unlike the movie business," says Nguyen. "Certain shows or games are big hits, and in between you can have jagged business. You can't just rely on a big hit."

He and his partners are looking to repeat IDG's winning performance in China, with Tencent delivering the highest investment return among dozens of its Chinese deals. IDG Ventures China invested $2 million for a 20 percent stake in Tencent in the late 1990s and made $300 million on the deal after the Shenzhen startup went public on the Hong Kong Stock Exchange in 2004.

Tencent became a minority investor in VNG, following a partnership deal in 2007 with Tencent to bring its QQ chat and casual games to VNG. Tellingly, Tencent's former mergers and acquisitions director Johnny Shen joined VNG in 2008 as chief financial officer and executive vice president of strategy and development. Also brought in as investor is prestigious investment banking firm Goldman Sachs, where, it so happens, IDG's Nguyen once worked as an associate in equity research.

VNG is the market leader in Vietnam, partly due to its home field advantage but also because of an international perspective. VNG has borrowed from the profitable gaming experience of China's Shanda. VNG became cash flow positive soon after its launch largely by relying on a prepaid card for playing games at

Internet cafes. The startup is highly profitable and hasn't needed to raise additional financing to invest in expansion. "It's almost like bragging, but at the beginning it was kind of like printing money," beams IDG's Nguyen, 38.

The well-connected Nguyen helped to mold VNG from the start. Shortly after meeting Le through a friend, he teamed him with Bryan Pelz—that serial entrepreneur from Los Angeles—who had moved to Ho Chi Minh City eight years ago and was working with IDG on building businesses. Pelz signed on as a co-founder and advisor to VNG and remains on its board. "Bryan is the big picture, higher-level strategic partner with strong international experience, and Minh is the day-to-day manager with strategic execution," observes Nguyen. "They are very complementary."

Le takes pride in the company culture he has created as CEO at VNG. He prefers to share the spotlight with his inner circle of six managers. Le had to be nudged to pose solo for a photograph.[17]

In a sign of his financial savvy, Le has adopted the Silicon Valley stock ownership model and granted shares to 150 key managers among his 1,400-plus employees. All employees have 15 days of vacation, health insurance, and free, catered lunches. They party together, too, and there have been at least 10 weddings among staffers. Every year on the day of the company's anniversary, the team celebrates with a camping trip, complete with bonfires and dancing. "We go crazy for one night," says Le.

One constant concern for social media startups such as VNG in Communist-controlled Vietnam is political criticism on the Web. Social media such as Facebook are sometimes blocked—as I discovered during my visit of Vietnam. Some games in Vietnam have been taken down, mostly because of violent content. In its early days, when online games were new to Vietnam, VNG faced being shut down by the Department of Information and Communications two or three times, according to Le. But it has remained unscathed.

"There is quite a lot of ambiguity about what's acceptable and what's not. It's a different job with every company, to figure out how to manage content and if it meets community standards—is it a violation or contradiction to explicit or implicit laws or unwritten community standards? The gray area is the hard part," says investor Nguyen.

The tech entrepreneurial spirit I see in Vietnam reminds me of the supercharged scene I've witnessed in China over the past decade. Many of the same forces—a young, switched-on population, a dedicated group of venture capital investors eager to fund enterprising startups, and a fast-expanding marketplace newly opened to commerce—provide a good base.

And while the scale of this tech surge underway today can't compare to the supersize statistics of China or the rise of India, the memory of Vietnam as a war-torn nation is quickly fading, and in its place is a new digital communications revolution.

PART II

Road Map to Hot Sectors

A detailed portrait of entrepreneurs at 25 leading-edge startups shows how they are perfecting tactics to cash in on Asia's booming market sectors, one progressive step at a time. The setting is the Asian tech centers of China, India, Taiwan, Singapore, and Vietnam. The characters are the local and expatriate founders, plus the scores of investors from North America, Europe, and Asia who seek to capitalize on these startups' growing riches and horizons.

These chapters start with an exploration of three of the hottest market sectors in Asia. Chapter 4 is mobile—of course, it's Asia, home to the world's two leading cell phone centers. Chapter 5 is cleantech, maybe a surprise, but it's happening here just like in Silicon Valley. Chapter 6 is one you might not expect: consumer. Chapter 7 winds up with a look at Chinese startups' strengthening hold in outsourcing.

Profiles and case studies of startups in social networking, currently the hottest area for entrepreneurship and venture investing, are interwoven in the Part One chapters on China, India, and Vietnam, largely because Twitter, Facebook, Google+, and their Asian counterparts are so integral to these markets.

The entrepreneurs who are profiled in Parts Two and Three were not just lucky. They were not just in the right age group, 30s and early 40s, when careers are typically made or broken.

All are smart, for sure, some with classier university degrees than others. Many have serial startups, too, to their credit. A few have managerial experience at multinational companies. Many are returnees and a growing number are locals. What all do have in common is an ability to "think different," that phrase made famous by Apple's Steve Jobs. Each and every one is creative, imaginative, and independent-minded; personality traits that can't be taught in a classroom or gained even through years of professional experience.

Altogether, these case studies and principles for success provide a road map for navigating Asia's unique and diversified sectors in the world's fastest-growing region and the globe's largest mobile and Internet markets.

CHAPTER 4

Catch the Mobile Boom

From Vietnam's fast-scaling game startup **VinaGame** to mobile search **JustDial** in India to China's mobile advertising winner **Madhouse** to India's own rising star **inMobi**, mobile is where it's at. **Google** angel investor **Ram Shriram**, **Kleiner Perkins** dealmaker **Ajit Nazre**, and **BlackBerry** maker Research in Motion have all made bets on mobile startups in Asia. As the Internet moves from the personal computer to the mobile phone, entrepreneurs are scaling their startups quickly as the mobile communications market surges in the region and they find and focus on the right business model to emerge profitably. Two of the mobile players profiled here— inMobi and JustDial—are benefiting from a surge in mobile advertising and look likely to go public before the end of 2011.

In northern Mumbai, close by the film studios of Bollywood, I drop in on entrepreneur V.S.S. Mani, the founder and CEO of JustDial. His startup has none of the glitz of its starlit neighbors. JustDial is a new-fangled yellow pages, offering free 411 calls to operators to find local business services, quickly receive a text or e-mail with five options, and get connected to the service at no cost.

His innovative startup bridges mobile search with traditional call centers, and it's a new twist on outsourcing as well, using low-cost Indian workers. The service has become a popular way to get easy answers and recommendations within 60 seconds. Customers call 1-800-Just-Dial, eliminating the need to search the Web or thumb through yellow page directories of tiny print listings to find restaurants, florists, plumbers, and pharmacies. Mani, who is a

JustDial founder V.S.S. Mani in Mumbai

natural salesman, says JustDial is a "100 percent toll-free service that is like having your own personal Yellow Pages, Free Directory Assistance, and Concierge Service. And, there's never any tipping."

In India, some 500,000 customers use the service daily, amounting to 180 million search queries in the most recent year. JustDial launched in the United States in May 2010 with a full-page color ad in the *New York Times* and a Facebook page, then followed up a year later with a national campaign on CNN. "We want to make JustDial into the world's number one search service," says Mani, who started the service during the depths of the dotcom bust in 2002. "Our ultimate goal is to launch in all English-speaking countries."

Mobile is the hottest market going for any budding tech entrepreneur. As multitask iPhones, BlackBerrys, and Android smart phones become more common, mobile communications and entertainment have caught on.[1] In many of Asia's emerging markets such as India, consumers have skipped an entire decade by buying handsets without ever first owning a personal computer and gone directly to the mobile Internet. Throughout Asia tech capitals, the mobile Internet is the default option to book travel, trade stocks, send messages, share photos, or play games.

Asian startups are springing up to capitalize on this mobile phenomenon, and in each country, the message is the same. Pick the right segment, get the timing and team right, and then ride the mobile boom, hopefully with enough financial support to tap the ever-growing market.

Clued-in venture investors have been quick on the uptake. Venture investment in mobile services nearly tripled to $6.1 billion globally in 2010—a significant chunk of the $38 billion venture market worldwide.[2] (See Table 4.1.)

Mobile businesses for e-commerce, payment, gaming, search, and advertising have sprouted. India's fast-growth mobile advertising service inMobi has emerged as the world's second-largest network, right behind Google-owned AdMop. In India, Apalya streams video on mobile handsets, 3DSoc builds interactive 3-D for mobile phones, PayMate links mobile to payments, Bubble Motion has launched voice blogging, and at least three startups—Kreeda Games, Nazarra Technologies, and Games2Win—have developed smart phone games. In Vietnam, Sobay offers mobile search, while VinaPay is providing electronic payments via mobile. In China, Borqs has developed a mobile operating platform that can work across multiple operators and handsets, 99Bill facilitates mobile payment, Pingco offers mobile chat rooms, and Papaya Mobile serves up social networking and games by mobile.

Sales of mobile communication devices are skyrocketing—up nearly 32 percent to 1.6 billion worldwide in 2010, or a quarter of the earth's population. Smart phones are the must-have gadget, and sales jumped 72 percent in 2010 to account for 19 percent of total mobile devices sold globally by Nokia, Research in Motion, Apple, Samsung, and Motorola.[3] By 2014, the global smart phones market will more than double to $150.3 billion from $69.8 billion in 2010.[4] Asia is the smart phone hotspot, predicted to top $45 billion by 2014. The drivers are 3G high-speed service, build-out of large cellular networks, and an influx of more mobile subscribers in China and India.

Table 4.1   Venture Investment in Mobile Services Globally

	2010	2009
Investment amount	$6.1B	$2.1B
Number of deals	416	269

Source: Rutberg & Co.

The mobile applications market is booming in lockstep. Worldwide revenues for apps will hit $15.1 billion in 2011—up threefold from $5.2 billion in 2010—and will reach for the sky at $58 billion by 2014.[5] The most popular mobile applications are search, commerce, video, e-mail, instant messaging, payment, social networking, and location-based services.[6]

As more ultrafast networks launch and consumers upgrade their wireless handsets, mobile is increasingly favored over traditional media. Watching videos and checking stock prices on tiny mobile screens isn't for everyone. But research shows U.S. adults spend 50 minutes per day on mobile devices. That's far more time than spent reading newspapers and magazines.[7]

Mobile advertising could become mainstream soon, too, from the current sliver. The growth figures are mind-boggling. By 2016, mobile ad campaigns are predicted to be almost three times larger than the current $2.7 billion expenditure.[8] Meanwhile, paid-search ads on handsets are becoming common, accounting for nearly 17 percent of worldwide mobile ad spending.[9] Tellingly, India and China will make up nearly a third of the $24.1 billion mobile advertising market worldwide by 2015.[10]

I see this mobile surge trend in action at JustDial, as I walk down the hallway with founder Mani past cubicles of office workers answering calls on their headsets and speed-typing into their PCs. Mani, who always seems to be in a hurry, is rapidly explaining how this search service works.

I try out JustDial once I'm back in the United States, ringing an operator and asking for a Chinese restaurant in San Mateo. Fielding my call is a heavily accented Indian male worker, who requested my city, state, and search category. He politely and promptly responded with a result, China Bee. Asking me if I want to be connected, he put my call through to the restaurant without charge. I confirm with the receptionist that the info is correct and find out it's located on B Street. Before I try out the restaurant, I'll be sure to take a look at the customer testimonials that are sent along by text message with each request. I guess I could have gotten about the same info online, but the key to this service is its speed and convenience, easily accessible anywhere—plus it's free to use.

Interestingly, JustDial's business model is based on paid search, the same concept that got Google out of the gate. Advertisers bid

to buy premium listings so their shops or services are given pref-
erence in the search results and answers. Loads of small-business
advertisers have signed up, and the service is gaining in popularity. JustDial has 5.4 million listings in India—up from 4 million in
2010—and 14 million listings in the United States.

The opportunity of the future for JustDial is obviously the
United States and not India. Mani estimates business search in
the United States to be $78 billion—150 times larger than his home
country's stake—although India's small-business ad market is growing by 7 to 8 percent per year.

As JustDial reaches beyond India, the startup is beating its
financial projections. For 2011, revenues are reaching $42 mil-
lion, up from $33 million the prior year. After-tax profits are run-
ning at $7.5 million, according to Mani. He sees no reason that
JustDial can't reach its target of $100 million in revenues in 2012
and remain profitable.

JustDial filed for a $79 million IPO in August 2011. Mani has
been jumping up and down to get an IPO in India before the end
of 2011, after several delays. Poised to profit are his venture firms
that have invested a total of $52.5 million for 55 percent of the
company. SAIF put in $15 million in 2006, followed by $20 million by New York hedge fund Tiger Global in 2007, $10 million by
Sequoia Capital India in 2009, and finally, $7.5 million from SAP
Ventures and Sequoia in mid-2011. SAIF partner Ravi Adusumalli
told me he's expecting to realize more than 20 times on his firm's
investment in the Indian mobile search startup.

Growing up in Calcutta in a middle-class family, Mani trained
as an accountant but forfeited a numbers-counting career for a bigger salary in sales. He worked two years as a sales director at a Tata
Yellow Pages firm. In fact, that's where he conceived the idea of
starting a search company that would give individuals an option to
access information by simply dialing a number.

In 1989, he started his own business, named AskMe, a precur-
sor to JustDial. Far ahead of its time, AskMe bombed after just two
years. Back then, the Internet and search engines didn't exist, and
AskMe operators relied on an in-house database that could be
searched by keywords. Very few Indians had a phone at home. "We
would apply for phone lines from the government and it could
take years to get a phone connection," recalls Mani. "We were way
too early with this business."

After that fumble, Mani did odd jobs in printing and publishing for a few years until he saved up enough money to try again with better timing. Easy access to landline phones came to India in 1996 with telecom liberalization. That gave Mani his entrée. He moved to Mumbai from Delhi, rented a 300-square-foot garage, and set up an office with rental furniture. Boostrapping it, he went door to door, collecting information on local businesses and collating the data.

But as luck would have it, by 1999–2000, the dotcom bubble burst. The odds for AskMe's survival looked slim. "I panicked a bit," says Mani, downplaying it.

The future seemed brighter once his business adviser, PricewaterhouseCoopers, hooked him up with successful Indian tech entrepreneur and executive Raj Koneru, the founder of entertainment portal IndiaInfo.com. Mani sold some shares in his startup for cash to Koneru, and the two companies merged. "I needed the cash for survival, and in the back of my mind, I didn't think it would work out. There was not much connectivity in India. It was a great time to cash out," says Mani, who pocketed about $2 million from the deal.

Mani spent the next 18 months on what he calls a spiritual sabbatical before he jumped back into the entrepreneurial pool to try his luck with JustDial in 2002. This time, he figured he had better timing.

He took advantage of the slowdown in the tech and telecom industries with the Internet bust and the 9/11 terrorist attack aftershocks, spending about a year fine-tuning the software for his new venture.

He seems to have the timing right this time to get rich. When he launched the business back in 2002, the Indian phone market

---

STRATEGY: JustDial

- Combine an old-fashioned business model with new technology, and leverage strengths of the home market—in this case, low-cost outsourcing.
- Timing is everything. Don't be too early or too late, but try to synch your service with the readiness of the local market.
- Come up with a name and description of the business that's easy to understand.

was landlines. Now more than two-thirds of the market is wireless, and smart phones are beginning to take off as third-generation phone service has arrived.

Ever the dreamer and the optimist, Mani sums up his company's positioning as "one-call solution for anything."

Another fast-moving Indian mobile startup I met with is advertising network inMobi. Founded in Bangalore by Harvard Business School graduate and ex-McKinsey consultant Naveen Tewari in 2007, inMobi has leaped swiftly from India to Southeast Asia and Africa and on to Europe, Japan, and the United States.

inMobi's exceptionally fast growth has put it in second place, right behind Google-owned mobile ad network AdMop. Headquarters for inMobi is a contemporary corporate park in a central business district of Bangalore. The energy in its tech-trendy open office space reminds me a lot of dotcom-era Silicon Valley.

What inMobi's technology does is help advertisers reach targeted consumers over mobile Internet sites run on hundreds of different handset models. It also measures the results of ad campaigns by tracking the clicks. As an example, Yamaha advertised a sporty, mid-size motorcycle to young men by placing mobile banner ads that clicked through to a commercial. Wallpapers of the bike on the road or the showroom could also be downloaded, and potential purchasers could exchange reviews of the bike. The highly effective banner ads were clicked by nearly 10 percent of viewers, and 7 percent of that group searched for the nearest store.

The supercharged mobile ad network space is loaded with global competitors. Google and Apple both entered the market, buying mobile ad businesses in 2010 to take advantage of consumers' increasing use of mobile devices to buy products and services. Google bought Admob for $750 million; Apple paid in excess of $200 million to buy Quattro Wireless. In the United States, Google ended 2010 with a 59 percent share of the mobile advertising market, while Apple grabbed less than 10 percent.[11] It's a sizable and fast-growing market to fight over. The Google-popularized Android mobile segment in the United States will top $1.3 billion by 2012.[12]

While Google and Apple are engaged in a turf war over advertising on the iPhone, iPad, and smart phones, inMobi is making inroads. In mid-2010, inMobi launched a promotion reaching out to Apple *and* Android mobile application developers. Within a few months, nearly one-fourth of inMobi's ads globally were displaying on these smartphones.[13]

Meanwhile, inMobi is working hard right in its own back yard of India, which is, according to the founder, now the largest mobile ad market in Asia. In India, inMobi overloads millions of Indian consumers with as many as 5.8 billion ads monthly.[14]

Like JustDial, what is truly significant about inMobi is how it has radiated out from India. In the third-world markets where inMobi has penetrated, the mobile net can reach people who can't read or write. Points out Ajit Nazre of Kleiner Perkins, a lead investor in inMobi: "A mobile device is the first thing that they want, not a personal computer or television."

Today, inMobi has more than 95 percent of revenues coming from outside India, with business across more than 140 countries and India as one of the top 15 geographies, points out Tewari, 33, a returnee to India. (See Chapter 12.)

That global perspective could come in handy if and when inMobi goes public, which looks likely in the third quarter of 2011. His investor, Kleiner Perkins partner Nazre, is upfront about the likelihood of a public listing on NASDAQ. He points out that inMobi can go public outside India since the company has an off-shore base in the Cayman Islands.[15] But Tewari deflects the possibility, hedging the timing and location. "An IPO is not planned anytime soon. We do not believe in going public unless we reach a specific scale in our business," he says.

The self-assured and polished Tewari benefits from an elite career and educational background, but at the same time, he has not been scared off by some harrowing bootstrap experiences. He graduated with a mechanical engineering degree from the Indian Institute of Technology Kanpur in 2000, then worked as a business analyst for McKinsey in Mumbai, where he had the opportunity to see Indian business magnate Mukesh Ambani in action as he launched Reliance Infocomm in 2002 and ushered in a digital revolution in India with a high-speed information technology network for homes and businesses.

Later, from 2003 to 2005 as an MBA student at Harvard, he did a stint in Boston with Charles River Ventures. To quench his thirst for entrepreneurship, following his MBA, Tewari spent a year in Silicon Valley working in small teams without pay and seeing if a business plan could be built on his colleagues' ideas. When those ventures didn't work out, Tewari went on vacation to India for one month and started to work on his own business plan. He never went back to the United States.

During his break, he became intrigued by the proliferation of mobile and came up with the idea of an SMS-based mobile search engine. Soon, he had teamed up with two former classmates: Abhay Singhal, now head of global ad sales, and Amit Gupta, who is inMobi's VP of business development. When a friend introduced Tewari to angel investors Sasha Mirchandani and Prashant Choksey in mid-2006, he and his co-founder got a chance to pitch an illustrious group of business executives who had formed an angel investor group, later known as the Mumbai Angels. The meeting went well, and the co-founders secured $500,000 to develop their brainchild. Working from bistros, an empty apartment in Mumbai, and office space in Bangalore, the team got their enterprise running by early 2007.

In the typically ups and downs of a startup's life cycle, the first approach did not fare well. A few months into the new venture, the team found there wasn't much demand for SMS mobile search in a place where people were used to trading information easily with one another at seemingly every street corner. "We didn't see how we could add a lot of value. We didn't have a lot of IP, and it didn't look like a long-term sustainable play," says Tewari.

The team began to focus on a fresh idea: a mobile advertising network. Out of money from the first failed business, Tewari and six developers in Bangalore worked for several months with no pay to develop the next product and take it to market. By mid-2008, the founding team had 12 credit cards maxed out, and everyone was worried about the venture's future. A stressed-out Tewari was dealing with a newborn baby at home and negotiating with venture investors over valuations to back his startup.

Then, the team got their lucky break. In April 2008, inMobi nabbed $7 million in funding from two savvy investors: Nazre of Kleiner Perkins and technology industry insider Ram Shriram through his global investing firm, Sherpalo Ventures. He got invaluable guidance as both joined the board. Shriram is well known for being one of the first investors in Google and a key exec in building online bookseller Amazon and Internet browser Netscape. Kleiner partner Nazre is a former top exec with leading business management software firm SAP.

A second stage of the build-out began after this initial funding, as the company faced the challenge of staffing up. Tewari decided to relocate the startup to Bangalore, where a pool of the best engineering talent in the country could be tapped. By the end of 2008, he had hired 50 people in four offices and, by early 2010, expanded the staff to 120 employees, 80 percent of them engineers and a significant number of them returnees to India. "We invested very heavily in our technology and hired the best engineers we could find at Google, Yahoo!, and MSN to be a part of the team," says Tewari.

Granting stock options to the entire team was another inducement to keep everyone united, spirited, and moving forward. Within months of raising the $7 million in venture financing in 2008, inMobi expanded to neighboring Southeast Asia countries, then ventured farther to South Africa and Kenya by 2009. In a remarkably swift time period, by mid-2009, inMobi turned profitable.

Thinking and acting globally, in 2009 Tewari smartly rebranded his startup. Its original brand name mKhoj signifies search in Hindi but is hard to pronounce in most Western markets. He launched the service in Europe in August 2009. The turning point was 2010. At the beginning of the year, a third of the ad network's revenues were coming from the United Kingdom and nearly half from Indonesia, Malaysia, and Thailand.

Angling into major developed markets, inMobi soft-launched in the United States in January 2010 and then rolled out nationwide in the United States by midyear, in synch with a Japan market entry. That same year, in July 2010, his two prior venture investors put $8 million more in inMobi, affirmation of the emerging company's progress. "InMobi has cracked the code on how to go international," says investor Nazre.

The backdrop to inMobi's latest flurry of new business is the U.S. mobile ad market,[16] pegged to more than double over the next three years to $2.5 billion by 2014[17] from a small percentage of current online ad spending.[18]

With all the forces aligned, inMobi celebrated an achievement perhaps Tewari hadn't imagined—in 2011, inMobi staked a claim as the world's largest independent mobile ad network. The network reached 194 million consumers worldwide, and the number of ads viewed soared fivefold over 2010 to 31.5 billion monthly.

Time to hire! The mobile ad network notched up to 230 staffers—most of them techies—with 55 employees working in offices in San Mateo, Tokyo, London, Nairobi, and Singapore. Former managers from Google joined the team in executive positions, most recently Isis Nyong'o as a VP and managing director in Africa and Atul Satija as VP and managing director for the Asia Pacific region.

Why inMobi isn't in China: Madhouse

About the only place inMobi isn't yet is China, and there's a reason. China is home to its own fast-growing mobile ad network Madhouse, founded in 2006 by Taiwanese native Joshua Maa, 43, and well-funded with approximately $20 million by Gobi Partners, TDF Capital, JAFCO, D2C Communications Docomo, and Nokia Growth Partners.

Previously the executive vice president responsible for the build-out of wireless services for Chinese Internet portal Tom Online and the founding CEO of mobile music entertainment service Rock Mobile, Maa brings more than 14 years of operational experience at leading companies in Greater

Madhouse founder Joshua Maa in Shanghai

China. He's built the Shanghai-based Madhouse to more than $10 million in revenues to become China's largest mobile ad network, with such big-time advertisers as KFC and Pepsi on its site, as well as local brands including China Unicom. Its CEO Maa says the Madhouse mobile ad network reaches more than 70 percent of the more than 300 million mobile Internet users in China. The startup is close to reaching profitability.

In my interview with Maa in Shanghai, he talked about his international ambitions. He already took Madhouse to Taiwan, and he's eyeing the large India and Asia Pacific mobile industry as the next frontier for expansion. "The mobile net will become one of the most important marketing platforms in the world," says Maa. "It will soon be bigger in China and India than the personal computer net because the mobile Internet is anytime, anywhere with Chinese consumers."

5

Get In on the Cleantech Boom

From electric cars, electronic waste-recycling facilities, and solar-powered lights in India to light-emitting diodes in Taiwan and China, cleantech startups in Asia with novel solutions are bubbling up to tackle the region's huge environmental issues. None other than swaggering **Tim Draper**—the investor who recognized the appeal of **Hotmail** and **Skype**—has put money into India's electric vehicle maker Reva to push it in the fast lane. He's also behind d.Light Design's solar-power lanterns to power third-world villages, and so is Silicon Valley star **Guy Kawasaki**. China's GSR Ventures is making a big bet on LatticePower and its advanced lightbulb for residences worldwide. **John Doerr** of cleantech investor titan Kleiner Perkins is backing an Indian solar equipment startup in India. Even Shanghai boutique hotel URBN is using green energy as a promotion to drum up business—well after the Expo.

I'm in a taxi heading to Attero Recycling, a cleantech startup in India funded by all-star financiers Tim Draper and Dick Kramlich and even the International Finance Corp. As we near the office in this gritty area of Delhi's Noida district, I see a cow meandering along our bumpy dirt pathway—heck, no surprise. Last time I was in Delhi, I saw an elephant ambling lazily on a city street.

Inside the bare-bones office of Attero, the contrast to this rough and tumble terrain couldn't be more striking. Here, CEO Nitin Gupta, 34, is somewhat impatiently taking time to describe to me his high-tech, novel mission to solve India's biggest and fastest-growing environmental problem: illegal dumping of computers, cell phones, and TV sets. His operation runs an e-waste recycling

Founder Nittin Gupta of Attero Recycling in Delhi

plant that extracts gold, silver, and platinum from electronics products for spot sales on the London and Indian metal exchanges. Seems rather intriguing!

It has the elements of success. The market is huge and expanding rapidly, the pain points are obvious, and Attero is here to make those aches go away with unique insights, clarity of purpose, and a groundbreaking sustainable business. Each year, 6 million cell phones, 8 million personal computers, and 80 million TV sets are dumped in India, Gupta says. E-waste equals about the same volume as plastic packaging—turning landfills into mountain ranges—but illegal dumping of such toxic substances as lead and mercury is much more hazardous. Much of e-waste recycling in this third-world country happens illegally, through operations that dip motherboards into poisonous cyanide to allow gold and all those other precious metals to float to the surface.

Worldwide, e-waste recycling is a $7 billion market, and it's growing by 21 percent annually.[1] Umicore in Brussels and Noranda Recyling in Canada are the kings in this business, but no one has claimed the throne yet in India. This is a market that isn't going to quit soon. Consumers are upgrading electronic products every day and discarding the old products without a second thought. E-waste is mounting and mounting, ballooning 500 percent over the next decade.[2]

Here to help fix the problem is Attero (which means "waste" in Latin), India's only integrated and automated e-waste recycling plant. It can process 36,000 tons of waste annually—that's a lot of e-trash. Attero makes it easy for customers. Call a toll-free number to request a pickup of disposed electronics goods. Then, Attero has garbage trucks collect the waste from premises in 20 cities and truck it to be processed at a state-of-the-art plant in Roorkee on the banks of the River Ganges.

The monstrous Roorkee facility covers two and a half acres. It has multiple patents pending for an internally developed metallurgical treatment process that turns up high heat to extract 12 valuable metals from electronic goods and safely gets rid of toxic waste. "It's a complex job. We're the only company in India with technology to extract metals from electronics waste," says Gupta. He explains the unique tech-intensive business model in a matter-of-fact way. "Some 1,000 kilograms of cell phones have an output metal value of $15,000. We get these metals out with 99 percent purity. Then we sell them on a commodity basis. That is the way we make money."

Gupta got the idea for Attero when he returned to his homeland in 2007 and was appalled by the environmental problems he saw. When he and his younger brother Rohan couldn't find a way to get rid of an old laptop, it was venture promise land—big problem, big market opportunity. Why not come up with an entrepreneurial solution?

Burning Gold

The Gupta brothers had enough training and experience to pull it off. Nittin is an electrical engineering graduate from the Indian Institute of Technology Delhi in 2000 and an MBA grad of New York University in 2006, with a London Business School exchange program. He worked as an engineer for two years at two U.S. computer software startups—Ishoni Networks and Ittiam Systems—and then was a vice president at Los Angeles–based technology incubator Lotus Interworks for four years before returning to Delhi in 2007. His younger brother Rohan, a chemical engineer by training, had tried his hand at entrepreneurship as the founder of online movie rental company Cinesprite and also had worked for two large companies in India, Infosys and SAP. Inspired by the example of their father, who had his own consulting business in the oil and gas industry, the entrepreneurial brothers set out to try something entirely new and established Attero in October 2007.

Nittin used his MBA smarts to put together a compelling business presentation and sent out e-mails to venture investors highlighting prospects for the enterprise. After getting turned down by two venture firms that were skeptical of the odds for success at a startup in an industry new to India, they eventually scored. In May 2008, Attero raised $6.3 million from Draper Fisher Jurvetson India and NEA-IndoUS Ventures.

With the investment, Attero gained two well-respected venture capitalists as board members: managing director Mohanjit Jolly of DFJ India and managing director Kumar Shiralagi of NEA-IndoUS. The understated Shiralagi, whom I met with during this trip, is the former Intel Capital head in India and doesn't exactly advertise that he has a PhD and 23 U.S. patents to his credit. "These are incredible guys to be on the board. They understood the risk of early stage venture," says Gupta, as we're eating the delicious Indian meal his wife has prepared. He brings in lunch every day from home since there are no nearby restaurants.

Shiralagi recalls when the two brothers showed up at his office with an Excel spreadsheet to outline the business model for their unique startup. "It's a core market and completely new," says the investor at NEA-IndoUS, a partner with Dick Kramlich's leading Silicon Valley–based venture firm NEA, which has done 23 deals in India.

"It's one of the rising stars in our India portfolio," echoes Jolly at DFJ India, which has three other cleantech deals in a broad Indian mix of 20 tech investments.

Getting the financing proved to be easier than the next steps: securing the licenses and clearances from the Indian government to set up, building the team, and finding a location for the plant. "We did extensive planning but everything was delayed. Not a single thing happened on time," tells Gupta. Attero eventually settled in Roorkee, 200 kilometers north of Delhi, a place close by his parents' hometown. There, Attero got a 10-year income tax break from the state government for his new $5 million plant. The facility relied on the local Indian Institute of Technology for access to equipment and leaned on PhD students to do research for making the recycling process more efficient.

Attero's recycling plant was finally inaugurated in January 2010 by former President of India Dr. A. P. J. Abdul Kalam. Since then, the milestones have piled up. Attero roped in $1 million in revenues in 2009, and Nittin was projecting $12 million revenues in 2010 and $50 million by 2013. Attero's clients include such large multinational companies as Visa, PerotSystems, KPMG,

Nokia Siemens Networks, and LG and numerous Indian corporations. Given the capital expenditures required, Attero is not profitable—yet.

In mid-2010, Attero dipped into the venture coffers again, raising $3 million from well-connected Granite Hill Capital Partners and its India Opportunities Fund, plus the startup's prior investors. Then, in early 2011, Attero gained credibility by drawing $5 million from the International Finance Corporation, part of the World Bank. An additional credit came as Attero picked up a prominent industry leader as an independent board member: Kiran Karnik, former president of India's influential tech association NASSCOM and current chairman of the outsourcing service provider Satyam Computer Services.

Attero is earmarking the money for strengthening the collection system and expanding recycling capacity. A key part of its agenda is raising awareness of safe disposal of e-waste. All in all, this young business is making important strides in recycling technologies that can help India transition to a green economy.

STRATEGY: Attero Recycling

- Tap into provincial government subsidies and local universities to reduce costs and strengthen the R&D base.
- Think big and bold. Develop a startup based on a huge and sustainable market need and opportunity.
- Don't forget that your own family can provide valuable managerial support and even help you start the business as a co-founder.

Cleantech emerged on the scene as a major investment trend with a nudge from former U.S. Vice President Al Gore and his 2006 documentary, *An Inconvenient Truth*. Cleantech investment globally shot up like a rocket, to $7.7 billion in 2010, a 28 percent rise over 2009.[3] North America took the lion's share at $4.9 billion.[4] Asia's share was tiny at $771 million, with China making up two-thirds of the amount, and India trailing.[5] (See Table 5.1.)

Cleantech ventures take years to produce investment returns, but financial results are accumulating. The year 2010 set a record for green IPOs globally, as 93 companies raised a total of $16.3 billion.[6] China accounted for 68 percent of the public offerings and 61 percent of the amount, plus racked up 8 of the top 10 largest

Table 5.1   Cleantech Investments Globally

	2007	2008	2009	2010
Global	6.55 billion	8.76 billion	6.09 billion	7.77 billion
N. America	4.15 billion	6.27 billion	3.65 billion	5.28 billion
Asia	609 million	620 million	655 million	771 million
China	386 million	479 million		
India	186 million	181 million		

Source: Cleantech Group.

cleantech IPOs in 2010. At the top of the list was China Goldwind, a wind turbine manufacturer that raised $917 million on a public offering on the Shenzhen Stock Exchange.

The impact of all those green dollars could be enormous. China and India are struggling with environmental issues and are often cited as the worst polluters in the world. Where's there a problem, count on entrepreneurs and venture investors to look for a solution. Entrepreneurs from Taipei to Delhi to Beijing are busily pumping up businesses to get rid of pollution and reduce greenhouse gas emissions. Several of the venture firms most active in this space in the United States—Kleiner Perkins, Draper Fisher Jurvetson, and Khosla Ventures—are also investing in Asian cleantech startups, from solar, wind, and biofuels to electric vehicles and the smart grid (Table 5.2).

Startups that monitor and improve energy use for telecom and utilities are understandably getting a lot of venture attention. In China, Prudent Energy Inc. was backed in 2010 with more than $22 million from a who's who list including Northern Light Venture Capital, Sequoia Capital China, DT Capital, and Draper Fisher Jurvetson. In India, its counterpart, ConnectM Technology Solutions, is a spin-off from Sasken Communications Technology and jointly funded with $6 million from IDG Ventures India in 2007.

Another focal point is energy-saving light-emitting diodes. These LEDs could replace conventional lights for streets, office buildings, and computer screens. Shipments of LED lights are forecast to triple to 166 billion by 2013 from 63 billion in 2009.[7] GSR

Table 5.2   Cleantech Investors in Asia

GSR Ventures

Keytone Ventures

Northern Light Venture Capital

Kleiner Perkins Caufield & Byers

Draper Fisher Jurvetson

Asia Vest Partners

Khosla Ventures

DT Capital

Sequoia Capital China

WI Harper

Source: Silicon Asia.

Ventures alone has made six investments in Mainland China LED makers. WI Harper has inked three LED deals in Taiwan: Testar Electronics Corp., NeoPac Lighting Group, and SemiLEDs.

Of the WI Harper deals, the one with the most interesting spin is SemiLEDs, which is based in Taiwan's Silicon Valley, Hsinchu Science Park, the home to mega semiconductor maker TSMC. The small company went public on NASDAQ in late 2010 and raised $89 million with its IPO. That's quite a long stretch from a start in 2005 in Taipei.

I first met the founder of SemiLEDs, Vietnamese native Trung Doan, on a trip to Taiwan in 2009. During a quick break, he related not only his own interesting international background and his growing number of patents but also the story of his firm's link to Boise, Idaho. Doan told me he immigrated to the United States in 1975 from Vietnam to earn an engineering degree from the University of California–Santa Barbara, worked at a series of tech firms in the United States and Europe, and eventually settled in Boise, working at Micron as a vice president. Micron got its start thanks to funds from J. R. Simplot of Idaho potato fame, and so did SemiLEDs.

Doan told me he chose the Dragon tech island as his company's base because of the goodies that were offered: no tax for the first five years and great high-tech infrastructure at Hsinchu. WI Harper's chairman Peter Liu put $7.5 million in SemiLEDs

SemiLEDs founder Trung Doan in Taipei

in 2007, following $10 million from the Simplot family. The innovative SemiLEDs has more than 60 patents to churn out chips based on copper for making long-lasting, bright, and energy-efficient bulbs sold mostly in Asia.

While its share prices have slid since the IPO due to disappointing financial results, it's hard to argue with its balance sheet for fiscal year 2010: a 209 percent revenue increase to $35.8 million and net income of $10.8 million. SemiLEDs has two plants in Taiwan and is ramping up operations in mainland China, leveraging a Greater China strategy and presumably lower costs. The six-year-old startup aims to triple its production from a new $350 million production facility in Foshan.

From Nanchang in Mainland China, an LED maker that is making its mark is LatticePower Corp.,[8] founded by Professor Fengyi Jiang, a physicist, in 2006. The venture investor behind it, Sonny Wu of GSR Ventures, is championing this breakthough tech innovator. He sent me an invitation to a signing ceremony with government officials at Beijing's China World Hotel in December 2010 to announce that the four-year-old startup had picked up a $55 million investment led by the International Finance Corp. That's on top of $45 million raised earlier by GSR Ventures, plus high-powered firms including the Mayfield Fund, Keytone Ventures, and AsiaVest Partners. The money for LatticePower will go toward building a new manufacturing facility to nearly double output of low-cost and well-performing solid-state lightbulbs and fulfill its mushrooming orders. I tried one of the company's lightbulbs at my writer's studio in California. It was bright but burned out faster than a standard GE bulb.

Delightful Solar Journey

About an hour's drive from Attero's recycling offices in central Delhi, I meet with yet another LED-related startup that's making headway thanks to funding from Tim Draper's venture firm DFJ and Guy Kawasaki's Garage Technology Ventures. Cranked up by Stanford University MBA grad Sam Goldman, 32, d.Light Design produces and sells low-cost solar-powered LED lanterns. Goldman tells me he got the inspiration to design these innovative lanterns after spending four years as a Peace Corps volunteer in a West African village where there were no roads, phones, or electricity. Kerosene lanterns were used but were dangerous, and Goldman's neighbor was severely burned when a kerosene lantern was knocked over. "I got really interested in what role business could play with social objectives," says Goldman.

On a social entrepreneurship mission, Goldman and his startup team designed safer and cleaner-operating lights priced at a bargain $10 to $45. Meeting at his office, Goldman shows me the nifty

Founder Sam Goldman of d.Light Design in Delhi

lanterns. There's a model that can be used as a spotlight for hikers, and another one has a feature for charging a mobile phone.

The market potential is huge. Goldman quotes World Bank figures that about 1.6 billion people worldwide are off the grid. Another 1 billion have intermittent access. That's one in three people globally, he figures. It's a short hop in logic to conclude that Goldman could reach his goal of selling at least 4 million lights and reaching 20 million people by 2015. The goal for 2011 is 5 million.

Goldman's entrepreneurial journey started in a Stanford business class where he, classmate Ned Tozun, and three engineers—Xianyi Wu, Gabriel Risk, and Erica Estrada—began tinkering with a design for a solar lantern. In classic Silicon Valley fashion, they worked nights and weekends and over summer vacation to build a prototype in a Mountain View garage. Then, once the business plan was finished, bingo! In 2007, the year he graduated from Stanford, Goldman and his team managed to win $250,000 in a business school competition for startups organized by leading Valley venture firm Draper Fisher Jurvetson.

By 2008, the co-founders formed their startup and secured $6 million in funding from superstars Tim Draper and Guy Kawasaki, in addition to Nexus Venture Partners, The Mahindra Group, and two social venture groups, Acumen and Gray Matter Capital. Partner Tozun soon had manufacturing set up in Shenzhen while Goldman, a world traveler who has lived in Pakistan, Peru, and India, established sales and marketing in the Noida section of central Delhi, a place Goldman knew well from high school.

In the first year of operation, some 100,000 lanterns were sold throughout poor villages in India and East Africa, bringing in nearly $3 million in revenues. The lights provide socioeconomic benefits, from helping moms work on handicrafts at night to earn income, to getting kids to study after sunset, Goldman tells me. "They got our products on an installment plan and were able to double their income by doing things like making banana leaf plates. They wanted to save up for a second light," says Goldman, whose manner and looks could just as well fit in on Wall Street.

By 2010, sales soared to 500,000, and revenues climbed to approximately $12.5 million. Goldman was eyeing two to three times that sales volume for 2011 and angling for profitability within a few years. In June 2010, he scored a coup by bringing in $5.5 million from his prior investors and Omidyar Network, the social fund run by eBay founder Pierre Omidyar.

By 2011, d.Light Design lanterns were being distributed in more than 40 countries, up from 28 in 2009. They're sold through local retail shops in rural areas, by entrepreneurs on commission, and by some microfinance channels. In the United States and the United Kingdom, the lanterns can be bought on Amazon.

In March 2011, Goldman stepped aside as CEO of the 60-employee company and turned the CEO reins over to his mentor, Donn Tice, a seasoned tech executive who had been chairman of the board since 2010. Goldman became chief customer officer, a position that brings him back to fieldwork. He enjoys seeing how the lights are being used and suggesting refinements, leaving Tice to take on the day-to-day responsibility of ramping up the business.

STRATEGY: d.Light Design

- Enter startup competitions to secure seed finance to get your project off the ground.
- Scale to the next level by bringing in professional management, and don't be afraid to step aside.
- Get out of the CEO chair and do fieldwork to find new consumer product uses.

While I'm on this cleantech tour in India, I figure I should check out a deal that Kleiner Perkins, the lead cleantech investor in the United States, has made here. It's Kotak Urja, an offshoot of Indian conglomerate Kotak Group, and Kleiner has funded it with $8 million, in concert with Sherpalo Ventures and Applied Materials. Here, on the outskirts of Bangalore in an industrial area of low-rise factory buildings, Kotak Urja churns out solar-powered gadgets to light up streets and gardens, heat swimming pools, and provide drinking water. Then CEO Srinivas Kumar,[9] a career engineer in Indian solar power companies and mechanical engineering graduate from India's National Institute of Technology, proudly showed me around the operation. We started with the sample showcase, toured the plant where the solar panels were being made, and wound up on the rooftop, where we saw the sun powering water pumps and heaters, streetlights, torches, and other industrial solar applications.

To demonstrate how this equipment can be put to good use, Kotak Urja recently installed a solar plant and electrified an entire village of Sikandapur in India's poor northern state of Bihar. For just five cents per day, 120 families in a remote northeastern spot have access to electric light and drinking water for the first time and enough juice to run a community-shared mobile phone, plasma TV, and an Internet connection to the world. The next step is to work with the United Nations Environment Program and take this pilot project to 80,000 villages that are not on the grid in India. All this sounds worthy of Kleiner's time and attention, even if it doesn't generate a lot of financial returns.

Revved Up Reva

Saving the most exciting clean technology startup for last during my green earth tech tour of India, I meet Chetan Miani, the founder of India's affordable, pint-sized electric car Reva.

A lot's happened with Reva since I first met Miani in February 2010. Indian conglomerate Mahindra & Mahindra snapped up a

Reva founder Chetan Miani in Bangalore

controlling 55.5 percent interest in Reva in May 2010. Subsequently, in 2011, General Motors dropped a plan to use its 200 dealers in India to sell a GM-branded eSpark car powered by Reva. Reva faces global competition from General Motor's recently launched $40,000-priced Chevy Volt. By 2020, maybe even 15 percent of all cars will be electric in this sizzling market.[10]

A tour of the Bangalore operation with the founder of Reva proved instructive—and was fun. Here at Reva, a 20-minute drive from the world headquarters of outsourcing giant Infosys, Miani, 42, showed me the electric-powered roadster that Reva was coming out with in 2012. Not wasting a public relations moment, Miani enthusiastically led me through the features of the stylish two-door hatchback Reva NXR car: a top speed of 130 kilometers, a range of 200 kilometers, an optional solar panel that can add eight kilometers of driving distance, a choice of 2,000 colors, and automatic transmission. As his tall, thin frame swerved around to catch my reaction, he smiled as he next told me about a clever, high-tech gadget add-on for Reva. It's a REVvie telematics system. Drivers who spot their car batteries running low can send a text message to a Reva customer support center and, within seconds, get access to a remaining backup charge to make it home or to their nearest destination.

While at Reva, I also had the chance to tour the new solar-powered plant not far from the business office. The Indian electric car maker was set to produce 30,000 of these vehicles here and sell them in Europe, Latin America, and Japan. The ambitious business plan looked for revenues in the $500 million range within a few years, up from $10 million in 2009.

A solar technology enthusiast who is passionate about his work, Miani sports a master's in engineering from Stanford University and an undergrad degree from the University of Michigan. It was at Ann Arbor where his breakthrough work on battery-powered vehicles began and flourished during the mid-1990s. Miani returned to his native India in 1999 to commercialize prototypes for stronger-powered and affordable electric hybrids. That year, he test-drove 40 cars over 1 million kilometers. In 2001, Miani launched India's first electric car in his hometown of Bangalore as a joint venture with the family-owned Miani Group.

By the end of 2006, his work caught the attention of Draper Fisher Jurvetson and the Global Environment Fund. They charged up Reva with an initial $20 million into further developing its patented technology, and later, with other smaller investors, ponied up $55 million. Mohanjit Jolly of DFJ India and Jeffrey Leonard, CEO and co-founder of the environmental fund, joined the board. "We have a strong space in the electric vehicle market because we started earlier. We had patents in the late 1990s, when we had early mover advantage," says Miani, who could afford more than his own well-used Reva parked nearby.

Not everything went according to plan. The operation never turned a profit, and only 3,500 of its two-seater models were sold, priced at $7,000 in India and an average $12,000 in the United Kingdom. Miani didn't make his goal of selling 1 million Reva cars. Dubbed the Nano of electric cars in reference to the $2,000 Tata Nano car sold in India, Reva's appeal was among well-paid professionals as well as adventuresome types looking for a second car. "We cater to 1 percent of the market, primarily in developed markets," says Miani, who speaks in a soft, diplomatic manner. "The requirements in India are different. The distances are smaller, the speeds are lower, and people are not willing to pay a premium for driving green."

The deal Reva has now made with Mahindra has several benefits and some drawbacks. Dealerships for the renamed Mahindra Reva have been increased to 25 from just Bangalore and Delhi before, and the blueprint calls for expanding to 75 distributorships by the end of 2011. On the downside, a plan to produce the cars in an upstate New York plant with Bannon Automotive has been delayed by a lawsuit. The suit, brought by Bannon in December 2010, accuses Mahindra of breach of contract for plans to launch the vehicle on its own or through a third party.

STRATEGY: Reva

- Develop patented technologies and reap the benefits of first-mover advantage before the market gets crowded.
- Partner with a big multinational with enough presence in the local market to boost distribution.
- If you're a technologist, stay true to your original mission and let others deal with the business hassles so you can focus on what you do best.

On the plus side, the deal with Mahindra frees up Miani from business hassles. A lifelong tinkerer, Miani has raced solar cars across Australia and from Michigan to Florida. Now he can focus his energy where he wants: research and development on the street and in the garage—and perhaps make electric cars go in the fast lane cross-country.

Admiring the sporty-looking cars parked outside Reva's headquarters, I kiddingly asked Miani why anyone would want a city car other than Reva. He answered, laughing, "Good question. Let the consumers decide."

If Reva ever gets to the United States, the cars are so neatly designed and affordable that I'd consider buying one for short hops to the grocery store or train station.

Ride the Consumer Wave

Online retailer **Redbaby**, rental car service **eHi**, and Indian fast-food franchise **KaatiZone**, founded by a former dotcom investor, are capitalizing on emerging Asia's consumer boom with western-styled business concepts tweaked to appeal to local tastes. Sequoia Capital, the venture firm that made Oracle, Cisco, and Yahoo!, is profiting in China and India with investments by savvy Neil Shen and Sumir Chadha in everything from a shoe retailer to an organic vegetable grower to the Siddhartha family's **Café Coffee Day**—the Starbucks of India. Asia's new consumerism is on display at crowded Ikea and Apple stores in Beijing and the Element Fresh cafes in Shanghai. Shopping for T-shirts to iPhones to cars is becoming a lifestyle. Enter the entrepreneurs who are seizing the moment to gain market leadership with consumer products.

In Beijing, on a late May day already sweltering with heat, I head out toward the northeast, reaching almost as far as the Summer Palace before I'm dropped off by my taxi driver at a corporate park with a row of buildings that all look the same. Here's where Redbaby is headquartered. Despite its innocuous surroundings, Redbaby is the talked-about consumer play in the e-commerce space because of its efficiencies, innovative approach, and huge potential. I find the founder and CEO of Redbaby, Xu Peixin, to be pretty impressive, too—though his chain-smoking throughout our interview was difficult to take.

Say Redbaby to well-informed venture investors in China and the United States, and their eyes light up. NEA venture leader Dick

Kramlich sparkles when Redbaby is mentioned. Investors Feng Deng of Northern Light Venture Capital and Joe Zhou of Keytone Ventures get pretty enthusiastic, too. They've all signed on as investors in Redbaby, to the tune of $35 million for a collective 60 percent stake in the startup. Deng and Zhou are on the Redbaby board, and Xiaodong Jiang from NEA's Shanghai office is as well. The plan? Take Redbaby public in the United States.

Both the entrepreneur—a 40-year-old former real estate investor from Beijing—and his business have them revved up. In just six years since its start in 2004, Redbaby has climbed to $230 million in revenues and reached profitability on an operational level. Most profits are being poured back into upgrading information technology and expanding supply warehouses and distribution.

Business-to-consumer e-commerce is a huge growth area in China that has been pioneered by such startups as Amazon look-alike Dangdang. Redbaby's strategy follows the same direction that Dangdang took of expanding from selling books online to marketing all kinds of merchandise. Like the name suggests, Redbaby is China's biggest online retailer for diapers, strollers, and pacifiers. But it's a bit of a misnomer. Redbaby also peddles cosmetics, housewares, food, and health supplements. That gives this retailer an advantage over would-be rivals whose expansion has been constrained by narrow specialization in fast-growth China.

A second prop is that Redbaby sells goods and wares directly to consumers, by catalog and over the Internet—again, a strategy similar to Dangdang. Redbaby started out selling through printed catalogs and only later transitioned to online sales. Off-line sales gave Redbaby a head start in developing internal systems to handle logistics, distribution, and customer service. The company's streamlined distribution cuts down the number of intermediaries to two or three from the typical five to seven channels to reach consumers.

"Today's Internet companies in China don't have the back office operations but Redbaby is an exception," says venture investor Deng, who led the first financing of Redbaby in 2005. "They are very strong in execution and logistics because they have this backbone. You really need two strengths—the Internet and the back office operation—instead of pure Internet."

The entrepreneurship wave in Asia's emerging markets began with Internet startups but has caught hold now in consumer fields, too. Everything from fast-food chains and coffee outlets to Chinese hotel brands to e-commerce retailers are positioned for China's new discretionary spending consumers. This is no surprise to those who have seen the crowds at Ikea, Starbucks, McDonald's, or Apple stores in Shanghai and Beijing or observed city malls on a weekend afternoon in Singapore, Hong Kong, or China's top-tier cities, glowing with neon lights and loaded with young families and couples window-shopping or filling their shopping bags with purchases.

Emerging Asia's high-growth consumer businesses cover a wide range of fields. There's fast-growing eHi's vehicle rental business based in traffic-jammed Shanghai and founded by returnee Ray Zhang. There's the Starbucks-like coffee chain in India, Café Coffee Day, started by wealthy businessman V. G. Siddhartha. Then there's a fast-food Indian restaurant group, KaatiZone, founded by former venture investor turned entrepreneur Kiran Nadkarni. All are backed with venture capital, and all are scaling up like there's no tomorrow.

The rise of a middle income class in Asia's boomtowns is the backdrop to this shop-till-you drop phenomenon we know all too well in the West. Both China and India are rapidly urbanizing with

Founder Ray Zhang of eHi Auto Services in Shanghai

households that have spending power for necessities but also entertainment, convenience, and even luxury goods. By 2025, China will add 400 million to its urban population, accounting for 64 percent of its total, while India will gain 215 million, bringing the percentage of city dwellers up to 38 percent.[1] More significantly, the number of urban households with discretionary spending power in these emerging nations is climbing rapidly. By 2025, China will more than quadruple this tally to nearly 280 million, compared with a sevenfold increase for India to 89 million.

That means a consumer class in these populous nations that's larger than the total population of the United States. It's no wonder that China and India startups plus their venture investors are seizing this opportunity. Not that long ago, say 2005—a lifetime in China's private enterprise history—Chinese shops were poorly lit places with merchandise almost hidden in counter displays. It's still mostly mom-and-pop shops along the side streets of urban Shanghai, Beijing, and Hangzhou, but colorful franchises are starting to appear. The same goes for India.

It doesn't take a lot of brainpower to determine what might be a winning concept to draw shoppers. Again, it's as easy as looking to the West, figuring out what works, copying it, and tweaking a few items in the local mix of merchandise. The potential of this wide-open and fast-growing consumer market in China is why Sequoia Capital China leader Neil Shen has funded dozens of consumer-oriented startups, from hotel brands to sportswear makers to organic vegetable farms.

Sure, it requires more capital to put bricks and mortar into building a business rather than expanding an online venture run virtually by software. But several are already producing big-time results for entrepreneurs and, soon, their investors.

Venture investors talk about the importance of team over business model in building successful startups. At Redbaby, they may have found a maestro in Xu Peixin, the startup's hardscrabble, homegrown Chinese CEO and founder. Meeting with Xu in late spring 2010, I go through a series of questions, from rudimentary business 101 to more personal questions about his background and influences. Throughout, he's direct, blunt, and opinionated.

Where's the biggest opportunity and challenge for Redbaby? I ask. Without a blink, he's back with an answer. The huge market in China and the need to overcome inefficiencies in a fragmented retail model with varying regional rules and competitors. That's the only way Redbaby can build a nationwide business.

What's the next milestone? Xu pauses for a microsecond before answering in his deep, gruff voice, "To be the top 10 retailer in China. Right now, we are among the top 100."

Why get into e-commerce now? "Within three years, it will be chaos. All the original factories, suppliers, warehouses, and traditional retailers will be trying to get into e-commerce," he says, estimating that e-retailing will comprise 3 percent of the consumer market by 2014, up from about 1 percent currently.

How about distribution? Xu says Redbaby reaches 700 million people in China with distribution in 35 major cities and its own sales team. Franchise partners help the retailer cover 60 more cities. It's definitely not Walmart. Many goods are delivered by motorbikes, and payment is cash on delivery.

Online-off-line sales mix? Right now, about 40 percent of sales are made online, but in five years, he sees that percentage growing to 90 percent and catalog sales becoming a small subsector. With a new megaround of financing that came in late June 2011, he plans to soon develop a three-dimensional, online shopping experience.

Biggest surprise? He answers the startup's very fast growth and correlating challenges in training employees quickly enough to keep pace. To fill the gap, Redbaby set up its own management school, which has rotated in 300 of 2,000 staffers for training sessions. Shares in the company are granted as incentives to continue improving quality, with all top managers and 10 percent of the blue-collar workers, such as delivery teams, receiving an ownership stake in the company. "A lot of times they become satisfied with what we have achieved. We have a spirit of improvement every day," Xu says.

Is going public in the cards? That's not the ultimate goal, he replies. "Our goal is to be the number one business-to-consumer e-commerce site in China and the top 10 retailer in China. We want to change the retail market landscape, but there are a few factors to consider. First, we want to lay the infrastructure. Before going public, we want to see a strong increase in profitability."

If there's one disappointment, he admits that he wishes Redbaby could have been ready for an IPO sooner, to build the business more quickly and not face limitations in scale. "We could have been a legend by now if we had done an IPO in 2007 or 2008," he says.

I should point out that Xu and I are conversing through an interpreter, the very capable business development manager Rebecca Qiu from Northern Light Venture Capital, who has volunteered to help out. As she interprets, I learn that Xu majored in marketing at Tianjin Commerce University, then after a successful career as a real estate investor, became a producer of a TV drama series for China's national television network, CCTV. Xu says he was brought up in Beijing by his grandfather, a successful businessman before the Communist Revolution. From his grandfather, he says he learned business, ethics, responsibility, and the courage to dream big. The strong-minded CEO begs off more questions about his upbringing, urging me to focus instead on his vision in shaping the company into a market leader by improved efficiencies and infrastructure.

"The opportunity in China is very obvious, and we will have continuing GDP growth for 30 years. The economic and political window is getting more and more open," he adds, "and that brings more and more opportunities."

We finish up with Xu offering his advice for up-and-coming entrepreneurs. "Dream big. It's not enough to have perseverance; you have to stick to your dream. To build a business, it's not always about profitability. It's about contributing to the efficiency of society, to making a structural change to a business to help society. It's a combination of dream and responsibility."

STRATEGY: Redbaby

- Build a base first in off-line sales with procedures for orders and distribution, then use those strong fundamentals to ramp up online business efficiently.
- Stress continual improvement by setting up an in-house training center for employees to learn the basics and take refresher courses, then reward staff with corporate shares.
- Perseverance is not enough. It also takes keeping the vision and the big dream, guts, and willpower.

A Smooth Ride in Shanghai

Turning next to Shanghai, I meet with Ray Zhang, the serious-minded entrepreneur behind a service that's booming in China's heavily trafficked cities. Zhang made it easy to meet him. He had a chauffeur-driven car pick me up at the Sheraton hotel in the Pudong district where I'd been staying and then drop me off at his office—all of which makes perfect sense. Zhang runs Shanghai-based startup eHi Auto Services and he wanted me to experience the ride in the fleet that he manages. The courteous driver, who knew some English, took me over the new bridge spanning the Huangpu River and straight on the overpass past People's Square to Zhang's high-rise office. Though no doubt the driver was briefed, I was impressed by the quality of the service, which included having the door opened for me.

Zhang's all-in-one Hertz rental, Carey limousine service, and Zipcar-like car-sharing business is in the right place at the right time. Zhang saw the opportunity to jump into China's burgeoning car market soon after returning with his young family to Shanghai in 2002 after being away for 17 years. Cars were only beginning to replace bicycles then, but already everyone wanted to learn how to drive.

A classic returnee, he had technology smarts from computer science studies at Shanghai's Fudan University and California State University. He also had entrepreneurial experience from 1990 to 2002 as the founder of Aleph, Inc., a Silicon Valley–based software startup for logistics management—the same company that powers dispatching of corporate black cars in New York City. Plus, he had that altruistic outlook—the extra chromosome common among the most sophisticated returnees I've met. "I really wanted to come back and do something for my country," says Zhang, as we met in his office. "In my 20s and 30s, I learned the Western technologies, culture, and value system. Down inside, I am still Chinese. I was born in Shanghai, and I wanted to do something at the macro and the personal level for this country."

Zhang set off on a journey to combine his thirst for entrepreneurship, smarts in business, and technology know-how. The year after he graduated in 2005 with an executive MBA from the well-regarded China European International Business School (CEIBS) in Shanghai, he formed eHi. "I like being in control of things instead of being controlled," says Zhang, 47, who has an intense electricity about him. "I like to create more value with my ideas and innovations while I also like to execute." He adds, "Running a car rental service like this demands precise execution and information technology innovations, which fits my personality very well."

The son of a schoolteacher and scholar on Sino-U.S. relations at the Hoover Institute on the campus of Stanford University, business didn't seem to be a natural path for Zhang. But then how many opportunities come along to be in the driver's seat looking out over a wide-open terrain in the world's fastest-growing economy? "Auto-related services are relatively new in China, and we are still at the tip of the iceberg. This is a service that is needed very badly. Not everyone can afford a car like in the U.S.," he says, pointing out there were more cars sold in China last year than in the United States. He notes that if every family owned a car in China, it would destroy the environment and lead to a dependence on oil imports. "If there are 300 million to 400 million cars on the road in China, it would be a disaster. My mission is to make sure we don't make the same mistake that some other developed markets did," says the president and CEO of eHi.

His timing for the world's largest auto market couldn't be much better. As a way to reduce traffic, both Beijing and Shanghai have introduced lotteries and auctions to apply for a license to buy a car. The licenses can cost as much as $7,000. At the same time, a shortage of parking spaces in China's crowded cities, low labor costs, and the prestige of being driven around in a chauffeured car all have contributed to the growth of car rental services. Every venture capitalist I know in Shanghai and Beijing and many leading entrepreneurs enjoy the luxury of a chauffeur-driven vehicle. It's a stress saver, for sure.

When Zhang founded eHi in 2006, he didn't have to wait long for the venture capitalists to arrive. In May 2008, he raised $5 million from Chinese venture firm Qiming Venture Partners and its U.S. affiliate, Seattle-based Ignition Partners. Then in July 2009, Zhang collected $19 million from prominent China investor CDH plus JAFCO Asia and his two prior investors. "Ray is an impressive entrepreneur with a budding star in eHi car rental," says Hans Tung, a managing director with Qiming. "It's potentially the category leader for the foreseeable future."

With CDH in tow as an investor, Zhang has a connection he probably wouldn't have with an international fund. CDH owns a chunk of auto manufacturer Chery Automobile Co., so it's a no-brainer: Zhang is expanding his fleet with locally made, lower-priced city cars, as well as adding late-model stylish cars.

Gearing up for the next stage, in 2010 eHi picked up a whopper of a financing deal. Goldman Sachs led a $70 million investment as the next step toward a probable IPO soon. The investment bankers have been trying to knock on his door—Goldman Sachs, Deutsche Bank, Barclays Capital, JP Morgan—eager to take eHi public on NASDAQ or the NYSE. "This is a capital-intensive business, and every year, we are fund-raising," Zhang relates. "We wanted to do one last pre-IPO round and that's it. We will save it for the rainy days in case the market is not in our favor, in case of a double or triple dip."

Who's to argue with close to 200 percent compounded annual growth over the past four years, from 2006 through 2010? Comparable to U.S. rentals, eHi charges an average rental rate of $30 per day, and vehicles can be booked online, by phone, or by e-mail. The business had been operating profitably since 2007, but fast expansion has eaten into profits. The company posted gross revenue of $26 million in 2010 and $9.7 million in the first quarter of 2011. Revenue for 2011 could likely double the 2010 figure, given how fast the fleet is expanding.

The auto service market in China is highly competitive. Primary rivals for eHi are local state-owned enterprises—hardly sleek marketers like Hertz or Avis. The first to introduce car sharing and a hybrid electric vehicle to its fleet, eHi currently claims market leadership of the car rental franchise business, with a network of 216 service locations covering 45 cities and 4,400 vehicles.[2] Additionally, eHi counts nearly half of the Fortune Global 500 companies in China as corporate clients and a high-powered list of financial firms including Deutsche Bank and Morgan Stanley.

Now that Zhang has accelerated into the fast lane, what's his advice for newcomers? "Make sure you understand a market and industry well and be fully prepared before starting," he says. Zhang also cautions would-be Chinese entrepreneurs to watch out for me-too rivals. "There is no shame to be a copycat in China."

STRATEGY: eHi Auto Services

- Leverage core software technology that worked in one field and carry it over to the next business. No need to reinvent the wheel each time.
- Tap a market with an unmet need that can be ramped up against not so savvy rivals.
- Go for leadership by raising significant sums, execute on the plan, and anticipate change with innovations.

Certainly Zhang has little chance of becoming bored in one of China's most dynamic sectors. "I like the uncertainties, the challenges, the unknowns," he says. "I would feel very bored if I already knew where and who I will become 30 years from now."

India: Fast-Food Nation?

On a busy street corner in Bangalore, I get a tour of Café Coffee Day, India's Starbucks, courtesy of founder V. G. Siddhartha, an aristocratic gentleman who grew up on his family's vast coffee plantation in south India. Born into wealth, that automatically gives him some edge in Indian business, but Siddhartha still has that entrepreneurial drive.

We've just come downstairs by private elevator to his flagship coffee shop from his plush office on the top floor of this building. As Siddhartha is discreetly pointing out the cafe's highlights, not too many people seem to notice he's here, although his distinguished bearing might give him away. In the retail shop are cheery-looking red and white matching cups and saucers, and contemporary furniture spaced at a comfortable distance. There's also a broad selection of coffee beans grown on his family's own plantations, neatly eliminating intermediaries and keeping costs lower than Starbucks' premium. You could easily spend an afternoon here, sipping coffee and surfing the Net on Wi-Fi connections.

It's amazing that Siddhartha has popularized Café Coffee Day, an upscale version of Starbucks, in third-world India. Now that Starbucks is entering India through a partnership with Indian conglomerate Tata, Siddhartha could face some tough competition, judging by Starbucks' success in China.

Siddhartha set up his first coffee shops in 1996. It wasn't until 10 years afterwards that he looked outside his organization to raise financing from a venture firm. Sequoia Capital India invested $20 million in Café Coffee Day, and $200 million in funding four years later came from storied New York–based private equity firm Kohlberg Kravis Roberts,[3] no stranger to India.

Café Coffee Day shops number more than 800 in India and are ubiquitous in the better areas of Bangalore and other India cities. International expansion is next on the horizon. With the new capital infusion, Siddhartha, 50, has his sights set on expanding abroad beyond the shops' initial outreach in Vienna, Prague, and Karachi to as many as 10 markets overseas. "I want to make India proud by making Café Coffee Day into one of the top three coffee brands internationally," he tells me, with no trace of doubt.

His success at popularizing coffee in what has traditionally been a tea-drinking nation and his flair for business are springboards for diversification. His parent company, Amalgamated Bean Coffee Trading Co., has expanded into real estate development, financial securities branches, tech investing, and even hospitality with its own hotels.

This is far from the typical path of most tech entrepreneurs. So is the story of former venture capitalist Kiran Nadkarni and his Indian fast-food chain KaatiZone, a first for India. I met with Nadkarni in Bangalore at one of his restaurants. As we sampled Kaati Rolls, Indian bread wrapped around mixed vegetables, cheese, chicken tikka, and other tasty fillings, Nadkarni told me how his career had taken a big turn. It turns out that he used to be a venture capitalist during the dotcom era, before getting the entrepreneurial bug himself and coming up with this idea to bring a restaurant franchise concept from the West to his homeland.

Nadkarni returned to the happening scene and mild climate of Bangalore in 2005 from the San Francisco Bay area. He used to be a partner at Draper International, investing in both India and the United States, and he was also a co-founder of JumpStartup, one of the earliest cross-border investment firms in India. Knowing

KaatiZone founder Kiran Nadkarni in Bangalore

STRATEGY: KaatiZone

- Tap an unexplored retail niche, and tailor the products to local tastes.
- Make your brand seem larger than it is by reaching out to the community with local events that generate word-of-mouth promotion.
- Consider franchising operations as a way to expand, rather than costly owned operations.

---

something about venture capital, Nadkarni, 59, was able to attract $1 million in finance from Draper as well as Accel Partners to get started with his shops. Today, they number 15, with a base in Bangalore and additional locations in Mumbai, Chennai, and Hyderabad.

Thanks to launching a franchise operation, KaatiZone outlets also are popping up quickly in the southern and western regions of the country. Nadkarni says his goal is to have 50 kiosk-size stores in high-traffic areas nationwide by the end of 2011. The kiosks are based on a modular plug-and-play format that can be set up in just three to four weeks, he adds.

Scaling up to the next level is his goal, and he's recently completed a second round of financing with a goal of building out 100 stores in two years' time. With few fast-food chains in India, it appears he stands a chance of claiming some space in this virgin territory. "I believe we are a pioneering player in the quick service restaurant business," he says.

In the Silicon Valley fashion of the dotcom era, KaatiZone's founder played host to a gathering of techie enthusiasts in Bangalore, including the well-connected Indus Khaitan of Morpheus Venture Partners. We enjoyed a relaxed evening of networking here while consuming lots of those yummy sandwiches. It was the kind of event that used to happen back in the late 1990s at the dotcom hangout Buck's Restaurant in Woodside, California. I suggested to Nadkarni that he should think of expanding to the San Francisco Bay area. I think his restaurant concept—which combines McDonald's-type décor and service with tasty Indian fast food—could work well in the Valley, but first he needs to conquer the India market.

Now that's the reverse of the way ideas usually travel cross border! So long, West to East? Hello, East to West?

CHAPTER 7

Create a Niche in a Proven Sector: Outsourcing

Outsourcing powerhouses Wipro and Infosys supercharged India's economy. Now a league of startups is making a run to claim title to this fast-growth market by offering specialized services and their own call centers and R&D labs to corporate customers nearby and abroad. **Sumir Chadha** previously with **Sequoia Capital India**, **Peter Hsieh** of **AsiaVest**, and **Lip-Bu Tan** of **Walden International** were in early on this trend and put tens of millions of capital into startups that powered up to become publicly listed firms, such as **MindTree** in India and a host of Chinese outsourcing firms, including **Neusoft**, **VanceInfo**, and **iSoftStone**. While India outsourcing offers natural advantages, this new group of well-equipped and amply funded China contenders is edging onto the turf of their Asian neighbor by tackling the technical jobs they do best.

In northeastern China's grim industrial city of Shenyang—enlivened by bright, colorful, LED-lit streets and buildings—I meet with Liu Jiren, the CEO of Neusoft Corp. He's the founder of China's largest outsourcing company, which in 2010 topped $710 million revenues with 18,000 employees and 15,000 corporate customers, pint-size compared with India's powerhouses but a symbol of China's progress in gaining a foothold in outsourcing. To give an idea of Neusoft's incredible growth—even by emerging market standards—in 2009, the company had $540 million revenues, 15,000 employees, and 8,000 corporate customers.

Neusoft's corporate campuses are at Disney World proportions and signal the ambition of its CEO and founder. I travel from

Neusoft headquarters in Shenyang by car to its regional campus in Dalian, supposedly the San Francisco of China. The journey takes a half day but it's a comfortable ride, zooming along a superhighway empty except for a few trucks speeding by. We stop at a newly built, sparkling-clean roadside rest that tops any along the Pennsylvania Turnpike—the only thing missing is McDonald's and Sbarro. Reaching Dalian, the site of China's own World Economic Forum each summer, we drive up to a regional campus that looks castlelike high over seaside Dalian. The landscaped acres filled with training institutes, design centers, and R&D hubs would be a landmark anywhere, even along the corporate strip of Route 1 south heading to Princeton, New Jersey. Neusoft's operations are mammoth, with six software research and development bases, in addition to a marketing and service network in 40 cities across China.

Neusoft grew fast by concentrating on customers from China's own homegrown businesses and nearby Japanese corporations. It's a contrast from India's outsourcing giants that focused on serving corporate clients in the Western world. The majority of Neusoft's

Founder Liu Jiren of Neusoft in Shenyang

business today comes from China and Japan, with an enviable client list of Toshiba, Sony, Motorola, Philips, Symantec, and a host of smaller Chinese firms.

Even as Neusoft's stature grows, Liu expects the home market will continue to be dominant for several years. Currently, international operations account for 30 percent of its total corporate revenues. "We think China will be our great opportunity for the next 20 years," say the charismatic chairman and CEO Liu, who is 56 years of age. He speaks English well and has raised his own profile by appearing at annual gatherings of the elite World Economic Forum in Davos. "We hope to be five times bigger than today. But this is not just a dream. It is a reality. We are ready for this level of expansion," says Liu, with his broad smile.

Neusoft has come a long way since its humble beginnings at Northeastern University in Shenyang, where Liu studied computer science, earned his PhD in 1987, and became a professor. The campus is where Liu, with two young teachers, set up a research lab for computer software and network engineering that was the seed for Neusoft. Their resources were limited, just $4,000, three computers, and—Liu recalls—a broken table and a stinky toilet in a corner of the room.

Liu's vision was expansive. From the lab sprang a research and development business center and its first corporate job, development of a software package for Japan's Alpine Electronics, a maker of premium audio units for cars. That work led to a $300,000 contract from Alpine. For the first eight years of the startup's short history, Neusoft doubled in size every year, as its work became known in other vertical markets such as telecom.

Neusoft went public on the Shanghai stock exchange in 1996, the first listed software company in China. Liu never lost sight of the company's origins. The brand name Neusoft is meant to suggest its origins at Northeastern University, which continues to hold a 15 percent stake in the company.

Neusoft's success is due in part to cultivating team spirit. Nearly 20 percent of employees own shares in the company for a total 14 percent stake. The employee turnover rate currently averages 7 percent, low for fast-growth China.

New hires are carefully selected and groomed. In a page out of the McDonald's book, Neusoft runs its own educational and training centers. Each year, some 25,000 students enroll in its center, where the lessons home in on technical training in information technology but also extend to liberal arts. Of the graduating classes,

---

STRATEGY: Neusoft

- Don't forget your company's heritage and use it to advantage.
- Conquer the home market and stay focused, despite better-seeming opportunities abroad.
- Keep equity in a startup that has been spun out from a university.

---

up to 500 students are selected to join Neusoft. Once on board, the most promising new hires get mentoring in leadership development. "It's like a human resource supply chain," says Liu. "We train them to join our practice."

When I met with Liu in 2009, he ticked off the reasons he believes Neusoft is well positioned for accelerated growth. First, the Chinese companies it primarily serves are only at the beginning stages of maturity, and as they grow, so will Neusoft. Second, multinational corporations are continuing to set up research and development centers in China and need local support. Third, China is moving from a manufacturing-based economy to more innovative digital services, creating an increasing need for more sophisticated information technology infrastructure.

China's Melting Pot for Outsourcing

Neusoft is hardly alone in advancing China's push into the vast, varied outsourcing market. While not exactly the sexiest business, China has gone after outsourcing big-time. In just a few years, China has claimed its stake in outsourcing with dozens of venture-backed startups specializing in all kinds of outsourcing—from software development to multilingual customer service centers, insurance claims processing, and more complex engineering design feats for mobile applications, digital cameras, and car navigation equipment. These young Chinese outsourcing companies are about to break through on the global scene as more go public and score multinational corporate customers. The businesses share several attributes. They've homed in on serving new vertical niches in the outsourcing market, handling work, for instance, for utilities. They've been able to shift from low-end jobs to more innovative reengineering work and to cloud computing. Then, too, they have high-level professional managerial talent at the helm, well-educated and trained Chinese returnees or locals, plus expatriates from top schools in the West.

Neusoft stands out as a symbol of China's ambitions to claim a major chunk of the outsourcing market. The Chinese outsourcing market is increasing by 25 percent annually, according to China's Ministry of Information and Industry. KPMG, which has built up a practice in China around serving outsourcing corporations, predicts this Chinese market will reach nearly $44 billion by 2014. That's a fairly sizable portion, compared with India's $60 billion market in 2011.[1]

China has the opportunity to shake up India's hold on outsourcing in a couple of ways. Infrastructure is one plus. The Haidian tech district of Beijing is home to several challengers, all with the syllable *soft* in their name—Beyondsoft, iSoftstone, ChinaSoft—headquartered in sprawling office parks. In Shanghai's Zhangjiang Science Park, state-of-the-art structures resemble Versailles, complete with moats and landscaped gardens, plus sports facilities, too. The scale of these zones is far larger than those in Bangalore, home to Infosys and Wipro.

The minus is that China needs to develop a global reputation for outsourcing. It's a factor that Neusoft CEO Liu readily acknowledges, and one reason he's initially focusing on getting customers closer to home. Most Chinese outsourcing vendors rely on a large percentage of their work within the region or domestically. By contrast, India derives the bulk of its business from abroad.

Chinese outsourcing startups have scaled up by focusing on a fast-growing niche and capitalizing on benefits the home market can offer. One big selling point: cost. Compared with India, pricing for this labor in China is generally 30 percent less. Plus, China has a large talent pool of skilled workers who can handle basic tasks, such as processing insurance claims and mortgage loans, as well as more technically advanced information technology jobs. China's work for multinational companies tends to be concentrated around software development and R&D, where language barriers can be overcome.

Not to be dismissed is China's ambitious quest to lead the outsourcing ranks. Name another country in the world that would craft a $1 billion program of subsidies, incentives, and training like China has to boost outsourcing. In a grand fashion that recalls successive five-year government plans, this $1 billion program seeks to develop 1,000 vendors, attract 100 multinational customers, and foster the growth of 10 hubs nationwide for outsourcing. The goal is to create 1.2 million jobs in China by 2013.

China's disadvantages compared with India are real, though. First, India has a natural advantage with English language skills. Second, India is considered less risky in the realm of intellectual property protections. India also has an edge in managerial skills to tackle more high-end projects. Despite newcomers such as China and the Philippines, India has grown its dominant share of the $500 billion global market, forecast to rise to $1.6 trillion by 2020.[2]

Such obstacles don't get in the way of Chinese outsourcing upstarts such as Neusoft and VanceInfo Technologies. I caught up with VanceInfo CEO Chris Chen at a hastily arranged meeting between flights at the Beijing airport. Over a cup of coffee at the brand new Terminal 3 in 2009, he told me he's determined to make the business he founded in 1995 "become the biggest outsourcing firm in the world." That's a long shot, but he's making progress, counting Microsoft, Hewlett-Packard, and IBM as clients.

Chen has jumped through hoops before. An engineering graduate from China's well-regarded Tsinghua University and a former China project manager for IBM, Chen dug into his bank account for $30,000 and borrowed money from a friend to set up VanceInfo. It wasn't until 2005 that he secured venture capital, lassoing $30 million from DCM, Legend Capital, and Sequoia Capital. By focusing on serving U.S. corporations, VanceInfo ramped up quickly and profitably. For 2010, revenues increased 43 percent to $212 million, while net income climbed 39 percent to nearly $30 million.

VanceInfo also earns kudos for a well-timed listing on the New York Stock Exchange in December 2007, "just months before the financial crisis hit. It wasn't until 2010 that two more venture-backed Chinese outsourcing companies followed: HiSoft Technology on NASDAQ and iSoftStone Holdings on the New York Stock Exchange.

Founder Chris Chen of VanceInfo in Beijing

MindTree: From Roots to Branches

India has its own share of startups, such as Bangalore-based MindTree Ltd., that have prospered even in the shadows of giants Infosys and Wipro, which established India's stronghold in outsourcing more than two decades ago. Like the Chinese startups in this sector, MindTree has climbed up rapidly from its start in 1999 by drilling down to what it does best: higher-end information technology work for companies in the West. MindTree bulked up to $301 million in revenues in 2011,[3] more than 9,000 employees, and 18 locations in India, the United States, Japan, Europe, and the Middle East.

It helped that founder and chairman Ashok Soota was the former vice chairman and president of Wipro. Another bonus was ample venture capital. MindTree raised $9.1 million in capital from Walden International at inception and then $14 million from such big names as Franklin Templeton.

Soota's goal was to crank up MindTree to be a $1 billion company, but he never came close to that milepost. In February 2011, Soota, 70, stepped down as chairman after a split in strategy over an acquisition to jump into costly research and development for the fast-expanding mobile handset business. The project was canned. The struggles showcased the importance of clearly mapping out directions to successfully ramp up an upstart company in an emerging market.

How China's high-growth outsourcing businesses will fare long-term in grabbing a chunk of India's stronghold is a bit of a question mark. Currently, China is a hodgepodge of outsourcing choices. Services come in all varieties, from firm size to location to pricing and specialty. That makes it difficult for a manager in charge of a corporation's outsourcing strategy to pick and choose. It takes localized on-the-ground insights to figure out, for instance, that Nanjing is making a claim as one of the country's most promising biomedical hubs for outsourcing of pharmaceutical research and development and clinical trials. That's in spite of outreach efforts by China to promote the sector to multinational corporations and encourage investment—which I saw in action in both Nanjing and Hangzhou.

I was at an opening ceremony in May 2009 for the establishment of a biotech outsourcing center in a Nanjing high-tech park. In the ballroom of a luxury hotel downtown, several high-level municipal officials welcomed a group of investors, biomedical experts, entrepreneurs, technologists, and real estate developers—even a doctor from Minnesota's renowned Mayo Clinic—to their city.

Later, we toured several sites at the biotech-focused software park: a lab that is working on research to standardize herbs for use in Chinese traditional medicine and still empty facilities for clinical testing of new drugs on lab animals. In the next building, Chuck Zhu, CEO of NJ PharmaTech, beamed as he showed us around the contemporary office space he's leased for his startup that does contract pharmaceutical research here.

In Hangzhou, Deputy Mayor Tong Guili is a powerful and attractive figure as she hosts welcoming dinners for foreign executives. She's an effective spokesperson in a bid to attract more outsourcing business to the city, known for its scenic West Lake and the home of China's leading Internet player, Alibaba Group.

Several China representatives from management consultancy KPMG were on hand for the dinner to hear her pitch. Sitting next to the deputy mayor was KPMG partner Egidio Zarrella, who heads up the firm's innovation advisory practice from Hong Kong. He's spending time coming up to speed on outsourcing in China, a big growth area for the firm. Zarrella says he's seen China make several major strides in developing a diverse and successful outsourcing market. "It's remarkable how fast the vision is becoming a reality," he notes.

Former Chinese government official Roc Yang leads Beijing-based China Data Group, an outsourcing firm he co-founded in 2005 to specialize in financial services. When he is not running the fast-emerging business, which has $32 million in venture capital support from leading Chinese private equity firm CDH and others, Yang is leading the charge for Chinese outsourcing firms to develop a unified voice and higher profile. He and other leaders in the business would like China to have an industry-wide association like India has had for years, with its influential NASSCOM. That would be a good step forward.

It took years for Korean cars to be regarded for high-quality engineering and manufacturing. Likewise, it will take at least a few more years before China gains a spotlight in outsourcing. But its rapid rise, with several startups founded by capable managers and with funding from the West, proves that Chinese outsourcing is not to be belittled but is just one more sign of the Dragon's power.

PART
III

Toolbox for Success Strategies

Part Three explores the tactics that startups are using to get ahead. These are the handful of strategies that belong in every entrepreneur's reading list—proven ways that young businesses gain traction.

They start with a look at how to get a handout from Singapore to launch a business, and progress from there. Chapter 9 delves into cloning, a well-known art form among Chinese entrepreneurs that has spread to India and Vietnam. Chapter 10 takes it to the next level, examining a few startups in Singapore, India, Taiwan, and China with that platinum standard: breakthrough technology.

Chapter 11 is not for the fainthearted. It's about going to Wall Street or Times Square for a big-time IPO—the risks and the rewards.

Finally, Chapter 12 wraps it up by taking it to the next frontier: the global landscape. Asian startups are beginning to make noise beyond their own national borders. This chapter contains case studies of startups that are making this international journey in record time and with no regrets.

These chapters showcase entrepreneurs who are proving to be the envy of startup founders anywhere. They are getting ahead by:

- Picking markets and regions that offer the best growth prospects.
- Assembling teams with specialized financial, technical, and managerial experience.
- Raising ample finance from western-anchored venture firms.

- Appointing astute board members.
- Doing spin-outs from university research labs.
- Managing for quick growth to beat competitors to new sectors and become the market leader.
- Looking to neighboring countries and the West for business models that can be successfully transplanted.
- Occasionally developing patented technology that can lead to a breakthrough business.
- Bringing in more experienced managerial talent to run their startups.
- Shifting the business model to a more promising segment and dropping a flop quickly.
- Figuring out to how to conquer the going public process without tripping over accounting issues, financial readiness, and market timing.

The founders and CEOs of Asian startups are increasingly sophisticated, internationally-minded leaders. They don't hesitate to find out what works and what doesn't. The following chapters highlight their progress in taking these startups from scratch, to IPOs, and global horizons.

CHAPTER

8

Tap into Government Incubators

Singapore's sweet spot in the Asian tech story is the amount of nurturing it gives to young startups that wouldn't otherwise have a hope in this island nation. Singapore has so many government-supported programs for budding entrepreneurs that the mix of acronyms for all of them can get confusing. Animation house **Sparky** dipped into Singapore's handouts for new digital media businesses and now competes with Lucas Films in startup zone Fusionopolis. **Soo Boon Koh** of **iGlobe Partners**—one of the few female venture partners in the business—has moved her shop from Silicon Valley to Singapore and is pouring investments into Sparky and others that are leveraging this Southeast Asian tiger's formula for advancing entrepreneurship. Walden International's Asian VC pioneer **Lip-Bu Tan** and **Lawrence Tse** of **Gobi Partners** also are funding Singapore-based startups that got a jumpstart here.

Michael Yap is leaning back in his swivel chair almost to the point of tipping over, his colorful tie askew. We're in a darkened studio at Fusionopolis, Singapore's would-be Hollywood and Silicon Alley all in one. It's one of several such techie spots—Mediapolis is another—that make Singapore seem more with it than its Asian neighbors.

Yap has just finished making an animated pitch using a giant video screen that fills the wall in front of us. The presentation is meant to demonstrate how Singapore is becoming a digital media hub, thanks in part to the center he runs: the Interactive Digital Media R&D Program Office, or IDM as it's known in Singapore, where

153

Michael Yap of Interactive Digital Media in Singapore

every organization, including its parent, the Media Development Authority, or MDA, has an acronym.

Singapore has thrown a lot of resources toward fostering the creative spirit of enterprise, arguably more than any other Asian nation. Sure, Hong Kong sports its Cyberport to house digital media startups and offers prize money of up to $13,000 for five startups annually. But Cyberport feels almost like a ghost town. Yes, the Hong Kong Science and Technology Park runs an incubation program for about 80 technology and design startups with a package of benefits worth $65,000 for legal aid, training, facilities, and tech support, but it's had a slow start.

Taiwan has the Industrial Technology Research Institute and other government-funded programs to spark breakthrough ideas in nanotechnology and solar power that can be turned into leading-edge startups and multinational giants. Taiwan wants to be a mini Silicon Dragon tech power radiating out from Taipei's Hsinchu Science Park and Tainan's Southern Taiwan Software Park. Credit has to be given to Taiwan for aiming to go beyond a traditionally powerful base with such industry leaders as TSMC in semiconductors and Acer in electronics production. One of the world's leading solar cell producers, Motech Solar, at the island's software park in the south, is a showcase example of its forward march to diversify. But Taiwan isn't really known for its startups.

Here in Singapore, the government initiatives to ripen the metropolis for entrepreneurship and propel its economy are just countless (Table 8.1). One of them is a weeklong series of venture and entrepreneurial programs and startup competitions I've attended regularly

Table 8.1   Singapore's Jump-Start Programs for Entrepreneurs

Interactive Digital Media Research & Development Office (IDM)
- Jam microfunding
    Selected projects in digital media, tech, and innovative businesses get an average-size grant of $40,000 to cover research, marketing, equipment, patents, and advisory expenses; recipients get allowance of $490 monthly.

National University of Singapore (NUS)
- NUS Enterprise provides seed financing to startups and access to government grants, plus funding by venture or angel investors.
- Runs the Overseas College Program and Start-up@Singapore business plan competition, with prizes for winners at $25,000 and runners-up at $4,000 to $8,000.
- Operates NUS Technology Holdings to seed new technology companies to commercialize university research.
    NUS Entrepreneurship Centre
    - Provides support programs including incubation facilities, seed funding, and mentoring
    - Offers entrepreneurial learning internship called iLead or Innovative Local Enterprise Achiever Development for NUS undergraduate students
    - Runs the Extra Chapter Challenge for PhD students to learn how to commercialize their research
    NUS Enterprise Incubator
    - Provides entrepreneurs of early startups with mentoring, advice on fund-raising, and access to office space and Internet connectivity
    - Open to NUS students, alumni, and faculty

Economic Development Board (EDB)
- Startups in clean energy and environmental sectors can receive up to 85 percent of costs for R&D, manpower, equipment, and training, with support capped at $408,000.

SPRING Singapore
- YES Start-ups!
    Matches four times the amount raised from outside sources up to a limit of $41,000 to cover business development expenses for young Singaporeans under the age of 26.
- TECS (Technology Enterprise Commercialization Scheme)
    Selected scientific and tech projects get funding of R&D efforts to develop proprietary ideas and carry out proof of concept tests. All qualifying costs are covered up to $200,000. Additional funding to double that amount is available for selected recipients to carry out research to develop a project or prototype.
- SPRING SEEDS Capital
    Coinvests in commercially viable local startups, matching amounts from third-party investors up to $800,000.
- Business Angel Funds
    Matches investment made by three business angel funds in local startups, up to a maximum of $1.2 million. Angel groups are BAF Spectrum, Sirius Angel, and Accel-X.

Note: Amounts converted to US$ from SG$.

Hsinchu Science Park Director-General and tech booster Randy Yen in Taipei area

that is collectively themed Globalentropolis. How's that for imagination? Yet innovation is more than a government policy or budget. It's about culture and education, and it takes years to change.

This notion of making Singapore sing with innovation still seems a stretch for a place I've been to as a journalist more than a dozen times over the past decade for interviews and assignments. With a population of only 5 million, the Singaporean market is just too small to attract many tech-savvy entrepreneurs—though the comfortable lifestyle here is suitable for raising a family, and several other amenities, such as low tax rates, have drawn many multinational corporations, Hewlett-Packard included, to put their regional headquarters here. The comparatively high pay and secure jobs that young talent can draw from banks, research labs, and publishers in Singapore has detoured many would-be entrepreneurs.

For sure, Singapore is advanced with its use of information technology for such purposes as monitoring street traffic, collecting tolls, and managing libraries. But its government-supported venture capital community is tiny and limited in scope, with several of the early venturers who got their start here tempted by China. Tina Ju of TDF Ventures now runs Kleiner Perkins from Shanghai. Finian Tan, formerly with ePlanet Ventures, works from Shanghai with Vickers Capital Group.

The most ambitious students I've met at Singapore's well-regarded universities have trouble resisting the call of China's bigger pastures to the north. Singapore may be a good launchpad for them because of all the handouts, academic institutions, and modern infrastructure, but it may not put them over the rainbow.

A former British trading post that gained sovereignty in 1965, Singapore under the leadership of Prime Minister Lee Kuan Yew developed as a financial center, logistics hub, and research and development center—and more recently, a tourist destination, with its two new casino resorts. But despite its status as one of four Asian tigers—the others are Hong Kong, Taiwan, and South Korea—Singapore seems stuck in creating a culture akin to Silicon Valley and has few successful, well-known startups to its credit. Singapore's homegrown digital entertainment maker Creative Technologies, which was founded in 1981 and listed on NASDAQ in 1992, is one exception, with its sound system that pioneered multimedia for the PC market. Air-conditioned shopping malls, the humid tropical climate, strict rules like no chewing bubblegum, lush urban greenery, Singapore Airlines flight attendants, the busy seaport, and landmarks like the world-famous Raffles Hotel, where I've had the pleasure of staying, are more memorable reflections of this Southeast Asian city-state.

Over lunch at Raffles, I spoke with K. C. Wong, the dynamo who heads up Sparky Animation. He's just the sort of entrepreneur that Singapore wants to encourage—and does so by offering his startup several government subsidies, such as lower rent at Fusionopolis. Moving Singapore along toward an aim of becoming an animation hub, Sparky is coproducing with the Jim Henson Company a hit children's TV series called the *Dinosaur Train*, which airs on PBS. Several of its kids' programs, such as *Fleabag Monkeyface*, based on a hugely popular children's book, and *Mr. Moon*, are televised in the United Kingdom, Canada, and Australia.

Wong, who looks a little like a cartoon character himself, with his round spectacles, big eyes, and unruly, wavy hair, explained that Sparky coproduces shows and uses nifty technology to expedite production from several days to a few hours. "In the long run, I think we will be fairly profitable because of these two pragmatic business models in parallel," he says, adding that Sparky combines his interests in technical work, artistry, and business. Wong founded Sparky in 2006 after teaching graphics and imaging technology for 13 years at Singapore's Nanyang Technology University. His goal? "In the next 10 years, I'd like Sparky to become the most successful entertainment enterprise in all of Asia. The challenge is to grow from a small enterprise to a medium- or mega-size studio, like Dreamworks or Pixar."

This is the kind of big, visionary thinking that Singapore hopes to see more of in the future.

Sparky's venture backer is Soo Boon Koh, founder and managing partner of iGlobe Partners. She scoped out Sparky early on and invested in the animation producer in January 2010. Sparky is a great fit for her firm as she plays a role in trying to develop Singapore's tech entrepreneurship culture.

She established her iGlobe tech investing fund in 1999 and had plenty of connections and experience to do it. Koh had logged 12 years with Singapore Technology's venture arm Vertex Management, which had sponsorship from the Economic Development Board of Singapore and a mandate to invest in emerging tech companies in Silicon Valley, China, and Singapore. Now Koh, a crackerjack who blends rare experience from the Valley, Europe, and China, has raised a new fund and is investing primarily in Singapore tech sectors where there is local expertise, including digital media and wireless technology. Since early 2010, her Platinum Fund has invested in two local startups, Sparky and Anacle Systems, a cleantech startup that makes software for improving energy efficiency in commercial real estate properties. "We have board seats at both companies and good influence in mentoring the founders and CEOs of the companies," says iGlobe founder Koh.

Singapore might be best known for the Singapore Sling drink at Raffles, but it sure wants to be regarded as the knowledge capital. Slapping together government resources and infrastructure to become an Asian hub, the Singapore government has coined a memorable term: "technopreneurship." As one prong of that multifaceted effort, the Ministry of Finance–supported TIF Ventures acts as a fund of funds, pouring money into indigenous venture firms, which in theory will fund local startups and entice Singaporeans and foreigners to set up shop here and stay. That would certainly be a switch from the past. Singapore fund managers are known for having a conservative approach to investing, and entrepreneurs often hop on planes to source funds elsewhere.

New forward-looking venture funds keep on coming, formed with an assist from Singapore government initiatives. Early-stage tech investor Gobi Partners from Shanghai set up an $81 million fund in 2010 with Singapore's MDA to back emerging companies in digital media and tech. The idea is to milk synergies between the two markets, and in fact, the fund can invest in either the Chinese currency renminbi or Singapore dollars. In 2011, the MDA joined with the National University of Singapore and the Innov8 fund run by local telecom company SingTel to launch another incubation program. This one is called Blk71, in a reference to its office space in Mediapolis.

Ignite the Fuse

Here at Fusionopolis, I can feel the flow of creative energy as Yap describes his mission to put Singapore in the center of an interactive media revolution. Toward that aim, his organization has formed partnerships to lure prestigious universities worldwide to do leading-edge research here, including the Massachusetts Institute of Technology, Keio University in Tokyo, and the Indian Institute of Technology in Mumbai. This endeavor isn't such a foreign concept, since Singapore is already the Asian campus for the renowned European school INSEAD. He's seeking to spur development of a digital innovation ecosystem in Singapore by bringing together research, entrepreneurship, and startup funding to, as Yap words it, "ignite grassroots innovations."

Previously the head of Oracle Singapore and a tech entrepreneur before that, Yap has the background and enthusiasm to help his government-funded center, set up in 2006, put Singapore on the digital media map. Its multiple initiatives are beginning to make a dent in changing this island nation's buttoned-down culture.

The program Yap has run for five years has funded 300 entrepreneurial projects in all the most popular sectors: mobile games, rich media, e-publishing, and social networks. For first-time entrepreneurs starved for cash, this is music to their ears. There are the normal hoops to jump through, of course, to collect the cash, but the amounts can make it worthwhile.

To be eligible, startups naturally need to be based in Singapore and have at least one full-time local founder on the team. Once selected as a promising startup, the center's funding scheme— known as i.Jam, another acronym!—match up the entrepreneurs with local incubator teams for mentoring. Each handpicked project gets a grant from IDM to cover costs, with an average size of $40,000. Founders also get a subsistence allowance of $490 per month. Some research expenses and patent costs are covered as well.

These grants carry more weight with matched funding from regionally based incubators, angel investors, or venture capital firms, including some better-known players such as Walden International. Each, in turn, is expected to invest 10 percent to 25 percent of the project's cost and then get an equal equity stake in the startup. But it's not just a handout: Entrepreneurs are supposed to repay the center once their startups turn a profit of more than $800,000 or their shares are sold to a third party for more than $400,000.

The long-term vision of the IDM program is to not only put Singapore at the forefront of the media age but also keep the nation's economy going, creating 10,000 new jobs by 2015.

As a sign of its commitment, the Singapore government plans to spend $13 billion on research, innovation, and enterprise over the next five years.

Yet another government entity, Spring (short for Startup Enterprise Development Scheme), is available to help young entrepreneurs get over the hump. Spring has pumped $51 million into 185 new firms since it was introduced in 2001. Results are good. Of those startups, 30 have recorded revenues of more than $800,000 in 2009 and 2010,[1] says Tan Kai Hoe, deputy chief executive of Spring Singapore. He further notes that some 53,400 enterprises were started in Singapore during 2010, a 6 percent increase from the prior year. "I would like to think that a part of this is due to the pro-business environment in Singapore and the variety of support provided by various government and private-sector agencies for startups," he says.

Maybe Singapore really is changing. If indeed it is, then the one individual who has done more than anyone else I know to transform it is Professor Poh Kam Wong. He is in a constant state of motion as he darts from business classes he teaches at the National University of Singapore to the school's Entrepreneurship Centre, which he leads under the direction of another impressive booster, CEO Lily Chan of the all-encompassing NUS Enterprise.

NUS Enterprise

This leading Singapore university tries to replicate some of that Stanford spirit by providing NUS-seeded startups with office space in stacked containers that are vaguely reminiscent of the Silicon Valley startup in a garage. It also invests in the startups and takes an equity stake. The approach has spawned imaginative work, judging by several entrepreneurs I met with on campus.

One beneficiary is 2359 Media, which has designed a customizable mobile ad platform. Started in 2009 by two NUS grads, Zhou Wen Han and Wong Hong Ting, 2359 Media has collected about $55,000 from government grants, not including the NUS-subsidized space. In early 2011, the Singaporean startup went up another notch when it drew about $1 million in investment from the Singtel Innov8 fund and hatched plans to launch in the United States soon.

Another startup that is an outgrowth of NUS school spirit is multimedia e-books maker Koobits, founded by China-born entrepreneur Stanley Han with NUS professor Sam Ge Shuzhi and researcher Chen Xiangdong. Like many other fledgling enterprises here, Koobits has swept through most of the government-sponsored programs from MDA and NUS Enterprise, plus received about $1 million in funding from local venture capital firm Accel-X. With Koobits software, users can create and organize their e-books, digital photos, and the like, plus publish and share them on social networks. Koobits is working with several book publishers on taking content and turning it into a suite of related multimedia and digital wallpapers, posters, games, and even mobile phone apps.

Professor Wong's credentials are solid, extending from his PhD at MIT, to Silicon Valley, where he's done research for the Stanford Project on Regions of Innovation and Entrepreneurship, to the World Bank, where he has consulted. His international perspective is a plus for the school's entrepreneurial-minded students. At NUS, this brainiac has pioneered a minor in technology entrepreneurship and advised on the establishment of an overseas program for students to do a one-year internship at tech startups in such hubs as Silicon Valley, Beijing, Bangalore, and Stockholm.

Wong is identified as a cheerleader for Singapore-style tech entrepreneurship, and he practices what he teaches in a no-nonsense style. Professor Wong is an angel investor in seven startups in Singapore, India, and the Valley, including several that have sprung from the NUS. He's also the founding chairman of a Business Angel Network in Southeast Asia. Further, he helps PhD students with promising discoveries learn how to commercialize their research. He's invited me to lecture at his classes and university forums, which I have done.

Not everyone is satisfied with the Singapore system of sparking entrepreneurship by putting programs in place to make it happen. Virginia Cha, an experienced tech executive who teaches and mentors budding entrepreneurs at Shanghai's Fudan University and at NUS, speaks up about the shortfalls. She says the concepts of the programs are well-intentioned, but the drawback is the

administration of the programs. She complains the system is bureaucratic and mired in paperwork requirements to obtain and put the
money to work. "One of the startups I work with here took one year to
get the financial support when it should have taken three months,"
she notes.

Moreover, some of most active venture capital firms—such
as Tina Ju's TDF Capital—have left Singapore for deal making in
China, she notes. "The venture capitalists in Singapore are relatively risk averse. A lot of inexperienced entrepreneurs are at a
huge disadvantage by venture investors who take controlling shares
in the company and don't trust the entrepreneur," observes Cha.

Still, the Singapore government has kept at its long-term goal
by providing funding for entrepreneurial endeavors to make the
city-state a magnet for scientific and tech innovation. For instance,
Singapore's National Research Foundation led an initiative to support venture capital firms by investing $6.5 million in six funds,
which then raised a matching sum to back local startups. A unique
part of the program allows fund managers an option to buy out
NRF's share at the price of 1.25 times the government's original
investment.

Highly respected cross-border Pacific tech investor Lip-Bu Tan
has his PhD from Singapore's Nanyang University and has raised
the firm's Seed Ventures IV fund through the NRF program. As part
of this initiative, Walden International put $1.3 million in a local
startup, Brandtology, an online branding consultancy and specialist
in social media.

Besides Walden, the five venture firms participating in the
NRF initiative are health care investor BioVeda Capital II, nano-
technology investor Nanostart Asia, Israeli cleantech fund Tamarix
Capital, Singapore-focused VC firm Upstream-Expara, and Raffles
Venture Partners, a new firm founded by investors from Singapore
government-backed TIF Ventures.

The proactive work in Singapore has caught the attention of
neighboring countries that would like to emulate the island nation.
One is Brunei, which is eager to lessen its dependence on oil as an
economic driver and turn to tech as an economic engine. Under
the direction of NUS and the Brunei government, a sleek new
iCentre incubator lab has been built in the capital city. The facility,
which I toured courtesy of director Hui Kwok Leong, is outfitted
with meeting rooms, office space, broadband access, and shared

Brunei Minster of Commerce Pehin Abdullah with author Rebecca Fannin in Brunei

faxes, printers, and telephones. About a dozen fledgling tech businesses have set up shop here.

The center is one rare sign of a bustling entrepreneurial environment in this small, wealthy country. The Sultan of Brunei has recently granted $1.3 million to the iCentre for nine projects to lift off from the incubation lab.

The highest-profile initiative the Brunei iCentre spearheads is with publishing partner Asia Inc. Together, they host the annual Think Big Tech forum, which features entrepreneurial thought leaders and multinational executives as guest speakers. At the forum, I sat next to Brunei's Minister of Commerce Pehin Abdullah, as he thumbed through his BlackBerry before I went on stage to deliver the lunchtime keynote speech at a packed ballroom of the ultraluxurious Empire Hotel and Country Club. This experience was definitely the highlight of my tech tour through Southeast Asia.

Back in Singapore, after a comfortable flight on Royal Brunei Airlines, I met with more alumni of Singapore's bootstrap support and training. The biggest success story is Tencube, a mobile security service started in 2005 by four classmates at NUS and acquired in 2010 by Santa Clara, California–headquartered McAfee Inc.—now owned by Intel—for approximately $16 million.

From Tencube to McAfee's

Tencube's innovative software, called WaveSecure, offers a recovery and backup plan for stolen mobile phones. Thieves attempting to log on get locked out and then tracked via a SIM card in the device. If the phone is not recovered, then the software wipes the data clean and restores it on a new phone. This handy software, priced at $20, was the brainchild of one of the company's founders, who discovered a market gap when his own expensive phone was stolen, and he had no chance of retrieving his contacts and e-mails.

When McAfee came calling with its acquisition offer, the chance to gain experience by working in a large American tech firm seemed like a good idea. Before accepting the deal, the co-founders consulted with Professor Wong. He advised them to negotiate with McAfee over pricing and then take the best offer, yet look toward future building opportunities. Today, the four founders all work at McAfee, in a separate mobile business unit that folds in their WaveSecure software. The young team has a noncompete clause for two years, which will soon be up.

I'm hearing the story of Tencube as I'm interviewing former chief technology officer Rishi Kumar, who is now the McAfee unit's chief of engineering, and the startup's CEO, Darius Cheung, director of strategy at the McAfee group. Their success came about partly because some of the founding team went abroad for a dose of entrepreneurship, courtesy of the NUS overseas college program in Silicon Valley, and got the courage to do a startup.

Relaying the story, Kumar, 29, tells me he was a 2003 computer science graduate from NUS who had spent six months at a software job with business technology service Avanade Singapore before he linked up with his mates to form Tencube. The team, including NUS grad and now McAfee chief architect Varun Chatterji, lived on a shoestring for the first three months while designing a prototype of the software. Things began to look up when they received seed funding of $25,000 after winning first prize in a local business plan competition. On a pitch to NUS Enterprise for financial support to develop their concept into a product, Tencube pulled in the larger amount of $245,000, which was matched by government initiative Spring.

All in all, Tencube drew $800,000 in financial support from Singapore government-connected groups, including NUS. To keep

---

STRATEGY: Tencube

- Go overseas to broaden your perspective and raise the bar on developing a first-rate startup.
- Build your team with like-minded internationally trained and experienced colleagues.
- Stay close to home while the startup is young to soak up all the nurturing you can.
- When you get a reasonable offer from a big tech brand, take it—and then look forward to the next venture!

---

going, the startup raised nearly another $1 million in early 2010 from One97 Communications, an Indian mobile value-added service provider, which took a 25 percent stake in the startup.

Keeping close to home base, for three or four years Tencube was incubated at NUS, where access to computers, fax machines, and copiers was handy. Moving into larger space as 15 to 20 fellow graduates were hired from the overseas program at NUS, the cofounders landed their first deal—a big one, to preload software on 20 models of Nokia phones sold in India. That contract brought in close to 500,000 customers, Kumar recalls. Singapore's telco SingTel came calling next with a big order. Business really took off when Tencube launched its direct-to-consumer portal, lassoing another 500,000 customers.

Becoming a millionaire is not the only thing Kumar got from his days at the university. He also met a mechanical engineering student who later became his wife, Pranoti Nagarkar Israni. Today, she, too, is an entrepreneur with her own startup, Zimplistic Inventions.

Roll It with Rotimatic

Thanks to financing from a government-sponsored Spring grant and incubation space from NUS to build a prototype, plus her own considerable ingenuity, Israni has come up with a machine to automatically make the Indian bread roti. She's lined up potential licensees and hired a lawyer to file a patent for her invention, called Rotimatic, naturally enough. She plans to launch the roti maker commercially in 2012.

Rotimatic founder Pranoti Nagarkar Israni in Singapore

"I've always had an engineering mind-set, and I come from a family of engineers," explains Israni, who is poised and slender. "I wanted to be an inventor when I grew up, and at home, we were encouraged to do things like break open a TV set to see how it works."

The industrious engineer got started on her entrepreneurial path after working for two years with Philips on a design for an automatic vacuum cleaner. When that product ultimately didn't get launched, she went out on her own, looking for new ideas. Why not bread making? After all, rice cookers already existed, and making handmade rotis was a lot more tedious. Rotimatic takes care of the mixing and baking automatically, and all that needs to be done is add in flour and water.

Winning prizes for her machine-made rotis proved to be fairly simple. All she had to do was let the judges sample the Rotimatic-made Indian bread. She won first prize in a Startup-up@Singapore competition and third prize at an Intel Berkeley Entrepreneurship Challenge in 2009. Her skills also resulted in two Singapore government-sponsored grants totaling about $80,000. Now, angel and venture investors are circling round, so it may not be long before this 29-year-old female entrepreneur finds a way to make her own dream come true.

Her story is the kind that Singapore wants to duplicate many times over. Singapore may not have that tech-jazzy formula down 100 percent, but it can't be blamed for trying. In these minihops for entrepreneurs, Singapore excels and makes its emerging Asian neighbors want to figure out how to emulate its success.

CHAPTER 9

Become the Next Twitter, LinkedIn, or Groupon for Asia

Vietnam has search site **Socbay** and e-commerce brand **Peacesoft**—localized versions of **Google** and **eBay**. India has four local versions of **Expedia**, MakeMyTrip among them. China has clones of **LinkedIn**, **Wikipedia**, and **Groupon**. But getting the right formula locally isn't easy. Sites just can't be blankly copied but need to be fine tuned for the local culture. Some of the most seasoned venture investors from the West, like **Bill Tai** of **Charles River Ventures** and **Feng Deng** of Northern Light Venture Capital, are funding young founders as they scale their Asian startup look-alikes quickly while the market is hot. The cloning craze is not over yet! It's an almost foolproof way to get a quick start.

China already has a Facebook, Google, and Twitter, so how much longer was it before a LinkedIn look-alike arrived? That would be Ushi.cn, the Chinese equivalent to LinkedIn, the popular social network for professionals.

Pronounced "you shuh," it means "outstanding professionals" in Chinese. Ushi is the brainchild of Dominic Penaloza, a Chinese-Canadian serial entrepreneur and former private equity investor in China and Hong Kong. Started by Penaloza in February 2010, the Shanghai-based Ushi is China's most popular social networking brand for professionals. It boasts a 200,000-strong membership—not bad for one year of being in business.

Ushi founder Dominic Penaloza in Shanghai

Penaloza relied on an old trick to boost his new site: word-of-mouth promotion from an exclusive group of go-getters. He invited 100 influential charter members to join, many of them venture capitalists, investment bankers, lawyers, ad agency execs, and Web developers. In turn, these members—many of whom I know, such as VCs Lawrence Tse of Gobi Partners, Eric Li of Chengwei Partners, and entrepreneur Frank Yu of Kwestr—invited their connections to join. Penaloza invited me to join fairly early on, and I've found Ushi, which is available in both English and Chinese, a handy tool for connecting with locals or expats in China's tech and venture circles.

Ushi is definitely onto something good, but how long it can stay tops with a whole bunch of competitors coming after it is a reasonable question. Not only are there two other early copycats of LinkedIn in China—Tianji and Wealink, which rank below Ushi in traffic[1]—but social networking powerhouse Renren introduced its own brand, Jingwei, in 2011. Now that LinkedIn has gone public, Ushi may face competition from the original brand if and when LinkedIn enters China with a Chinese-language version of the site. But getting the right formula for China won't be easy.

It requires more than just uploading translated copy for China. Localization is key.

For young entrepreneurs heading to Asia for professional opportunities, doing clones was an easy way to get started. Copycat models of popular Western brands first arrived in China with the Internet sites early last decade. This cloning craze hasn't gotten tired out, and maybe it won't. More clones keep coming to match an ever-growing number of new types of sites and business models.

Venture capitalists have favored copycat models because they've already proven to work in larger markets. They've also green-lighted them because most of the early ones were created by returnee entrepreneurs with sophisticated experience in the West. China was the frontier market for clones, but now the duplicating trend has spread to other Asian hubs.

Numerous well-funded and high-profile clones of Western businesses have cropped up in China, India, and Vietnam. Facebook has copies in Renren and Kaixin001; Twitter has Weibo in China and SMS GupShup in India; Amazon has Dangdang in China, FlipKart in India, and VinaBook in Vietnam; eBay has Peacesoft and Vatgia in Vietnam; Expedia has Ctrip in China and MakeMyTrip in India; and so on. Several of the best-known Chinese sites have gone public in the United States at high market valuations, proving that this well-worn business approach in Asia's emerging markets still carries clout.

The biggest current cloning craze is localized versions of daily coupon site Groupon. In China, there are more than 1,500 Groupons, at least 10 exist in Vietnam (NhomMua, Hotdeal, and Phagia), and India has 30 Groupon-esque sites (Snapdeal and Taggle are two of them). Moreover, Groupon has acquired sites in many locales: SoSasta in India, Beeconomic in Singapore, Atlaspost in Taiwan, Groupmore in Malaysia, and uBuyiBuy in Hong Kong. Even the original Groupon, which entered China as Gaopeng and has had a bumpy ride, was rumored in April 2011 to be acquiring another Chinese Groupon with the name, if you can believe it, Groupon.cn.

With so many replica sites out there, sufficient venture funding to ramp up fast and kick back attackers can definitely pay off. Of the Groupon clones in China, Lashou stands out. Its CEO Bo Wu, a serial entrepreneur with one IPO and one acquisition to his startup credits, turned down an acquisition offer by Groupon in late 2010 for his months-old startup and instead picked up $166 million in venture capital over the next few months from a host of investors, including Milestone Capital and GSR Ventures, the largest shareholder in Lashou. The number of Groupon look-alikes that have sprung up in Asia proves how easily the business model can be copied. But how much money will be lost on this sector is another matter. Valuations for these deals are in the $1 billion-plus range.

Clones of all kinds in Asia have caught on as multinational brands, eBay and Google included, have stumbled. These regional replicas have proven so popular that even the original brands have tried to snap them up, with mixed success. After failing with the Chinese clone Eachnet in China in 2003, eBay is trying its luck with a Vietnamese look-alike, Peacesoft Solutions. (See Chapter 3.) Google invested $5 million for a slice of Chinese search engine Baidu back in 2005 but later sold it for a solo entry to the market. That same year, Google made a failed bid to acquire Vietnamese search engine Socbay.

In China, the world's clone capital (see Table 9.1), former Google China president Kai-Fu Lee is stirring the cloning pot at his incubator and venture fund, Innovation Works. Many of the start-ups Innovation Works is backing are almost foolproof bets, localized remakes of Web 2.0 brands from the West such as Tumblr, Yelp, Getjar, and iTunes. (See Chapter 1.)

In India, the most pronounced example of copycating is in the online travel market. There are as many as four clones of the model perfected by Expedia and Travelocity in the United States and Ctrip in China. All four have targeted India's rising middle-class population with their increased spending power. All four also have in common first-class international venture capital.

MakeMyTrip had venture funding from SAIF, Helion Venture Partners, and Sierra Ventures to the tune of $39 million. Cleartrip was backed with $3 million from Kleiner Perkins and Google founding investor, Ram Shriram. Yatra was financed with $5 million from Norwest Venture Partners. Travelguru had $15 million from Battery Ventures and Sequoia Capital India.

MakeMyTrip has out-distanced the trio of rivals with stellar operating results and and a successful NASDAQ IPO. Meeting a different fate, Travelguru was sold in 2009 to Travelocity for $12 million, in a money-losing deal for the investors. The other two

Table 9.1   Copycat Models in China: Cloning Craze

Categories	United States	China
Social networking services	Facebook	RenRen, Douban, Qzone, Kaixin001
Message boards	Yahoo Message Boards	Tianya, Mop
Blogging	Blogger, WordPress	Sina Blog
Microblogging	Twitter	Weibo, Sohu, QQ
Blog hosting	Tumblr	Diandian
Mobile chat	WhatsApp	Feixin, Weixin
Instant messaging	MSN Messenger	QQ
Video sharing	YouTube	Youku, Tudou
Photo sharing	Flickr	Bababian, Babidou
Online music	Spotify	Top100, Xiami
Wikis	Wikipedia	Baidu, Hudong
Q&A	Quora	Zhihu, Tianya, Zhidao
Review	Yelp	Dianping, Fantong
Check-in	Foursquare	Jiepang, Digu, K.ai
Deal of the day	Groupon	Manzuo, Meituan, Lashou
Online trade	eBay	Taobao, 360Buy
Professional social networking	LinkedIn	Ushi, Tianji, Wealink, Jingwei

Source: Ogilvy, Silicon Asia.

contenders have tapped new funds to expand. Cleartrip drew a $40 million strategic investment in April 2011 from NASDAQ-listed travel management Concur in Redmond, Washington, while Yatra sold a stake in the company for $45 million to Norwest, Intel Capital, and Valiant Capital Management.

What set MakeMyTrip apart? It wasn't just copying the original formula. It was all about tailoring the service to the local market and executing on the plan with a clear vision. The startup team led by CEO Deep Kalra relied on a multi-pronged strategy to get ahead in this jungle of rivals. They tailored the service to the local culture by offering travel tickets at both retail shops and online, allowed cash payment options versus credit cards, and offered a short-text messaging service keyed into India's booming mobile market. Finally, they emphasized travel packages and mom-and-pop hotels over lower-profit-margin airline business.

In China, the most fruitful area of cloning has been in social media. Sites in this fast-developing area have caught on quickly and gained traction here for one key underlying reason: censorship and blocks of popular Western sites such as Facebook and Twitter. Even professional networking site LinkedIn, which boasts 100 million members worldwide, has been blocked occasionally in China. Such restrictions have allowed local Chinese sites Ushi—the LinkedIn of China—and Hudong—the Wikipedia of China—to gain entry.

It is LinkedIn's limitations in China, for instance, that have given entrepreneur Penaloza the window to launch Ushi. "We had the know-how and the competence to do something like LinkedIn and got tired of asking ourselves, why is there no such thing in China," says Penaloza, 41, who grew up in Toronto, returned to China in 1992, and has formed three Internet startups since 2000.

China's LinkedIn: Ushi

Of Chinese-Filipino ethnicity, Penaloza is from a three-generation family of entrepreneurs. His grandfather established the elementary school in his hometown, and his father ran UBC, a China startup that distributed bearings and industrial parts nationwide. Penaloza worked with his dad on starting UBC for a year, then in 1994 left to pursue a career in investment banking and private equity. He worked as an associate for Smith Barney in Hong Kong and as an assistant director for a leading private equity investment company in Asia, PAMA Group. In 2000, at the peak of the dotcom boom, Penaloza turned up the entrepreneurial juices and did his first of three Internet startups. "The idea of becoming an Internet entrepreneur was irresistible," he recalls.

His first startup, Hungry-For-Words.com, was designed to teach Japanese and Chinese people how to speak English, by learning a new word each day for free with a flash card service and built-in audio. The service gained 200,000 users, but when NASDAQ crashed and ad support fell, Hungry-For-Words closed the China business. Thanks to a lifeline thrown from maverick investor Masayoshi Son of Tokyo-based Softbank Corp., the brand was revived as a moneymaker in Japan with high-priced social events and parties, plus English lessons as an aside.

Building on that experience, in 2003, Penaloza launched World Friends, a cross-cultural networking service for a monthly fee of

$24.95 that blends Facebook for connecting with friends and pen pals, plus Match.com for finding dates.

To fund World Friends, Penaloza relied on finance connections from Hong Kong and raised $9 million from an enviable list of high-profile investors, including Danny Lui, founder of Lenovo Hong Kong; Timothy Chia, chairman of UBS Investment Bank Asia; Henry Cornell, a senior partner at Goldman Sachs; and former PAMA colleague, CEO Michael Kwee. Within five years, WorldFriends reached profitability, racked up nearly 2 million users worldwide, and managed to seal a partnership deal with Yahoo! Japan. WorldFriends—which has office space down the hall from Ushi—more recently has partnered with Tencent's QQ instant messaging service as well.

As a spin-off from World Friends, Penaloza launched Ushi in 2010 in style. He held a ceremony at the newly opened Waldorf-Astoria Hotel in a landmark heritage building along the famous waterfront Bund promenade. Charter members were on hand to see him pick up a check for $1.5 million in venture financing from prominent investors, including philanthropist and fund manager Peter Kellner of the social capital nonprofit Endeavor.org and Jose Cheng of Li & Fung's private equity group.

I caught up with Penaloza in Shanghai in November 2010, a month after he had deposited that $1.5 million check. Sitting in his tech-trendy office in a complex that houses numerous techie start-ups, he seemed relaxed and confident that Ushi would make it.

Ushi copies LinkedIn's popular features for networking, groups, event listings, and messages, but it's layered in extras, including a job-posting service, virtual currency, badges, microblogs, mobile check-in for business conferences, and networking parties to socialize with professional contacts. Ushi also has a unique feature for mobile phone users to check into an event and see if peers from the Ushi network are there. The business model is similar to LinkedIn, with monthly and yearly subscription charges for sending messages and getting introductions outside a circle of connections. At $8.50 per month for 10 messages and unlimited introductions, Ushi is a bargain over LinkedIn pricing of $49.95 monthly. Ushi's invite-only formula filters out hangers-on and helps to keep the network exclusive. "It's like you don't want to build a golf course and then allow everyone to play for free. It can ruin the golf experience. You need quality filters," says Penaloza.

STRATEGY: Ushi.cn

- Network with VIP business influencers who can endorse your service, pro-mote it, and even help you raise venture capital from leading sources.
- Take the learning from one startup, even if it crashed, and apply it to get-ting the right formula for the next startup.
- Seek advice from mentors with parallel experience in more mature markets.

Penaloza has a competitive advantage with his tech-savvy con-nections. His co-founder is former Yahoo! China product manager Zhang Yue, who also designed rival site TianJi, acquired in 2007 by French business networking site Viadeo. Penaloza relies on that useful tool, mentoring, from Bill Liao, the co-founder of Xing.com, a German business social networking service. Penaloza credits Liao for advising him on how to jump-start Ushi as an invite-only service. "We meet on Skype every two weeks," says Penaloza.

Given his circle, Penaloza has generated a high profile for Ushi without spending a ton on advertising and promotions. As one attention-grabbing customer incentive, Ushi offered members a free drink at Starbucks as a thank-you for inviting business contacts to sign up. Ushi also launched a cobranded marketing program with the *Wall Street Journal China*, inviting subscribers to join Ushi and boost their white-collar careers.

A deal for additional venture finance is in the works for 2011, but Penaloza isn't disclosing details or revealing financials for the still-young site.

"Our mission is very aligned with the nation's mission to con-tinuously evolve as an advanced economy. We are no longer just the world's low-cost factory. China needs networks of professionals and entrepreneurs, and we can accelerate that process," says Penaloza, sounding like he was making a pitch. "At the same time, we're also helping to solve every Chinese CEO's top challenge: recruiting experienced talent."

China's Wikipedia

Haidong Pan first captured my attention at an annual conference of the entrepreneurial networking group Hua Yuan Science and Technology Association (HYSTA). It was his sense of humor I was

drawn to, as he described how in his
early 30s he was able to get financing
for his first startup—a Chinese version
of Wikipedia—from Silicon Valley VC
Tim Draper.

In an animated manner, Pan told
the story of how Draper latched on to
his nickname, PHD, and figured that
Pan must be as smart as his PhD degree.
That pun helped Pan weasel his way
into a meeting with Draper and jump-
start his business with Draper Fisher
Jurvetson money.

Pan has the gift of gab, which has
served him well. With his outgoing personality, he has managed to forge connections with well-placed achievers and
gotten ahead. Through an introduction
from a classmate, he persuaded DCM's

Founder Haidong Pan of Hudong
in Beijing

Hurst Lin to sign on as an investor in his Wikipedia-styled site, then
nabbed Feng Deng of Northern Light Venture Capital and raised a
total of $30 million in early 2008. He went back to the till in August
2011 and raised $15 million from investors including Draper Fisher
Jurvetson.

A returnee to China, Pan, 36, follows in the footsteps of the first
wave of Ivy League–educated Chinese Internet entrepreneurs who
came back to their homeland to do startup clones. He is equally
comfortable in the East or West. Pan picked up and moved to
Beijing shortly after graduating in 2002 with a doctorate in systems
engineering from Boston University. It was a homecoming for Pan,
an overachiever who grew up in Sichuan province and earned a
bachelor's degree in mechanical engineering from Beijing Science
& Technology University and a master's in manufacturing engineering from Tsinghua University.

Pan had debated whether to stay in the United States or return
to China to start his career, but friends convinced him to look
eastward. He had some publishing managerial experience under
his belt, having run the monthly student magazine *Harvard China
Review* and its related annual forum. "My friends in the U.S. and
China were all about 10 years older than me, and they said, 'If you

are going to do something, you should go back to China because that's where the opportunities are,'" Pan relates, as we're meeting in his funky loftlike office in Beijing in 2009.

Pan's first job in Beijing was in 2004, as chief information officer of AsiaEC.com, an e-commerce startup that was acquired a year later by Office Depot. Pan didn't own shares in AsiaEC.com and didn't benefit financially from the sale.

He made sure that didn't happen again. Influenced by the emergence of Wikipedia as a contributor-generated reference source for all things encyclopedic, he launched the Wikipedia of China—Hudong.com—in July 2005, in both Chinese and English versions.

Hudong, which means "interactive," can't compare to the expanse of the global Wikipedia, with 281 languages, 69 million articles and images, and 28 million contributors. But it is the leader in the Chinese marketplace, with a 95 percent market share.[2] Hudong has accumulated more than 5 million entries from 3.6 million contributors.

Unlike the nonprofit Wikipedia, Hudong is a profit-making enterprise with 210 employees. Hudong generates revenues from targeted advertising on its site and specifically packaged content for businesses.

Pan, who is chairman and CEO, estimates revenues of $20 million and profits of $5 million for 2011. The biggest challenge, he says, is recruiting local talent to build his team. "We are on our way to success. It's much more of a challenge to find talent here than in the U.S.," notes Pan, who has a wiry build and a friendly face. "They don't know basic things, like how to write e-mails, use the copier or the fax."

Like other successful look-alike sites, Hudong goes beyond the original with features designed especially for local customs. The user-friendly site, which runs on open source Chinese wiki software, has colorful graphics and icons to click on imaginatively designed sections. Social media is baked into the site. There's a knowledge club for sharing info about science, groups for getting acquainted with like-minded friends, and centers for exchanging copyrighted images. Hudong has its own frequent user plan, where contributors can accumulate credits to redeem gifts. Information is categorized to be more readily accessible as well. For instance, there's a section called Leaderboard, where rankings of lists from the fields of science, history, geography, and the economy are published. Among its most creative features are a museum info platform and a cutting-edge entry list sent out every five minutes. "We are scientific and serious like Wikipedia, but we also have entertainment and very up-to-date content," says Pan.

Another innovation Hudong is popularizing is a package of expert content for business, called *Baike* ("encyclopedia"), which can be ordered on demand. "The quality is improving fast as more and more real-world experts are getting heavily involved in the collective writing," says Pan, adding that the coverage is moving from "what" and "why" to "how." He notes that the content for *Baike* is contributed by specialists in their field.

Running a site with social media content in China can be risky. While Hudong hasn't exactly incited a social revolution, it's been known to shake things up for the public good. Pan, who has been recognized as a "Young Global Leader" by the World Economic Forum, tells me the story of the "cheating horse" or *Haidong* as an example.

STRATEGY: Hudong

- Use your natural charm and a winning idea to tempt investors to write big checks.
- Think out of the box to come up with imaginative features not yet seen elsewhere but ideal for the local culture.
- Bake social media into a tried-and-true business model.

A sports car driver speeding in Hangzhou hit a man and was about to get off with a small fine when one of the witnesses submitted an entry on Hudong to report the incident. The witness scolded the arresting police for listing the speed of the driver at 70 miles per hour—a lot slower than the actual speed. The contributor used the imagery of the cheating horse, which is pronounced like "70 miles" in Chinese, to describe the incident. That submission soon popped up all over China, Pan says. The driver was subsequently fined 1.3 million renminbi, the equivalent of $200,000.

It's a good example of how the Internet is enabling civilian paparazzi—not exactly what Pan had in mind when he created the site. Still, he's pleased. "I am a risk taker, and I want to do good for society," says Pan, repeating a common refrain I've often heard from Chinese entrepreneurs raised in a collective society. "Money is not the final thing."

To be sure, Pan is making a difference, keeping social networking as a communication option where foreign sites such as LinkedIn and Wikipedia are sometimes blocked or censored in China. His and other Chinese copycat brands like Ushi are offering Chinese citizens content they couldn't otherwise tap.

As long as clones can continue to bring in Web traffic and profits for their founders and investors, they're here to stay in Asia's emerging digital communications hubs. The next generation of tech leaders is likely to become bolder and venture out into new space with more original ideas. Already, that's beginning to happen with localized features, some more advanced than seen in the West. Disruptive technologies that break up the standard ways of doing things that have been the hallmark of Silicon Valley will still take some time to appear at full scale in Asia.

CHAPTER 10

Originate a Breakthrough Discovery

Not too much technology innovation is truly the kind of revolutionary, breakthrough work that has the potential to change the world. It's refinement of existing concepts and incremental innovation to lower costs, improve efficiency, or appeal to local tastes. Yet some Asian startups are advancing as spinouts of research from leading universities in Singapore and Bangalore. Others are getting ahead by recruiting knowledgeable teams from multinational corporations for their helm. From clean energy to mobile communications, Asian entrepreneurs are moving up the ladder of invention. Venture investors well positioned to capitalize on this "invented in Asia" trend are **Sonny Wu** of **GSR Ventures**, who has backed six innovative LED makers in China and **Ashish Gupta** of **Helion Venture Partners**.

China has been criticized as the clone capital of the world. India has been faulted as primarily a service center for the West. Entrepreneurs in both markets don't have the world's respect for earth-shattering originality that can compare with Silicon Valley's much-heralded record. It's still mostly about made in Asia and not about invented in Asia. But change is coming, as I found through a discovery of leading-edge startups in Bangalore, Singapore, and Beijing, several of them spinouts from university research.

On the world stage for technology and science research, the United States continues to be the world's superpower. A look at the Nobel Prizes awarded in medicine, physics, and chemistry dating from 1950 to recent years shows that American scientists claimed 58 percent of the 257 prizes awarded in these categories.[1]

Cleantech maverick Sonny Wu of GSR Ventures in Beijing

The United States leads the world in patent filings, too, with more than a quarter of applications globally. Of the top 20 universities applying for patents in 2010, all but four were from the United States, with Japan and Korea at two each.[2]

But several indicators of a shift in the balance of scientific power to the East are cropping up, from academia to the corporate world to research and development labs. One sign of the tilting scales can be seen in international patent applications. Globally, filings increased by 4.8 percent in 2010, led by strong gains from China and South Korea, offsetting mixed performance in European countries and a continued decline in the United States. (See Table 10.1.) Of the top 20 corporations filing for patents—a list led by Japan's Panasonic Corp. for two years in a row—the United States had only four: Qualcomm, Microsoft, 3M, and Hewlett-Packard.

In the academic world, Chinese scientists from top American universities are being lured back home. Biologist Shi Yigong left the faculty of Princeton University in 2008 to become the dean of life sciences at Tsinghua University in Beijing. Rao Yi, a biologist at Northwestern University, departed in 2007 to become the dean of the School of Life Sciences at Peking University.

The brilliant PhD Qian Gao, who had been teaching and conducting research at the Yale School of Medicine, has come back to China and is now dean of the School of Medicine at Nanjing University. I observed a graduate-level biology class of Gao's in Nanjing. As guest experts lectured in English about their biomedical research—among them an oncologist from Mayo Clinic and a senior VP from pharmaceutical company Merck—I noticed the students listening politely. But no one was curious enough to ask a follow-up question, and all piled out of the classroom afterward. Anyone who has lectured in a traditional Chinese classroom

Table 10.1   Top 15 Ranking for Patents

Ranking	Country	2006	2007	2008	2009	2010 Estimate	2010 Percent	2010 Growth
1	United States of America	51,280	54,043	51,637	45,618	44,855	27.5%	-1.7%
2	Japan	27,025	27,743	28,760	29,802	32,156	19.7%	7.9%
3	Germany	16,736	17,821	18,855	16,797	17,171	10.5%	2.2%
4	China	3,942	5,455	6,120	7,900	12,337	7.6%	56.2%
5	Republic of Korea	5,945	7,064	7,899	8,035	9,686	5.9%	20.5%
6	France	6,256	6,560	7,072	7,237	7,193	4.4%	-0.6%
7	United Kingdom	5,097	5,542	5,466	5,044	4,857	3.0%	-3.7%
8	Netherlands	4,553	4,433	4,363	4,462	4,097	2.5%	-8.2%
9	Switzerland	3,621	3,833	3,799	3,671	3,611	2.2%	-1.6%
10	Sweden	3,336	3,655	4,137	3,567	3,152	1.9%	-11.6%
11	Canada	2,575	2,879	2,976	2,527	2,707	1.7%	7.1%
12	Italy	2,698	2,946	2,883	2,652	2,632	1.6%	-0.8%
13	Finland	1,846	2,009	2,214	2,123	2,076	1.3%	-2.2%
14	Australia	1,996	2,052	1,938	1,740	1,736	1.1%	-0.2%
15	Spain	1,204	1,297	1,390	1,564	1,725	1.1%	10.3%
	All Others	11,531	12,595	13,725	12,659	12,909	7.9%	2.0%
	Total	149,641	159,927	163,234	155,398	162,900		

Source: World Intellectual Property Organization.

has seen the blank conforming stare of pupils. Gao later took me aside in the hallway outside the classroom and earnestly explained how he wants to transform China's educational system of learning by memorization toward critical thinking. Only by shaking up this long tradition, he says, can a critical mass break out of the mold and provide momentum for further advances.

Signs of China's emerging technological edge can also be seen in scientific research output from China. Over the past decade, Chinese scientists quadrupled the number of scientific papers published per year, ranking second only to the United States. In the intensely competitive and emerging field of nanotechnology, an important driver of the knowledge economy among industrialized nations, China doesn't lag far behind the United States. Chinese and U.S. researchers are authoring roughly the same number of papers, though the work is increasingly collaborative across borders and the United States retains the lead for truly innovative research.[3] As China seeks to close the gap, nanotechnology has been prioritized as one of China's key fields for science and technology development, and about 5,000 Chinese scientists are conducting nano-research at institutions, universities, and enterprises.[4]

Away from the ivory towers and in the thick of Asia's startup tech clusters, I absorb the buzz of creativity that makes things happen, that gives rise to sometimes little, and sometimes major, transformations. It's the same energy I've felt in Silicon Valley and Cambridge. Charles River partner Bill Tai, a veteran investor in China, India, and the United States, observes that new business models and innovations happen faster and travel farther than ever before due to high-speed digital information flows. As one example, South Korea's always-on digital communications market developed an innovative social networking service named Cyworld, which has a bit of Facebook, LinkedIn, MySpace, and YouTube. Cyworld, invented in 1999, soon was replicated in China, Vietnam, and the United States. A second example is Tencent's popular QQ instant-messaging and chat service that started in Shenzhen in 1998 and has been copied in Vietnam by social networking startup VNG.

In Bangalore, Helion's Ashish Gupta, a self-described technologist, tells me he's convinced a strong tech-based infrastructure in India will evolve over the next five years and produce an economic payoff. Gupta adds that he's betting his venture investing career on India technology making "real change happen."

Deep in the trenches of Asia's boot camps, a spark of originality can be seen in a wide array of fields, from clean energy to biomedical

Helion's venture honcho Ashish Gupta in Bangalore

to mobile communications and e-commerce. Medical device maker Perfint Healthcare from Chennai, which has a patent for robotics to do highly precise biopsies, is one stand-out example. (See Chapter 2.) From Nanchang, LatticePower spins out high-energy, long-lasting LED lightbulbs, while Taiwan's SemiLEDs does the same. (See Chapter 5.) Others highlighted earlier in this book include Borqs and Prudent Energy (Chapters 4 and 5). A sampling of several more inventive startups that caught my eye during my Asian tech tours in 2009 and 2010 follows.

In his ground-floor office space and over the noise of horns honking from the nearby street in Bangalore, engineer Janesh Janardhanan is showing off a robotic-powered vacuum cleaner powered by chips he's designed. He's applied for 14 patents in India for the device made by Robhatah Robotics Solutions, a spin-off from research he developed with a professor from his alma mater, the National University of Singapore. Placing the circular, bowling ball-size machine on the table, he switches on the robot. We watch it go round and round the table, whirring and sensing the edge before turning in a new direction.

The fanciful, hands-free vacuum cleaner is made possible by a startup team of 15 engineers in India and a group of PhD students at the university, funding of $500,000 from an angel investor network in Delhi, plus a cross-border invention and manufacturing chain, leveraging designed-in-India chips and made-in-China labor.

As we're meeting in February 2010, Janardhanan is telling me he wants to commercialize the robotics cleaner and take it mass market. His goal is to sell 600,000 to 700,000 of these cleaners within one year. At a price of $140, the robot-powered device is affordable for most average income workers in the developed world, though I haven't seen it at Wal-Mart yet. His sales estimate seems reasonable enough, given that its chief rival, iRobot, which costs about three times more than Robhatah, passed 6 million in sales in early 2011. "The challenge is to make something affordable," says Janardhanan, who is husky and has a big smile framed by a black mustache and beard. "This is the first mass consumer product. We are going for high volume and low margins."

Assuming that Robhatah makes it to consumer shelves, the next objective is to launch an upright model priced at $500 and meant for tougher jobs, combining the hands-free benefit of a robot-powered model with the power of a commercial cleaner.

Robhatah Robotics founder Janesh
Janardhanan in Bangalore

"This next product will make a new category for vacuum cleaners. It's a game-changing product and will go straight from the lab to the consumer market," claims Janardhanan, who has that sort of eccentric quality of a mad scientist and once worked on research at Johns Hopkins University to develop a three-dimensional imaging system for virtual plastic surgery.

Five years from now, Janardhanan sees robotics research entering a new dimension where robots can skate or dance and sport unique personalities shaped by the individuals powering them. He says such far-out work is already going on at the National University of Singapore.

"It is the dream of every robotics company to see its products used by consumers, to be a part of life and not just a gadget, from the mundane to interactive experiences, like a pal—for instance, to design toys that can be loved, to express distinct behavior with a basic set of features that can be differentiating," says Janardhanan, who combines his mechanical engineering degree with an MBA from the Singapore university.

Picking up on my curiosity about these science fiction–like possibilities, Janardhanan is on a roll and demonstrates his most-loved project: a cricket match played by teams of robotic-powered toys, relying on artificial intelligence to move the players. This is definitely a fresh realm for artificial intelligence.

In case the robots don't go commercial, Robhatah has developed a secondary business plank. The high-tech startup is taking its advanced research into Robotics 101 classrooms in India as a way for students to test their programs and ideas on educational robots.

> **STRATEGY: Robhotah Robotics Solutions**
>
> - Spin out R&D from a university lab to work on commercializing a product with advanced technology.
> - Have a long-range vision but work on implementing the plan a step at a time without breaking the bank.
> - Leverage high-end engineering work from India with low-cost labor from China.

Bubble Talk in Motion

From Singapore, a leading edge startup with the memorable name of Bubble Motion and a service cleverly called Bubbly has repositioned its service and brought in a new CEO with Silicon Valley experience. Best described as an audio version of Twitter, Bubbly is a pioneering social communication tool for mobile phone users to share updates with friends and contacts.

As with Twitter, a person can send a message to their followers, from an intimate few to thousands. Users dial in to check voice-recorded messages on the service, similar to going online for a Twitter status update. The startup's advanced routing technology makes it possible for these voice messages to go out instantaneously in files as large as 1 megabit, without crashes like Twitter's Fail Whale messages when the service gets jammed with too many updates at the same time.

Bubble Motion has filed for five U.S. patents to protect the intellectual property that goes into its voice tweets service, developed by engineers hired from the United States, India, China, the Philippines, and Malaysia, many of them relocated to Singapore. "The service allows one-to-many routing. It isn't a cure for cancer, but this is a huge engineering feat," says Tom Clayton, CEO and president of Bubble Motion.

Amazingly fast, within one year of its spring 2010 launch, Bubbly has blown up to 8 million users across four Asian countries: India, Indonesia, Japan, and the Philippines. Bubbly has fans from the Bollywood elite, as well as girl bands in Japan.

Enter the venture capitalists. Bubble Motion nabbed $10 million in capital from the SingTel Group's corporate venture capital fund SingTel Innov8 in the first quarter of 2011 and was joined by prior investors: the Singapore government-affiliated Infocomm Investments,

Sequoia Capital India, Palomar Ventures, and NGC. Altogether, Bubble Motion has raised the significant sum of $45 million.

"In many ways, Bubble Motion is the first company to introduce this messaging paradigm," says Mohit Bhatnagar, a partner at Sequoia Capital India, which, together with Sequoia's U.S. fund, has a $15 million investment riding on its success. "The market is very large because this service can run on all kinds of wireless-connected devices," Bhatnagar points out.

Making sure Bubble Motion stays on track, in 2007 Sequoia Capital dug into its bag of tricks and recruited serial entrepreneur Clayton, 34, from Silicon Valley to run Bubble Motion. Clayton previously managed the worldwide telecom business of BEA Systems, acquired by Oracle for a stunning $8.5 billion. The Harvard MBA has started up five companies in networking software, systems integration, and high-end audio manufacturing, plus served as a broadband policy consultant to the White House.

Clayton took over from the startups' Indian serial entrepreneurs Sunil Coushik and Venu Sriperumal, who had co-founded the service in 2005. The new boss initially thought he would move the startup to the Valley, but he's kept it in Singapore—sensibly enough, because the customer base is Asia. Two markets being skirted for now are Vietnam and China. Monitoring the voice tweets to wipe out politically sensitive content in these Communist-controlled nations would be too problematic, Clayton says.

Not wasting time as the startup's new CEO, Clayton took action to put Bubble Motion on a path to profitability, with an upgrade of the technology to a more advanced service. An original peer-to-peer service named Bubble Talk was sidelined by an innovative one-to-all Bubbly talk service. Clayton notes that "Bubbly has 25 million lines of code compared to 2.5 million lines for the peer-to-peer service."

STRATEGY: Bubble Motion

- Invest capital to upgrade technology, and launch more innovative services with mass-market appeal.
- Keep an eye on the cash burn rate, and balance with high revenue growth.
- Hire high-end engineers from multiple locations, and relocate them to headquarters to achieve fast, world-class results.

Bubble Motion makes money by sharing revenue with mobile phone carriers such as Bharti Airtel, Reliance Communications, and Vodafone that charge users a small fee, typically five cents per message. With the upgrade, Bubble Motion has upped its revenue share with carriers from a previous 20 percent to at least 40 percent and as much as 70 percent.

The new service has helped revenues double each quarter since a launch in early 2010. Clayton projects Bubble Motion will reach $11 million in revenues for the full year 2011. Though on a roll with growth, Bubble Motion was burning cash at the rate of $200,000 per month in early 2011. With tech-centered startups that require large sums of capital, reaching profitability lickety-split is rare, even for bubbly brands with consumer appeal like this one.

The final startup I meet with on the tech frontier is 3DSoc. The Bangalore-based startup has patented technology to bring rich, interactive 3-D content to your mobile phone. It doesn't seem all that novel until you see how it can be used to make cool, personalized greeting cards with messages and visuals that come alive over the screen.

I shake hands with Krishnan Ramaswami, a co-founder and managing director of 3DSoc—by the way, Soc is shorthand for "solid compression." Started as a joint research project more than a decade earlier at Stanford University and the Indian Institute of Science, 3DSoc was spun off into a commercial venture in 2006.

The startup is housed nearby the research-centric, postgrad-focused Indian institute where Ramaswami got his master's degree. Ramaswami cowrote the software guts for 3DSoc at Stanford University, where he earned a PhD. At Stanford, the brainy software developer worked with Professor Fritz B. Prinz on this technology called virtual interactive solid (VIS) format.

STRATEGY: 3DSoc

- Collaborate cross-border on breakthrough technologies, and let necessity be your guide.
- Work with professors on research, then spin the technology out into a commercial venture with equity stakes for the universities.
- Figure out ways to take your complex technology and make it useful for business as well as consumers.

Their India-U.S. collaboration grew out of a frustration with uploading 3-D models over the Internet and sharing the large files over low-bandwidth speeds. Necessity being the mother of invention, the startup team got a patent in 2004 for the technology, which Ramaswami says can condense files by more than 1,000 times. This works wonders for browsing three-dimensional content, animated graphics, text, and audio on mobile phones without sucking up too much juice.

Always on the lookout for new and exciting technologies, IDG Ventures India invested $1.2 million in 3DSoc in December 2007 and got two board seats, including one for managing director Sethi. Both universities also have an equity stake in the startup, with co-founder Professor B. Gurumoorthy representing the Indian Institute of Science. Working with a software team of 23 in Bangalore and just $400,000 in up-front costs, Ramaswami codeveloped a mobile phone application based on the technology that works on multiple handsets, including Nokia, Sony Ericsson, Samsung, LG, and Android phones.

He showed me a demo of one customized app they've developed: a little, yellow chicken cartoon that clucks and dances in 3-D. The dancing chicken was downloaded more than 1 million times in dozens of countries within nine months of its April 2010 launch. The chicken is just the egg of a whole bunch of applications for this technology beyond rich media. Imagine the possibility for e-learning manuals, for instance, as well as mobile games and avatar designs.

The business plan when I met with Ramaswami in February 2010 was to reach 5 million downloads by September 2011 and 10 million downloads by March 2012. The startup posted modest revenues of $50,000 in 2008, its first year of operation, and was aiming for $1 million in its second year. "The conciseness and interactivity of this app could be the key to mass adoption," he says.

That seems to be a reasonable expectation, since the mobile applications market is booming and was projected to top 8.2 billion downloads in 2010.[5] Moreover, Ramaswami estimates that the market for 3-D publishing is currently more than $18 billion, and the rich Internet applications market is worth billions more.

That might be more than Ramaswami had in mind when he looked out over the horizon. "I always wanted to come back to India. There is a lot of engineering talent here," says Ramaswami, 43, who grew up in Chennai and returned to India in 2002. "I wanted to show that you can build a product company out of India, and to showcase to the world that it's built from here."

11

Take Your Startup Public on the NYSE or NASDAQ

What entrepreneur doesn't have dreams of taking their startup public? The rush of Chinese tech startups, such as China's Facebook-plus **Renren**, holding court on Wall Street, set some new standards for drama. Stock market investors weighed the risks against the opportunities of owning shares in businesses that were marginally profitable at best but primed for liftoff as market leaders. Rumbles about fraud at some publicly traded Chinese companies led the stocks of several once-hot Chinese companies to tank below their IPO prices. For entrepreneurs and their venture investors, the pressure is on to get the business fundamentals in place for an IPO and then time the listing when the market is hot. The challenge is also to make sure the IPO is clean. India's **MakeMyTrip** provided some valuable lessons on going public with good timing and profitability, and showed up many of the newly listed Chinese startups.

As shares of Joe Chen's Renren—the Facebook-plus of China— began trading up on the New York Stock Exchange on May 4, 2011, I couldn't help but recall our interviews in Beijing a few years ago. Back then, he candidly shared his view of what it takes to win the Chinese Internet race.

"We gotta get big faster than rivals, and we're fairly fast in areas that really matter. We are land grabbing everywhere," he told me. I also remembered him telling me about his supercharged approach to building web sites: "In China, we just chunk it out. We just do it."

As I went down memory lane, I could hear Joe telling me what he'd learned from reading investment books about such business

IPO scorer Neil Shen of Sequoia Capital China, in Hong Kong

legends as Bill Gates, Larry Ellison, and Rupert Murdoch. He said then he was applying what he had learned from these masters to "buy companies of intrinsic value with a barrier to entry and then nurture them." And the biggest lesson he took away? "I want to make sure to have an ample supply of cash to do deals."

Chen's IPO delivered the capital required to duke it out in the Chinese tech race. Striking at a time when Wall Street was going nuts over China's YouTube Youku and its Amazon look-alike Dangdang, Renren raised $743.4 million in its debut, while shares soared 29 percent above the $14 IPO price. The lofty valuations for unprofitable Chinese startups recalled the mania of the late-1990s dotcom boom.

But within a few weeks, the initial euphoria faded, and the Chinese tech stocks were getting slammed. The China Internet growth story had cast a spell on Wall Street, but now sobered investors saw risks and not so awesome balance sheets. Renren lost money in 2010 but turned a profit in second quarter 2011. Still, its share price did not rebound much immediately after news of its first profitable quarter as a publicly-traded company.

Meanwhile, Chinese Internet stocks were getting hit as accounting irregularities led to investigations and trading suspensions among companies that had gained U.S. listings through shell companies— so-called reverse mergers or backdoor listings. Citing market conditions in mid-2011, Shanghai-based Nobao Renewable Energy Group, backed with $12.5 million by tech-focused private equity firm Silver Lake in 2010, scrapped a NYSE IPO. Chinese digital media company Xunlei, in which Google has a small stake, postponed a planned $200 million IPO on NASDAQ.

The turbulence showed that the whole going-IPO process is not for the fainthearted. It can be tricky and requires perseverance, plus fast growth plus profitability plus great timing. An IPO is the prize every Chinese Internet entrepreneur I've met wants. Who wouldn't want to pose in front of NASDAQ's Times Square headquarters like Robin Li did in 2005, when his Chinese search engine Baidu posted a first-day jump of more than 300 percent? The real challenge begins in delivering performance after the IPO, under the scrutiny of regulators and watchful stock market investors quick to buy or sell based on every strategy, tactic, market shift, or rumor.

Chen looked serious and stressed as he rang the opening bell at the NYSE to kick off trading in Renren. The May 4 date—coming on a Chinese holiday, Youth Day—matched well with Renren's youthful appeal (though "four" sounds like "death" in Mandarin, not a good omen).

No doubt, Chen was anxious after lots of sleepless nights dealing with pre-IPO problems. He had wanted to take his startup public a few months earlier, but it was held up by his CFO's maternity leave.

Just two days before trading began, Renren filed an amended prospectus to correct user growth in the first quarter, a mistake that Chen blamed on a typo. In the original prospectus filed April 15, 2011, Renren said its number of monthly active users increased 7 million monthly to 31 million in the first quarter of 2011. The amended filing reflected that 2 million of those 7 million new users were added in the fourth quarter of 2010, reducing the first-quarter 2011 growth rate from 29 percent to 19 percent.

The change highlighted the murkiness of data in China's fast-flying Internet sector.

As Seattle-based Harris & Moure attorney Dan Harris noted in his China Law Blog, the best-case scenario is that the Chinese social networking site had problems accounting for how many new users were actually active or else it inadvertently attributed two quarters of growth to one. The worst-case scenario: Renren thought no one would notice that its numbers were inflated.

On top of this, in the run-up to the IPO, some investors were raising questions about whether Renren was misleading the market by valuing the company on 131 million registered or activated users when only 31 million used the service at least once a month.

Meanwhile, another storm was brewing. Four days prior to the IPO, Derek Palaschuk, the chief financial officer of NASDAQ-listed Chinese software company Longtop, resigned as head of Renren's audit committee "to protect Renren." The step followed an accounting controversy at Longtop that had sent the company's shares plummeting the week before. David Chao, an independent director representing DCM's minority investment in the Chinese social network, replaced Palaschuk. The NYSE halted trading in Longtop shares on May 17 as the SEC opened a probe into accounting fraud at Longtop, and on June 1, Palaschuk resigned as CFO.

These incidents—coupled with the fact that Chen sold 13 million shares at the Renren IPO to reduce his shareholdings from 28 percent to 23 percent and cash out more than $50 million—prompted one China tech investor in New York to remark, "Renren is certainly not a clean IPO."

I spoke with Chen at lunchtime the day of the IPO, as the stock price was surging. "This is the beginning of the next chapter, a prelude to line one. We're very happy with the overall outcome and now it's time to execute on the promise of the prospectus," said Chen, who was cautious to avoid a flamboyant sound bite like he had once made about the evil BAT (Baidu, Alibaba, and Tencent), now that he was head of a newly publicly traded company. "Real name social networks like Renren are not just ordinary communications tools, but are recording the history of daily life and capturing human interactions and emotions as an archive," added Chen.

Asked about the pre-IPO saga, Chen admitted, "We had a few small stumbles." What lessons did he learn? "You have to make sure you legitimize everything and have the facts right," Chen responded. He added

STRATEGY: Renren

- Triple-check the facts, filings, and figures before the IPO to prevent any snags. Don't panic even when last-minute flare-ups happen.
- Going IPO is the easy part. Running a public company isn't. Different skill sets are required.
- Don't rush the IPO. Make sure the company has the business fundamentals in place and the market conditions prime.

that he would advise other Chinese entrepreneurs to be sure they are "very, very prepared in the filings" and "very transparent."

Standing behind Chen at the opening bell was venture capitalist and now audit committee chair David Chao, an early backer of Chen's startup. An active investor in Asia and the United States, Silicon Valley–based DCM has a 9 percent stake in Renren. Its shares are in lockup for six months following the IPO. Chao and I spoke the day of the IPO, and he indicated that DCM is a long-term shareholder. "Renren is the first social network site of a major magnitude to go public worldwide," he pointed out, adding, "It's a great long-term play like Facebook in the U.S."

MakeMyTrip: A Long Passage

While all the focus was on China, Indian travel startup MakeMyTrip was making the newly traded Chinese tech stocks look bad. Its shares were holding relatively steady one year after its IPO, in contrast to the roller-coaster ride for several of the money-losing China newcomers on NASDAQ and the NYSE.[1]

MakeMyTrip listed on NASDAQ in August 2010 and—no reverse merger here, as with some China listings—ranked as one of the top IPO performers. The Indian travel startup reached a market capitalization of $903 million on its debut, ranking sixth among 26 venture-backed Asian startups that went public in the United States during 2010. It was the only Indian company among those newly listed Asian startups and the first from India since 2007.

The financial results for MakeMyTrip looked comparatively strong, too. In its first fiscal year ending March 31,

MakeMyTrip investor Vispi Daver of Sierra Ventures in Menlo Park

2011, MakeMyTrip logged net income of $5.1 million and revenues of $124 million, a 49 percent gain over the previous year.

Years of getting the underpinnings in place for success were being rewarded for the pioneering Indian online travel site, formed in Delhi's exurban Gurgaon in 2000 by ex-banker Deep Kalra and two co-founders. (See Chapter 4.)

In the slower-moving evolution of the Indian Web (see Chapter 2) compared with China, it took MakeMyTrip 10 years to go from zero to IPO. Its China comparable, market-leading Ctrip, went public on NASDAQ in 2003, only four years after its start. Both are market leaders in their home country's travel sector.

Not only stock market investors but also venture backers have done well by betting on MakeMyTrip. Its venture investors—SAIF Partners, Helion Venture Partners, and Sierra Ventures—have profited handsomely from a combined $39 million in the deal. SAIF is making a 20 to 25 times return, according to partner Ravi Adusumalli, on a $10 million-plus investment in MakeMyTrip dating back to 2005. Sierra Ventures partner Vispi Daver said the firm's return on the India bet stacks up very well against those in its U.S. portfolio.

"The IPO gives MakeMyTrip stature, access to capital, and a lot more flexibility as a public company to develop as a global brand," Daver pointed out, adding, "MakeMyTrip was a landmark deal for India."

Meanwhile, MakeMyTrip's success is paving the way for more Indian companies to bulk up and seek IPOs. Kleiner Perkins–backed mobile advertising service inMobi was expected to file for an IPO in the United States during the third quarter of 2011. Also taking a cue from MakeMyTrip, in early August 2011, Indian entrepreneur, V.S.S. Mani, filed for a public listing in India of JustDial,

---

STRATEGY: MakeMyTrip

- Keep an eye on the business fundamentals and strategies to boost the bottom line and score an enviable IPO.
- Outwit rivals with a concerted focus on the core, money-making strengths of the business, and ditch unprofitable lines.
- Figure out what local customers want, and then tailor the service features to win them over.

his mobile search startup, frontloaded with $52 million from leading venture investors.[18]

Going public requires a fine balance of timing and terms, just like raising a round of venture finance. When I interviewed Ray Zhang, CEO and founder of eHi Auto Services (see Chapter 6) in Shanghai in November 2010, he was contemplating how to get that alignment right as he eyed an IPO in the United States. Several investment bankers had been trying to knock on his door, eager to underwrite the issue. The practical Zhang was taking the bankers' calls but keeping his own pace. He offered this advice on handling the ambitious dealmakers: "Better first judge where their eagerness is coming from. Is it just to lock in another potential IPO deal for business development or do they genuinely believe the timing is good and the company is ready?" Asked how Zhang and his team would mark the calendar for the IPO, he responded with a determined, "Our own readiness and the capital market's timing."

No doubt Zhang was carefully considering the timing, as more and more newly-traded Chinese stocks were getting hammered as the second half of 2011 began. The pre-IPO quiet period rules for new stock offerings were in effect, and Zhang was not talking.

China or U.S. Exchange?

No other market in Asia comes close to China's streak of startups on U.S. exchanges. During 2010, China accounted for 22, or nearly a third, of 61 venture-backed IPOs in the United States, according to institutional research and investment firm Renaissance Capital in Greenwich, Connecticut. It was a banner year for China IPOs globally, as both the number of IPOs and the amount raised surged over prior years. (See Table 11.1.) India's MakeMyTrip was the sole startup from the subcontinent in that tally. Taiwan had one: NASDAQ-listed LED chip maker SemiLEDS Corp.

Table 11.1   Venture-Backed IPOs Worldwide among China-Based Companies

	2007	2008	2009	2010
# of IPOs	23	11	45	138
Amount raised*	$2,855.8	$618.9	$4,447.7	$21,443.9

*In millions.

Source: Dow Jones VentureSource.

China has had no shortage of winners since 2003. Some 64 Chinese tech companies scored a market valuation of more than $1 billion with listings on NASDAQ, NYSE, and HKSE, as well as the Shenzhen and Shanghai exchanges,[2] from 2003 through third-quarter 2010. Amazingly, 21 of those 64 entered this $1 billion league during the third quarter of 2010. Moreover, five venture-backed Chinese companies reached a market cap of more than $1 billion on the opening day of trading on U.S. exchanges in 2010.[3]

On the flip side, post-IPO performance doesn't look so robust. Of the 10 worst-performing venture-backed U.S. IPOs in 2010, for instance, six were Chinese companies, based on returns from IPO date to December 31, 2010 closing prices.[4] Furthermore, if an investor bought every Chinese IPO since 2008, the average return through mid-June 2011 would have been a loss of 24 percent, compared with a 25 percent gain on the average non-Chinese IPO,[5] according to Renaissance Capital. These figures underscore the risks and volatility of investing in Chinese newcomers to U.S. exchanges.

Turning to India, some high achievers exist, but most have stayed below the news radar outside their home country. Indian startups are required by law to go public first within their home country. The exception is if the startup is structured offshore through a holding company. MakeMyTrip was set up with a domicile in Mauritius; inMobi is registered in the Cayman Islands. Venture-backed Indian startups typically go public on the Bombay Stock Exchange and the National Stock Exchange of India.

In contrast, most of the early Chinese startups financed in dollars by Sand Hill Road investors were set up offshore, usually in the Cayman Islands, allowing them to directly list on NASDAQ or the NYSE. This difference helps explain why IPOs of Chinese startups have a higher profile internationally than those in India. Have you heard much about some of the more successful Indian IPOs? These are SKS Microfinance (2010), financial service firm Edelweiss Capital (2007), Idea Cellular (2007), job site Naukri (2006), information technology outsourcing service MindTree Consulting (2007), and business processing provider Firstsource (2006). Probably not. These firms didn't make much headline news outside India because they listed locally. Change may be coming, as the Indian Venture Capital Association has been lobbying for an easing of this listing regulation so that Indian companies can first go public in the United States or elsewhere.

STRATEGY: Naukri

- Back off from taking the venture money if the investors are in too big a hurry to take the startup public.
- Keep building the core business, even through a downturn, and keep your eye on the IPO prize.

One flagship Indian startup that well exemplifies the going public within India pattern is job site Naukri, the Monster.com of India. Founder Sanjeev Bikhchandani beat the odds and outlasted the dotcom downturn of the prior decade before taking his startup public on the Bombay Stock Exchange and the National Stock Exchange in 2006. That perseverance paid off. Naukri ranks as India's eighth most highly valued technology exit, giving its venture investors a $311 million return on capital. (See Chapter 3, Table 3.2.)

What worked is not being in a hurry to list the Indian job site, despite prodding by venture investors and investment bankers. In fact, the startup maven even turned down venture capital from Silicon Valley investors eager to float Naukri on NASDAQ during the dotcom boom of 1999. His enterprise had just turned profitable. The financiers urged the founder to invest the startup's slim profits into advertising to expand the brand and then angle toward an IPO. But Bikhchandani turned his back. "I walked out of the meeting and said, 'I don't want your money, thank you very much.'"

Instead, he settled for a relatively small $1.7 million investment from a domestic Indian firm, ICICI Venture, in 2000, "right before the dotcom party was over," he recollects as we're speaking at his office in Delhi in 2010. Starting from a small base, Naukri put the building blocks in place for his small business until 2004, when, after waiting out the downturn, the economy began to recover and money was flowing again. By then, his startup was bringing in revenues of $2 million and profits of approximately $200,000, he recalls. Finally, in 2006, he and his advisers decided that the timing was right for Naukri to go public. It was a good decision, judging from the value that was created.

Shenzhen and Shanghai Exchanges

As more Asian startups—primarily of China vintage—head for IPOs, the NYSE and NASDAQ still rate as the premier exchanges for globally oriented companies and their investors. But, domestic Chinese exchanges are on the rise for a growing number of RMB-funded startups in China, as noted previously (Chapter 1, Table 1.10).

A local China exchange, ChiNext, dubbed as China's NASDAQ, launched to fanfare in October 2009 with 28 listings and 100 in the queue. The NASDAQ-style board for high-growth tech startups had been in the works for several years and long anticipated by investors and small-company founders seeking to reap the financial rewards of their hard work. ChiNext created an avenue for yuan-financed Chinese startups to go public in China. In 2010, ChiNext grabbed 63 of 152 venture-backed domestic Chinese IPOs.[6]

ChiNext hasn't been quite the godsend investors and founders were anticipating, due to stringent regulations, though better accounting transparency and fewer limitations on sales of stock after the IPO could heighten its appeal. Currently, Chinese startups must be profitable for two years before a ChiNext float. Venture investors can't sell shares in these newly listed companies before three years, and pre-IPO investors must wait two years before unloading stock in the enterprise.

Another option for founders to take their Chinese startups public is the Shenzhen board for small and medium-size enterprises, which launched in 2004 and drew 80 initial public offerings in 2010,[7] with good returns.[8] As a sign of its growing clout as an exchange, even the Chinese electric maker BYD backed by billionaire investor Warren Buffett made a turbocharged debut on the larger Shenzhen Stock Exchange in June 2011, selling yuan-denominated shares, in addition to shares the automaker already had listed in Hong Kong.

Meanwhile, trade sales really aren't where the action is in China. Apart from a few higher-profile deals, such as Baidu's buy into travel search engine Qunar in June 2011,[9] trade sales haven't produced numerous financial rewards in China like they have in India. Some 183 venture-backed Chinese companies merged or were acquired in the first half of 2010. But China placed only sixteenth in a ranking of the world's top 20 countries for value of cross-border mergers and acquisitions.[10] The United States led the list, followed by the United Kingdom. India surprisingly did not make the cut although, as noted in Chapter 2, mergers and acquisitions such as TutorVista's sale to Pearson are more common than public offerings.[11]

Flowers Wilting

As China startups began a parade to U.S. exchanges in fall 2010 after a two-year dry spell, the talk in investing circles was about a bubble forming for Chinese Internet stocks that might come close to the 1990s dotcom boom and bust. Both online video-sharing site Youku and e-commerce site Dangdang went public on the fortuitous date of December 8, 2010, the "8" symbolizing good fortune in China. Youku jumped 161 percent from an IPO price of $12.80 for a close of $33.44—the strongest first-day advance for a U.S. IPO since Baidu in 2005—and edged out its predecessor ChinaCache International as a record holder.[12] Meanwhile, e-retailer Dangdang surged 87 percent on its opening day to $29.91, over an IPO price of $16. The upward trend seemed unstoppable, as yet another Chinese tech startup, Qihoo 360, soared on its NYSE debut in the first quarter of 2011.[13] Interestingly, all of these China tech stocks were financed primarily by Silicon Valley venture money.[14] (See Table 11.2.)

At the same time Dangdang and Youku were red-hot in early 2011 so were Chinese portals Sina, Sohu, and Netease.[15] The hyped up action led Robin Li, founder and chairman of Baidu, to warn

Table 11.2   Top 10 U.S. IPOs among Venture-Backed Asian Companies, 2010

Company	Market Capitalization*	Exchange	Country
1. Youku	$3.443 M[†]	NYSE	China
2. Dangdang	$2.330 M	NYSE	China
3. Soufun	$1.365 M	NYSE	China
4. Tal Education	$1.117 M	NYSE	China
5. Mecox Lane	$ 990 M	NASDAQ	China
6. MakeMyTrip	$ 903 M	NASDAQ	India
7. Noah Holdings	$ 875 M	NYSE	China
8. iSoftStone	$ 842 M	NYSE	China
9. China Lodging	$ 820 M	NASDAQ	China
10. Xueda Education	$ 839 M	NYSE	China

*As of date of IPO.
[†]In millions.
Note: NASDAQ and NYSE were about evenly split for total number of Asian IPOs during 2010.
Source: U.S. exchanges.

Youku venture investor Len Baker of Sutter Hill Ventures in Palo Alto

founders of Chinese Internet companies against listing overseas in haste. He advised entrepreneurs to instead focus on developing and improving their products. "You must remember that listing is not a means to an end, it is only a means of business development," Li said, speaking at a Baidu summit in Beijing, as shares in the Chinese search engine were trading at 90 times earnings.

Despite the words of caution, the race was on to go public soon to catch the sun before it set. As April flowers began to bloom in 2011, stock investors were betting on the growth and potential of the Internet in China, where only about two-thirds of the population is online. But how long investors would fall for the growth minus business fundamentals was looking iffy.

Lots more Chinese startups, most of them financed with Sand Hill Road money, were lining up to go public in quick succession. By early June 2011, 15 China-based companies had filed for IPOs in the United States, and 10 had priced, according to Renaissance Capital. The volatility of the market was a constant backdrop, yet the action seemed unstoppable.

Among those in the queue in midyear 2011 were several more venture-financed Chinese companies, including social networking site Kaixin001.com, car rental service eHi, and video programming site PPLive. Chinese online video web site Tudou resumed plans to go public after an IPO in November 2010 had stalled over accounting issues (and while a divorce settlement was finalized between CEO Gary Wang and his ex-wife over equity interest in the video-sharing site). In the tough market of mid-August 2011, Tudou managed to go public and raised $174 million.

How long would the adrenaline rush last? Not long.

Indeed, one day after the listing of Renren on May 4, 2011, a Chinese maker of security software for mobile phones, NetQin Mobile, flopped with its NYSE debut. The stock closed at $9.30 a share, down a steep 19 percent from its IPO price of $11.50. Kids' entertainment site Taomee got through the NYSE IPO gate in early June 2011, though investors traded its shares below the opening price on the debut.

It was time for a reality check for entrepreneurs, venture capitalists, and stock market investors. A company's growth alone cannot sustain a high valuation; it has to be growth and bottom-line results, plus all the other managerial, governance, and market leadership factors that go into the equation. Money-losing Youku exemplified this new reality. Gains in the share price of Youku,[16] which had peaked in mid-April at nearly five times its offering price of $12.80,[17] were collapsing by late May and into August. The same scenario was being repeated at marginally profitable Dangdang.[18] Its IPO pricing pop was erased by mid-March, and the stock was trading well below its opening IPO price of $16[19] by mid-August 2011.

It was hardly the first time that the China IPO scene had turned theatrical. In what former Beijing Bureau Chief Gady Epstein of *Forbes* described as "bizarre behavior for a newly listed company's boss," Dangdang CEO Li Guoqing, who is married to Chairwoman Peggy Yu, wrote in a Sina microblog that the investment banks that took them public way underestimated the company's valuation, which reached $2.4 billion on opening day.

In "even more bizarre behavior," Epstein writes, a Sina user purporting to work for one of those banks, Morgan Stanley, fired back at Li in coarse language. Epstein noted that Morgan Stanley says she is not an employee of the bank, but her tweets did seem to indicate some inside knowledge of Dangdang's pre-IPO machinations. A good account of the heated exchange, in which the "banker" cautioned Li to be careful "if you continue to cook the book," could be found on iChinaStock.com.

Count on such drama on the China Internet and IPO stage to continue as a microcosm of China's opening up. The risks and challenges for both venture and stock market investors among

China newcomers on U.S. exchanges, the stepped-up regulatory watch over Chinese stocks, the allegations of accounting fraud and corporate governance issues, and the roller-coaster stock prices all add up to look before you leap.

For astute entrepreneurs contemplating this arduous process, the real fun—*hard work*—really begins once the company is public and it's no longer the founder's sandbox, with accountability to an all-new set of interest parties and owners. Words of wisdom: Treasure those bootstrapping moments and don't be rushed to the IPO altar.

12

Go Global from Asia

Indian startups are gaining with a think-global, act-global strategy that permeates the entire company culture. From India, **TutorVista** offers online lessons to students in the United States while **iYogi** provides a remote PC fix-it service. Chinese net startups Baidu, Tencent, and Alibaba are developing foreign-language versions to go outside country borders, too. The trend is escalating as venture investors such as **Ajit Nazre** of **Kleiner Perkins** and **Mohanjit Jolly** of **DFJ India** plus corporate backers **Intel** and **Pearson** finance emerging Asian startups that seek to extend their reach to developed regions of the world. Expanding across borders takes the right business model and precision timing. Most of all, it takes a CEO who has that global vision from day one.

The idea started with a cartoon on the cover of the *Economist* magazine. This was back in 2000, when outsourcing of business processes to India was fairly new and getting a lot of attention, negative and otherwise. The cover featured a U.S. customer dealing with an Indian service representative and saying, "Don't tell me you're in Bangalore!" The cartoon was underscored with the cover line, "The one thing you cannot outsource is your homework."

That cartoon captured the imagination of serial entrepreneur K. Ganesh. "Why not?" he asked. And so TutorVista, a business run out of Bangalore with Indian tutors for overseas pupils, was born.

It's a perfect example of the type of startups from Asia that can go—and are increasingly going—outside their country borders. India is at the forefront of this trend naturally, because of the commonality of the English language. But startups in other countries, too, like Tencent's QQ instant-messaging service from China, are edging into the global landscape. For decades, it's been a West to East phenomenon, with Apple computers, Microsoft software, Cisco routers, BlackBerry mobile devices, Coke, Pepsi, McDonald's, and you name it going across the Pacific. But the tides are changing. Chinese-language search engine Baidu has made it to Japan, helped by the commonality of Japanese and Chinese characters. Alibaba and Tencent are edging into the United States with acquisitions and English-language versions of their sites and services.

No one said Asian brands are incapable of competing on a world stage. People used to joke about Japanese, then Korean, cars. But quality, pricing, and efficiency got these models into the mainstream and then into the garages of upwardly mobile consumers. Take personal computers, cameras, and mobile phones: All have dominant Asian brand names, including Samsung, LG, Sony, Toshiba, and Acer. The travel business has some of the best examples of Asia's exceptional quality and service: airlines Cathay Pacific, Singapore Airlines, and Japan Airways, plus hotels Shangri-La, Peninsula, and Raffles. Of course, not every business can go global. An online matrimonial site named Bharatmatrimony begun by Murugavel Janakiraman in Chennai wouldn't travel well across borders.

But more Asian startups are being hatched by forward-thinking managers with transportable concepts, and these companies are going global. If accomplished, it's one sure way to scale the business and not be limited by the home country's smaller market. It helps to have a product or service that's easily understood and leverages the geographic base, typically low costs. Technology advancements are making ideas travel faster and farther than ever before. Sometimes tech products from Asia are even more advanced than those in the West.

TutorVista has universal appeal. Who doesn't want to bound ahead with a better education? Indian startup iYogi offers a remote help desk in India to solve personal computer problems—another common need the world over.

Both TutorVista and iYogi are startups with headquarters and staff within their home country of India, and both have reached out internationally. Both, too, have figured out a new angle on the traditional business model of outsourcing, long India's stronghold.

The trend is going deeper as more specialized businesses such as mobile ad network inMobi and mobile search service JustDial (Chapter 4) cross borders, open offices, employ staff, and gain customers abroad.

Developing an international culture begins and ends with the CEO, from the very first day of business, as inMobi's Tewari found. Although inMobi is now in most developed markets, going global was not something done with a snap of the fingers. It started with changing the corporate branding to a name that could be easily understood outside the home market.

Far more challenging than that was hiring people with the right mind-set who understood the go-global mission for inMobi. "We had to convince employees that we can go global and convince the whole team to think big," relates Tewari. "This is a set of people with a middle-class background. They are taught to think small. We want to encourage them to think big and don't be afraid; we will make it happen," he adds.

"We knew we had to think global and think big. Most companies that are emerging don't do that," says Tewari. "InMobi is one

inMobi founder Naveen Tewari in Bangalore

of the very few startups from India to be successful in becoming global," he emphasizes, pointing out that his startup took the untraditional route of "going East to West, not West to East."

In Bangalore, about a mile from the palatial Leela Hotel where I'm staying on an India visit in early 2010, I drop in on Krishnan Ganesh, the brains behind TutorVista, which British-based media and education company Pearson Group took majority ownership of in 2011. Ganesh, a postgraduate from the Indian Institute of Management in Calcutta, sports a mechanical engineering degree from Delhi University and is one of India's best-known serial entrepreneurs. His career has been spent in tech and outsourcing in India, and this former CEO, who turned around a British Telecom joint venture in India from near bankruptcy, has an international outlook. He's an out-of-the box thinker, and TutorVista is his brainchild.

"Our biggest challenge is creating a consumer brand from India. It takes a lot of time. Coke was built up over centuries. And here, we are talking about a very personalized service, not like iTunes," says Ganesh, who started TutorVista in 2005. With Pearson as a new parent company, his goal is to create TutorVista into a $1 billion global brand by 2016. He notes that the Pearson parentage gives the startup branding, positioning, resources, and a global platform. Ganesh is staying on as CEO at TutorVista while his wife is CEO and managing director of Pearson Education Services, a division that includes TutorVista.

At TutorVista's command center, it's enlightening to see dozens of teachers sitting in front of their PCs and communicating with students in the United States, using Skype to speak or chat and whiteboard for writing lessons. The pricing is a mind blower: $99 per month for unlimited tutoring, which is one key reason why TutorVista's customer base has expanded to more than 100,000 students worldwide. "We have a huge opportunity of marrying Internet technology and global teaching resources to provide affordable education. We want to scale that," says Ganesh, whose looks bear a resemblance to a thinner Buddha.

Don't be fooled that TutorVista would ever compete with an Ivy League university. Its niche is teaching basic math and language skills. Though the concept of tutoring the world from India might seem far-fetched, Ganesh has proven his idea is not off the mark.

The four-year-old startup brought in revenues of more than \$20 million and turned profitable in 2010.

TutorVista, which raised \$38 million from Sand Hill investors including Sequoia Capital India, Lightspeed Ventures, and Silicon Valley Bank, employs more than 3,000 tutors across India, most of them working off-site. Indian Army wives and retired workers make up the faculty, and each receives three weeks of initial training in how to use the online tutoring systems. Up to 70 percent of the lessons are in mathematics, with the remainder in English and science. All the sessions are recorded so they can be played back for quality control. TutorVista also operates 13 schools in southern India in locales where the Internet and personal computers are not widely available.

His first startup was a computer repair service he bootstrapped called IT&T Ltd.—a business frowned upon by his mother-in-law, who opposed his entrepreneurial endeavors. That startup went public in 2000, and later, parts were sold to information technology services company iGate Corp. in 2003 for \$10 million (so much for nay-saying). "These were the days before venture capital was present. At that time, to start any business you needed a license from the government, and you had to be part of a big industrial group or family-owned business," says Ganesh. "The only reason you started a business is if you were unemployed or unemployable."

By mid-2000, Ganesh was on to his second startup, Customer Asset, co-founded with his wife, Meena, as one of India's first and, later, largest outsourcing centers for handling business processes. Customer Asset, funded by Japan's Softbank and News Corp., was acquired for \$22 million by India's largest bank, ICICI, in 2002, then later merged with Firstsource Solutions, a business process outsourcing (BPO) firm that went public in India in 2006 at a high market valuation of \$605 million.

On a lucky streak and using his own capital, Ganesh started his third business, a marketing data analytics BPO firm with the brand name Marketics. That business was sold in 2007 to NYSE-listed WNS for \$63 million.

TutorVista marked Ganesh's fourth startup. His solid track record shows that experience counts for a lot in going this distance in a startup's journey and reaching the goal of going global with a novel idea.

STRATEGY: TutorVista

- Rely on your serial entrepreneurial instincts and knowledge to fine-tune the business model, and don't let naysayers get you down.
- Pick a business model that stands a good chance of catching on, and offer introductory pricing at bargain rates.
- Use an acquisition from a foreign company as a springboard to overseas expansion.

India's iYogi Stretches

It's a short taxi ride from the Trident Hotel, where I'm staying in Delhi's Gurgaon district close by the airport, before I arrive at the office tower headquarters of iYogi Technical Services. I'm here to interview Uday Challu, the co-founder and CEO of this startup that is making waves with a personal computer tech support operation for everything from software and hardware repairs to fast setups to virus removals.

Like TutorVista, iYogi is an Indian-originated consumer service brand with reach outside the home market. Both charge customers an inexpensive subscriber fee, with iYogi offering unlimited tech support at a low price of $169 yearly—a bargain for anyone dealing with a computer crash while on deadline.

The name iYogi suggests it isn't exactly from Jersey City. Actually, it's another Indian outsourcing service company that is leveraging low-cost, high-quality work in a new category.

Outsourcing of service jobs has sometimes gotten a bad rap in the United States for loss of work to India. But as you can tell from the company brand name, iYogi is pretty up-front about its Indian origins. The tech-smart remote service reps at the startup are called iYogis. Each is instructed to finish customer service calls with a good karma wish for the individual on the line from overseas. "We are an Indian company, and we didn't try to hide it. We said, 'Let's keep the face in front,'" says Challu, who is Bollywood movie star handsome.

The sleek, contemporary décor at iYogi gives a strong hint that the culture at this startup is outward-looking. Indeed, iYogi is one of the few Indian startups that engages a full-time media relations manager, and she's here during my interview with Challu. The role of public relations as a way to influence customer perceptions is

iYogi founder Uday Challu in Delhi

one of those Westernized business practices that has only begun to catch on at Asian startups with aspirations of going global.

Over a hurried lunch of gigantic pizza slices, we chat about the journey of iYogi and its international direction. "We know how to think global, act global, manage, and interact with media," says the suave Challu.

Yes, iYogi has a sales and marketing center in New York City. And yes, an initial public offering in New York could be in the cards for iYogi. No doubt Challu is encouraged by the stellar IPO of Indian online travel service MakeMyTrip in 2010.

The startup's sleek style and global-minded culture starts at the top with Challu. A serial entrepreneur with experience in both India and the United States, Challu, 49, has solid grounding thanks to his degree in economics from Delhi University in 2004. What also has given him a head start in business is failure. He's had nearly as many flops as successes—just like any serial entrepreneur in Silicon Valley.

Challu began his business career in 1985, selling personal computers into homes. He ended up closing the shop after realizing later on that it might be too risky and problematic to have technicians installing hardware at households when a housewife was home alone. The young entrepreneur spent the mid-1990s as a vice president of sales and marketing at an emerging data management supplier, Newgen Software Technologies, in Delhi. Then, he moved on to a managerial post at DnyPro Inc., a fast-growing information systems consulting firm with offices in India and headquarters in the famous Research Triangle area in North Carolina. That experience gave him his international passport. He leveraged that job after three years into starting his own cross-border management consulting boutique,

Concordia Consulting, mentoring startups and helping them raise capital in the Valley and in India. Two of the five startups he advised went under with the 2001 dotcom crash, but others ended up prospering, such as event management agency Wizcraft. Next, he put his business creativity to use as CEO and co-founder of IQ Resource, a niche outsourcing firm focused on business-to-business media, which was later sold to another entity in India.

Having tried so many types of businesses with checkered results, Challu put on his thinking cap and decided to try a fresh approach. This time, Challu took a month off and surveyed the landscape, trying to figure the best and biggest opportunities. He ruled out business process outsourcing because the profit margins were tiny, and he figured that the India low-price arbitrage wouldn't last much longer than 10 to 15 years. Building a startup around information technology outsourcing was also out because the space was already dominated by large players, with little room left for new entrants to squeeze in.

He set out on a six-month journey including a series of meetings with electronic goods suppliers and retailers in the United States and Europe. Through that grassroots approach, Challu eventually determined that tech support was a field that represented a huge market opportunity that could also be scaled internationally. He knew the industry trends: More people were buying personal computers for use at home and spending more time in front of their PC screens, but customers were getting less support from traditional electronics retailers or branded manufacturers.

Challu did his homework well in figuring out what business to pursue. A forecast by market research firm Parks Associates estimates that digital tech support services in the United States will increase from $2.3 billion in 2010 to $11.8 billion in 2015.[1] The monthly subscription portion of these services is projected to rise from $663 million in 2010 to approximately $4 billion in 2015.

Challu and his co-founder Vishal Dhar, a former colleague at IQ Resources, started the service in 2007 with the idea of offering a sort of concierge service for information technology support.

His new business was set up as an independent service provider handling multiple brands for third parties. It had a strong niche in India's giant outsourcing sector and was naturally international.

The startup's primary market is in the United States, but iYogi also serves the English-speaking nations of Canada, the United

Kingdom, and Australia. Challu has a much broader horizon in mind. Given the multiple markets, the operation is staffed to field service calls around the clock.

He plans to soon launch the service in the Middle East, and then if all goes well, Europe, and he may even motor back to the home market of India. If all this isn't enough outreach, a pilot service offering remote multilingual tech support in French, German, Spanish, and Italian is underway, too.

Some four years into the startup's young history, the initial indications are trending positive. With Dhar heading up marketing from New York City, iYogi has ramped up to 400,000 subscribers by early 2011, and growth is continuing strong despite the annual fee being jacked up by $20 from the prior year. The number of iYogi tech experts has grown to 6,000 from 1,400 the year before. Nearly half of those helpers have come from new dedicated centers set up by multinational corporate partners that include IBM Global Services, Genpact, Ventura, and Infinite Computer Solutions.

At iYogi headquarters in Gurgaon, the Indian staffers field service calls in well-lit, side-by-side cubicles on six floors of a contemporary building, one of six service centers that iYogi runs in its home country. To keep the quality of service at a competitive level, iYogi trains new hires for up to three months and bases a portion of employees' salaries on customer feedback.

The goal is to provide personalized service. Subscribers get an 800 number to dial in for tech expert solutions. One of the values that iYogi has built into the service is a database called iMantra. The database stores information, based on prior sessions, about customers' equipment and their PC headaches. This way, callers and representatives don't have to start from scratch each time a new complaint or question arises. The iYogi reps have been known

---

STRATEGY: iYogi

- Think and act global from day one, a culture reinforced by around-the-clock service.
- Hire a public relations professional to get press coverage, field questions, and raise your firm's profile.
- Train staff at an international level and reinforce attention to quality service by tying pay to results.

to spend as long as 45 minutes on one call. "The customer wants to be dealt with, and you need to spend time with them and allow them to vent, then guide them through the problem and build the trust," says Challu, sounding like a veteran salesperson. "Tech support is like the doctor visit, dealing with pain points."

Given the attention to detail, the financial side of the business could be better. At iYogi, revenue has skyrocketed to $53 million in 2010, more than doubling from the year before. The business is cash flow positive, though not yet profitable.

In the United States, the main rival to iYogi is the well-named Geek Squad, run by the large consumer electronics retailer Best Buy. It also competes with PlumChoice and Support.com. "Both Support.com and PlumChoice are smaller than us, have been around longer than us, and have raised more capital than us," points out Challu.

Determined to stay ahead of competitors, iYogi has recently stepped into next-generation tech support services for Android phones and the Apple iPad. The young business also raised the relatively large sum of $30 million in late 2010 to expand. Most of that capital is from investors from the West—Sequoia Capital India, with return investors Canaan Partners, SVB India Capital Partners, SAP Ventures, and Draper Fisher Jurvetson—another indicator of the founders' international perspective and goals.

Investor Jolly of DFJ India, which initially funded iYogi with $9 million in December 2009, says, "iYogi is leveraging India to serve the world and is growing very rapidly. This is a key example of how an Indian company can be a global company, even as a startup."

Look for more Asian startups to become global names, as a growing number of entrepreneurs from China, India, Singapore, Taiwan, and even Vietnam boost their confidence level and take their can-do attitude, combined with a new assertiveness, and a comfort level with both Eastern and Western cultures, to a bigger international stage. It's all a part of the entrepreneurial revolution that is fired up in Asia's tech capitals and threatens to take the edge from Silicon Valley.

Afterword

Today, we live in a globally connected world with lightning-fast communications 24 hours a day.

Not only does news travel across continents and oceans in split seconds, but scientific advancements, groundbreaking research, and tech innovations go around the globe as fast as the information superhighway. This connectedness, made possible by social media, television, mobile phones, and the Internet, is blending Western and Eastern cultures and lifestyles. Shopping malls, jammed highways, luxury hotels, and fast-food franchises that seem the same from Singapore to Shanghai can make it difficult sometimes to realize you're in a foreign place—particularly if you're jet-lagged.

When I was on the speaking circuit for my first book, *Silicon Dragon*, my message of China climbing the invention ladder didn't exactly go over that well with a resistant and defensive Silicon Valley. But today, some three years later, I no longer get that push back.

Entrepreneurial leaders from China—and some from India, too—have gotten on the radar with international expansion and Wall Street IPOs. It's becoming increasingly accepted that Asia's emerging economies and plugged-in digital communications markets offer a good launching pad for startups—some of them with features more advanced than in the West. In fact, Asia's tech rise is now more than ever viewed as a threat, as increasing numbers of young graduates and talented workers head to the region for better career opportunities, succeed, and don't return.

For sure, the pace is a lot faster, and the energy is turned up higher in the tech hotspots of Beijing and Shanghai. I'm no longer one of a handful of journalists covering this beat. Today, I have company. Fast-breaking news of all-star tech entrepreneurs such as Robin Li and Jack Ma is covered by CNN and the *New York Times*.

The success China is having on the tech frontier is a motivator for other dragon and tiger markets to push forward and prove their own entrepreneurial prowess. Venture capitalists are accelerating this trend by taking successful business models and technologies and establishing them in new frontiers. They're on the boards of these startup companies, too, to shape their progress and make sure they scale. Just about every winning idea from the United States or China is being copied and funded in the outer reaches, in countries never said in the same breath as innovative thinkers, game changers, or risk takers.

This is by no means a race where the winner takes all. And with the way that ideas cross borders today and the convenience of jumping on a plane and taking resources, talent, and concepts from one time zone to the next, tech entrepreneurship zones are no longer defined by nationality. Entrepreneurs and venture capitalists, plus their mentors and advisers, are increasingly collaborative and speak the same language.

This book has example after example of startups that have originated and grown by tapping into the best practices from anywhere in the world. Vietnam's social networking and gaming startup VNG borrows ideas from China's Tencent and Shanda. China is developing an entirely new business market sector in outsourcing, the area that India pioneered and has dominated for decades. Singapore's voice-messaging service Bubbly has software codes written by world-class engineers from the United States, India, China, the Philippines, and Malaysia. India's 3-D interactive mobile application was jointly designed at the Indian Institute of Science in Bangalore and the Stanford University campus. A robotics-guided medical device that can do highly precise biopsies originated from a startup team in Chennai that worked at GE.

With this sort of sharing, it's a win-win, not a losing proposition for the United States or for any other country that fails to keep up. While we may not all get richer, in the end, we all benefit by improved technologies to make our lives easier, healthier, and longer lasting.

Acknowledgments

Y ou'd think that writing a second book would be easier. Well, not really. What does help is having family, friends, colleagues, and a support network from East to West.

Startup Asia began in mid-2009, with a two-year series of interviews after my first book, *Silicon Dragon*, was published in 2008. My reporting for *Startup Asia* included more than 100 interviews with entrepreneurs and venture capitalists in Taipei, Tainan, Ho Chi Minh City, Hanoi, Singapore, Bandar Seri Begawan, Hong Kong, Beijing, Shanghai, Dalian, Chongqing, Shenyang, Hangzhou, and Silicon Valley—not to mention at least 50 more interviews with experts in law, accounting, investment banking, recruiting, and management consulting, plus data from several market research and publishing groups. It has been an exhaustive but exhilarating effort.

A book doesn't happen in a vacuum but requires collaboration. I wish to thank the entrepreneurs profiled in *Startup Asia* for taking time to meet with me for interviews, photos, and videos and for responding to follow-up queries about the progress of their ventures. A few characters deserve double thanks for being characters in books 1 and 2—Joe Chen of Renren for one.

Likewise, I'd like to thank the numerous venture capitalists I've tracked from Sand Hill Road to offshoots in Bangalore, Beijing, and beyond, as I've followed the money trail. They include David Chao of DCM, Sonny Wu of GSR Ventures, Dick Kramlich of NEA, Joe Zhou of Keytone Ventures, Gary Rieschel of Qiming Venture Partners, Bill Tai of Charles River Ventures, ex-Sequoia investor Sumir Chadha, Ajit Nazre of Kleiner Perkins, Tim Draper of Draper Fisher Jurvetson, Lip-Bu Tan of Walden International, Ta-Lin Hsu of H&Q Asia Pacific, and many others too countless to mention individually here.

Thanks to *Forbes Asia* editor Tim Ferguson and *Forbes* San Francisco bureau chief Eric Savitz for providing a platform over the past two years to cover entrepreneurship and venture capital in Asia's emerging innovation hubs. Thanks to *Chief Executive* Editor-in-Chief J. P. Donlon for an outlet to write feature stories about this topic and other global business trends. I would be remiss if I did not acknowledge associate editor Anise Wieckowski of the *Harvard Business Review* for publishing my work as well.

This book would not have been possible without the steadfast support of Leah Spiro, my first book editor. She stayed with me for the second book—this time as my agent at Riverside Creative Management, Inc. Her publishing instincts and smarts have helped to sharpen the prose and positioning. I'd like to thank John Wiley & Sons Associate Publisher and Editorial Director Pamela van Giessen for having the foresight to support this book. Nick Melchior, my editor, has my thanks for believing in *Startup Asia* and making it happen. So does Wiley publisher Nick Wallwork. Special thanks to Howard Krongard for his eagle eye in proofing my draft on tight deadlines and finding the fault lines. Senior Editorial Manager Emilie Herman at Wiley wins my praise for keeping me grounded during the book's production. Thanks, too, to Senior Production Editor Todd Tedesco.

I wish to thank these industry professionals who have supported my book writing, newsletter, and event projects over the past two years. They include Charles Comey, Sherry Yin, and Thomas Chou of Morrison & Foerster; Egidio Zarrella, Ning Wright, Gary Matuszak, Anson Bailey, and Patricia Rios of KPMG; Daniel Quon and Andy Tsao of SVB Financial Group; Howard Chao and David Roberts of O'Melveny & Myers; Robert Pietrzak of Sidley Austin; John Huber and Brad Smith of Wells Fargo; Curtis Mo and Steven Liu of DLA Piper; Chris Cooper, Christie Simons, and Clarence Kwan of Deloitte; Fred Greguras of K & L Gates; Barry Silbert and David Berger of SecondMarket; and Kai-Fu Lee of Innovation Works. Finally, thanks to several groups for partnering with my Silicon Asia group on events: Bruno Bensaid, Benjamin Joffe, and Frank Yu of MobileMonday; Barrett Parkman and Duncan Leung of the Great Wall Club; William Bao Bean of AngelVest; Sara Rauchwerger of the Chamber of Commerce International Consortium; Diamond TechVenture's Henry Wong of Chinese Software Professionals Association; Edith Yeung of BizTechDay and SFentrepreneur; Kai Lukoff of StartupDigest; Christine Lu of Affinity China; Janet Carmosky of The China Business Network; Bakul Joshi of the Global India Venture Capital Association; Lawrence Wang of Invest HK; and Bruce Pickering and Robert Bullock of the Asia Society. My thanks to Alan Campey and Todd Outhouse of the Rosewood Sand Hill Resort—the venue is great for our Silicon Valley events.

My thanks go, too, to Brunei's iCentre incubator lab for putting out the welcome mat for me. I'd also like to acknowledge Singapore's NUS Enterprise and Economic Development Board, the Taipei Economic and Cultural Office, and the Hangzhou and Nanjing municipal governments for their introductions to tech sights and sounds.

I wish to thank Cathay Pacific, Singapore Airlines, Air Canada, Dragon Air, Jet Airways, EVA Airways, and Vietnam Airlines for helping me stack up frequent flier miles and safely getting me to faraway places and back. Plus, I should mention the high-speed rails I traveled roundtrip from Shanghai to Hangzhou, Beijing to Tianjin, and Taipei to Tainan. My gratitude goes to these hotels for providing a comfort zone during my research and reporting trips: Tata, Sofitel, Leela, Marriott, Four Seasons, Harbour Plaza, Le Meridien, Shangri-La, Oberoi, Landmark, Sheraton, Trident, Fairmont, Howard Johnson, Langham, Hyatt, Peninsula, Mandarin Oriental, Ista, Best Western, Ritz-Carlton, and Home Inns of investor Neil Shen fame. A few boutique hotels should be recognized as well: URBN, Le Sun Chine, and Jia in Shanghai; Opposite House in Beijing; and Mira, Upper House, and Hullett House in Hong Kong. And how could I skip the way too many nights at hotels conveniently located close to airports: Langham in Beijing and the Regal and Novotel in Hong Kong. Thanks especially to the Empire Hotel & Country Club in Brunei for letting me stay in an incredible ocean-facing suite so I could be well rested for my keynote talk.

To the neighborhood of Burlingame, where I have a studio, thanks for providing a restful place to write this book in peace and quiet. The library, Mollie Stone's supermarket, and Il Fornaio restaurant in my little triangle here have become all-too-familiar stops. The close-by CalTrain has saved me the hassle of having a car here.

To John: Thanks for holding down the fort in New York City and Connecticut while I finished the draft for this book. Your trust, patience, and faith in me have made a huge difference and are much appreciated. The same is true of my mom in Ohio. You have been a great sounding board, as usual.

Finally, my thanks go to all those entrepreneurs in Asia and Silicon Valley who shared their inspirational stories with me. You have influenced me and had a considerable impact on my own endeavors as a journalist entrepreneur.

Notes

Introduction

1. *Asian Venture Capital Journal.*
2. Dow Jones VentureSource.
3. World Intellectual Property Organization (www.wipo.int/pressroom/en/articles/2011/article_0004.html).
4. Vivek Wadhwa, "Foreign-Born Entrepreneurs: An Underestimated American Resource," *Kauffman Thoughtbook 2009,* Ewing Marion Kauffman Foundation, www.kauffman.org/entrepreneurship/foreign-born-entrepreneurs.aspx.
5. AnnaLee Saxenian and Jumbi Edulbehram, "Immigrant Entrepreneurs in Silicon Valley," *Berkeley Planning Journal* 12 (1998): 32–49, www.ced.berkeley.edu/pubs/bpj/pdf/bidl1205.pdf.
6. Renaissance Capital, 2010 Global Market IPO Review and 2011 Outlook.
7. Renaissance Capital, 2010 Global Market IPO Review and 2011 Outlook.
8. MakeMyTrip scored a market valuation of $903 million on its opening day on NASDAQ, August 12, 2010, based on closing price first day.
9. Source: Dow Jones VentureSource, 2010. M&As were far more common among U.S. companies than with China-based companies, however. A total of 15 mergers and acquisitions of China-based companies garnered $866 million, compared with 445 mergers and acquisitions of U.S. venture-backed companies that raised $33.9 billion, according to Dow Jones VentureSource.
10. Sharon La Franiere, "After Brain Drain, China Is Luring Some Scientists Back Home," *New York Times,* January 7, 2010, www.nytimes.com/2010/01/07/world/asia/07scholar.html.
11. IDC Asia/Pacific, 2010 figures.
12. Dow Jones VentureSource, 2010 figures.
13. *Asian Venture Capital Journal.*
14. World Economic Forum and INSEAD, *The Global Information Technology Report 2010–2011.* Rankings are based on widespread use of mobile phones, Internet, and personal computers, as well as regulatory environment and IT infrastructure.
15. 2009 study conducted by econometrics firm IHS Global Insight.
16. National Science Foundation–supported study in 2008 conducted by the Georgia Institute of Technology.
17. "Nobel Science Popularization," Beijing Municipal Association for Science & Technology; Sharon La Franiere, "After Brain Drain, China Is Luring Some

Scientists Back Home," *New York Times*, January 7, 2010, www.nytimes.com/2010/01/07/world/asia/07scholar.html.

Chapter 1   China's Next Generation Tech Stars

1. Zero2IPO, China venture fund-raising, April 2011.
2. Dow Jones LP Source, January 12, 2011.
3. GSR analysis based on Bloomberg data, excluding some acquired companies.
4. World Intellectual Property Organization, 2010 figure.
5. Venture capitalists in China have broadened their mix of deals to solar, health care, financial services, retail, and consumer products, sectors that today comprise almost half of their China deals. CV Source, January 2011, ChinaVenture.com.cn.
6. Chris Evdemon, General Manager, Incubation Labs, "Technoentrepreneurship and the Early Stage Ecosystem in China," Innovation Works, April 2011.
7. Richard Robinson, "Startups in China," January 2010, for entrepreneur group EO (Entrepreneurs' Organization).
   The three companies were Web development agency Modem Media, Renren, and Mobile Interactive Games. Robinson cashed out from an IPO of Web development agency Modem Media, co-founded and took public the original Renren Chinese community site, raised $31 million from Murdoch's News Corp. for Renren, and watched Renren soar to a market cap of $1.5 billion on the Hong Kong Stock Exchange in 2000, then crash and almost be delisted before it was acquired in 2001. He also costarted MIG (Mobile Interactive Games), one of China's first text-focused mobile gaming companies, which was merged, then later acquired by NASDAQ-listed Glu Mobile in December 2007 for $40 million.
   The Renren listing was through a reverse merger or so-called backdoor listing, on the Hang Seng index in Hong Kong, purchasing a company in decline that had clean books and no debt and then making that company a subsidiary of the parent.
8. Richard Robinson, "Startups in China," January 2010, for entrepreneur group EO:
   "Theoretically, as a foreigner, you can act as the bridge between the Chinese and outside markets—in practice you are the cartilage getting crunched between the realities of the China market and the expectations of international markets. This is mostly a losing proposition if you can't have control, which encouraged me further to become an entrepreneur again."
9. Japan-China–focused investor Infinity Ventures.
10. Oak Pacific Interactive was renamed Renren in late 2010. Youlu's CTO is Peter Jiang, a leading software developer of a Chinese character input method at portal Sohu.
11. Fong helped to jump-start GSR Ventures in 2004 through a partnership with Mayfield Fund, where he was a managing director.
12. Zero2IPO Group research, April 2011.
13. Zero to IPO data.

14. In late June, Muddy Waters issued a critical report on NASDAQ-listed Chinese chip maker Spreadtrum Communications that suggested the company misstated financial results, and shorted the stock.
15. Rebecca A. Fannin, *Silicon Dragon* (New York: McGraw-Hill, 2008), Chapter 2.
16. See Silicon Dragon Video of Joe Chen, 2008, www.youtube.com/watch?v=aXCLa9msJic.
17. IPO prospectus, Securities and Exchange Commission filing, April 30, 2011 (www.slideshare.net/ichinastock/inside-renren-inc-nyse-renn-by-ichinastock-7648243).
18. See clip from Silicon Dragon Video interview with Cheng Binghao, 2010, www.youtube.com/watch?v=4EerSYm2ZHI.
19. Fannin, *Silicon Dragon*.
20. Chris Evdemon, General Manager, Incubation Labs, "Technoentrepreneurship and the Early Stage Ecosystem in China," Innovation Works, April 2011. Cites original data sources from CNNIC, iResearch, and www.pewinternet.org.
21. Alibaba's Chinese auction portal Taobao is a favored destination and claims 80 percent of China's $75 billion market, projected to double in 2011. China B2B Research Center.
22. Alibaba.
23. Now at the *Economist*.
24. Sina earnings statement, May 11, 2011.
25. Edison Research report, "Twitter Usage in America."
26. International Data Group research.
27. Known as MMORG or massively multiplayer online role-playing game.
28. Analysys International, China Internet Search Market, Q1 2011.
29. DCM's $100 million "A-Fund"—backed by Japanese mobile gaming social network GREE and mobile operator KDDI, plus China's Tencent and tracking Kleiner Perkins $200 million iFund for iPhone app developers—is likely to spur more startups to build on the Android open ecosystem globally and in China's giant market.
30. Beijing-based Zero2IPO Group. The trend escalated in the first quarter of 2011, as Chinese currency funds comprised 62 percent of deals and 48 percent of investment in China startups.

Chapter 2   India Emerges to Narrow the Gap

1. Plus the guilty verdicts against noted hedge fund manager Raj Rajaranam on 14 counts of securities fraud and conspiracy.
2. National Association of Software & Services Companies (NASSCOM), February 2011 (www.nasscom.in/Nasscom/templates/NormalPage.aspx?id=60499).
3. NASSCOM, February 2011, "India: On the Rise" (www.nasscom.in/upload/newsline/Feb2011/Newsline_Presidents_Desk.pdf).
4. India engineering graduates numbered 215,000 in 2005, third in the world next to the United States at 222,335 and China at 644,106, according to

research by Duke University professor Vivek Wadhwa: www.businessweek
.com/smallbiz/content/dec2005/sb20051212_623922.htm.

5. IDC Asia/Pacific, March 2011.
6. 74 million people or 6 percent of India's population had Internet access in 2010: IDC Asia/Pacific, March 2011.
7. Internet penetration could reach 19 percent by 2015 in India. Boston Consulting Group, "The Internet's New Billion," September 2010.
8. Wireless Intelligence, January 2011 report, GSM Media, www.wirelessintelligence .com.
9. Dow Jones VentureSource, Global Venture Investment, February 2011.
10. Rebecca A. Fannin, *Silicon Dragon* (New York: McGraw-Hill, 2008), Chapter 2, eBay case study.
11. World Intellectual Property Organization, 2010.
12. Vivek Wadhwa, "Foreign-Born Entrepreneurs: An Underestimated American Resource," Ewing Marion Kauffman Foundation (www.kauffman.org/ entrepreneurship/foreign-born-entrepreneurs.aspx). Saxenian is also the current dean of Berkeley's School of Information.
13. Vivek Wadhwa, "A Fix for Discrimination: Follow the Indian Trails," *TechCrunch*, February 21, 2010. He also notes that Indians started 6.7 percent of the U.S. tech and engineering firms.
14. Of exits, 32 percent reached a valuation of more than $100 million and 6 percent at more than $500 million. Indian technology deals lead all sectors, weighing in with 100 exits and far exceeding 42 exits in financial services, retail, and education from 2004 to 2010. Technology exits brought in the financial rewards, too, with 30 percent generating investment returns of more than a four times return and 15 percent achieving a 10 times return. Source: analysis of technology venture exits by IDG Ventures India research desk, with Venture Intelligence data, 2004–2010.
15. SKS was tarnished in scandal later that year in a microlending boom when as many as 30 loan recipients committed suicide over harassment by collection agents for high-interest loans, resulting in new restrictions for microlenders.
16. *Asian Venture Capital Journal.*
17. Calculation based on MakeMyTrip's closing price first day of $26.45 on August 12, 2010.

Chapter 3   Vietnam: The Next Frontier

1. Number of Internet users is 27 million, according to Vietnam's Ministry of Information and Communications, March 2011. The government has hatched plans to increase Internet penetration and hike the number of Internet users to more than 70 million by 2020.
2. Tech research firm International Data Corporation, based on April 2011 data.
3. Vietnam has 163 million phone subscribers, 91 percent of them mobile phone subscribers, according to the Ministry of Information and Telecommunication, January 2011 (www.vneconomynews.com/2011/01/booming-vietnam-telecom-industry.html). By March 2011, Vietnam had 174 million phone subscribers,

including 16.5 million fixed phone users and 158 million mobile phone users, a 28.2 percent over the same period the year before.

4. The Nielsen Company, "A year of 3G in Vietnam," December 2010, March 2011. Nielsen points out that 20 percent of Vietnam's population is between the ages of 15 and 24, and half subscribe to mobile services. Thus, adoption rates of 3G service should quicken.
5. Vietnam's Ministry of Information and Communications reported major gains in 2010 for several high-tech markets nationally: digital content was up 50 percent to $700 million, software grew 40 percent to $880 million, and telecom by 30 percent to $8.8 billion.
6. PricewaterhouseCoopers research, November 2009, www.pwc.com/vn/en/releases2009/press-release-en-09-11-2009.jhtml. PricewaterhouseCoopers, in July 2009 research, forecasts this segment will increase nearly 17 percent to $2.3 billion by 2013.
7. Rebecca A. Fannin, *Silicon Dragon* (New York: McGraw-Hill, 2008), Chapter 1, and Silicon Asia at Forbes.com.
8. Singapore Management University, DigitalMediaAsia, March 2011.
9. Socbay founder cited the 2 percent figure for its online market share, March 2011.
10. StatCounter Global Stats, July 2010, http://royal.pingdom.com/2010/07/29/google-undisputed-heavyweight-champion-of-mobile-search/.
11. Naiscorp company figures.
12. Vietnam's e-commerce market is predicted to boom over the next four years and grow fivefold by 2015, according to the government's E-commerce Development Master Plan.
13. Fannin, *Silicon Dragon*, Chapter 2.
14. Fannin, *Silicon Dragon*, Chapter 2.
15. Fannin, *Silicon Dragon*, Chapter 3.
16. Alexa measures web site traffic.
17. *Forbes Asia* article, VNG, February 2010.

Chapter 4   Catch the Mobile Boom

1. "Worldwide Wireless e-Mail Users to Reach 1 Billion by Year-End 2014" (Wireless e-Mail Market, Gartner, Inc., June 2010 report, www.gartner.com/it/page.jsp?id=1392716).
2. San Francisco–based boutique investment house Rutberg & Co., a specialist in mobile and digital media.
3. Information Technology Research Firm Gartner, Inc., *Competitive Landscape: Mobile Devices, Worldwide, Q42010 and 2010*, February 2011 report, www.gartner.com/it/page.jsp?id=1543014.
4. The market is growing at a brisk pace of more than 22 percent per year. (Global Smartphones Market, 2010–2014, MarketsandMarkets, www.marketsandmarkets.com/PressReleases/smartphones-market.asp).
5. Information Technology Research Firm Gartner, Inc., Forecast: Mobile applications stores, January 2011, www.gartner.com/it/page.jsp?id=1529214.

6. Gartner, Inc., "Ten Consumer Mobile Applications to Watch in 2012," February 2011, www.gartner.com/it/page.jsp?id=1544815.

7. Digital marketing research firm eMarketer, December 10, 2010 report.

8. Mobile advertising was $2.7 billion in 2011 and is predicted to rise to $6.6 billion by 2016. Mobile advertising is still a small fraction of the $412 billion in 2011 for media advertising globally. Source: Ad forecasting group Magna Global, owned by the Interpublic Group of Cos., December 6, 2010, report, worldwide ad spending forecasts, www.magnaglobal.com/c/global-2/. Overall advertising will be up by just 5.4 percent in 2011 and online advertising up 12.5 percent the same year.

9. eMarketer, "The Search Wars Are Going Mobile," July 17, 2007, www .emarketer.com/Article.aspx?R=1005083.

10. Informa Telecoms and Media report, November 2010, www.informatm.com/ itmgcontent/icoms/s/sectors/mobile-markets/; www.bloomberg.com/news/ 2010-11-23/mobile-advertising-sales-to-grow-tenfold-by-2015-informa-says .html. As India and China grow, Japan, South Korea, and more developed markets in Asia will tip to 21.7 percent of usage by 2015, downward from 43.6 percent in 2010.

11. IDC report.

12. The Android market segment generated $850 million in 2010 and will reach $1.3 billion by 2012, according to Piper Jaffray analyst Gene Munster. See Eric Savitz, "Google's Android. A Billion Dollar Ad Business by 2012?" *Forbes*, February 8, 2011, http://blogs.forbes.com/ericsavitz/2011/ 02/08/googles-android-a-billion-dollar-ad-business-in-2012/; Jason Ankeny, "Google Gets Aggressive on Mobile Advertising," *Fierce Mobile Content*, Feb. 9, 2011, www.fiercemobilecontent.com/story/google-gets-aggressive-mobile- advertising/2011-02-09.

13. By October 2010, some 5.8 billion ad impressions from inMobi were showing up on these smart phones, nearly one-fourth of the global ads inMobi delivers overall. Source: inMobi research, http://techcrunch.com/tag/inmobi/.

14. inMobi research, January 2011, www.inmobi.com/press-releases/2011/01/06/ india-now-the-largest-mobile-advertising-market-in-asia-pacific/.

15. See Chapter 2, offshore structure for Indian startup companies to list outside India.

16. Estimates of the U.S. mobile ad market size vary widely. See U.S. Interactive Marketing Forecast, 2009–2014, Forrester Research, Inc., http://blogs .forrester.com/interactive_marketing/2010/03/is-mobile-really-that-big-a-deal .html. Forrester Research, Inc., predicts U.S. mobile advertising to reach $1.2 billion by 2014, up from $560 million in 2010, www.forrester.com/rb/Research/ us_interactive_marketing_forecast%2C_2009_to_2014/q/id/47730/t/2.

17. Mobile ad spending in the United States is pegged at $1.1 billion in 2011 and rising to $2.5 billion by 2014. See "Mobile Search in the U.S.," *eMarketer*, July 24, 2007. Meanwhile, the mobile search market in the United States was projected to account for almost 15 percent of total mobile ads in 2011 (www .emarketer.com/Article.aspx?R=1005170).

18. While U.S. marketers spent just 3 percent of their online ad dollars on mobile in 2010, the proportion will increase to 5 percent in 2011. IDC pegs the U.S. mobile ad market at $2 billion in 2011, more than double the $877

million in 2010. See "Google Gains Market Share in U.S. Market," *Bloomberg BusinessWeek,* December 3, 2010.

Chapter 5   Get In on the Cleantech Boom

1. ABI Research provides market intelligence across a range of technologies from a base in Oyster Bay, New York.
2. United Nations Environment Programme study, "Recycling, from e-Waste to Resources." The February 2010 projection is for year 2020 from 2007 levels.
3. Market research firm Cleantech Group in San Francisco.
4. In the United States, clean energy ventures drew 68 percent of total venture capital invested in 2010, according to Clean Edge, a cleantech market research firm based in Portland, Oregon, and Oakland, California.
5. China ranked second worldwide with $479 million in cleantech venture spending, while India came in fifth place with $181 million. Source: market research firm Cleantech Group in San Francisco.
6. Cleantech Group.
7. Industry analyst iSuppli.
8. Rebecca A. Fannin, *Silicon Dragon* (New York: McGraw-Hill, 2008), Chapter 12.
9. Kumar has since left to start a solar business for Indian villages and turned the operation over to Chairman Sunil Kotak.
10. Frost & Sullivan study.

Chapter 6   Ride the Consumer Wave

1. McKinsey & Co. research based on a report by directors Richard Dobbs in Seoul and Shirish Sankhe in Mumbai, www.mckinsey.com/mgi/mginews/opinion_china_vs_india.asp.
2. eHi, March 31, 2011.
3. KKR set up operations in India in 2008 and has invested $1 billion in the subcontinent market.

Chapter 7   Create a Niche in a Proven Sector: Outsourcing

1. National Association of Software and Services Companies (NASSCOM) predicts India's outsourcing market will grow nearly 19 percent in 2011.
2. NASSCOM, 2011: India's share of the global market was 55 percent in 2010, up from 51 percent in 2009.
3. Fiscal year ending March 2011.

Chapter 8   Tap into Government Incubators

1. Results reported by Spring Singapore as of end of 2010.

Chapter 9   Become the Next Twitter, LinkedIn, or Groupon for Asia

1. Web research firm Alexa.
2. Chinaz.com, a Chinese Web analysis web site.

Chapter 10   Originate a Breakthrough Discovery

1. Nobel laureates by country (Nobelprize.org); Dennis Redovich, Center for the Study of Jobs and Education in Wisconsin and the U.S.
2. World Intellectual Property Organization in Geneva, February 9, 2011. At the head of the rankings were the University of California, Massachusetts Institute of Technology, University of Texas, and University of Florida.
3. 2010 study on nanotechnology by Professor Phillip Shapira, School of Public Policy at the Georgia Institute of Technology, www.nano.gatech.edu/news/release.php?id=5277. The United States retains a lead in the quality of publications, though the work is becoming increasingly collaborative across borders.
4. Denis Fred Simon and Cong Cao, *China's Emerging Technological Edge* (Cambridge: Cambridge University Press, 2009).
5. Information technology research firm Gartner, Inc., forecasts 17.7 billion mobile app downloads in 2011, up 117 percent from an estimated 8.2 billion downloads in 2010. By 2014, Gartner projects 185 billion downloads and a market size of $58 billion, an increase from $15 billion in 2011. See Gartner, Inc., "Gartner Says Worldwide Mobile Application Store Revenue Forecast to Surpass $15 Billion in 2011," www.gartner.com/it/page.jsp?id=1529214.

Chapter 11   Take Your Startup Public on the NYSE or NASDAQ

1. In June 2011, Renren shares were off 49 percent from the IPO opening price in early May, while Dangdang was down 25 percent from its IPO opening price in early December 2010.
2. Wind, Bloomberg.
3. Silicon Asia analysis based on NYSE, NASDAQ, OMX data.
4. 2010 Global IPO Market Review and 2010 Outlook, Renaissance Capital, January 2011.
5. "What's Wrong with Chinese Stocks?" Renaissance Capital.
6. CVSource, January 2011, ChinaVenture.com.cn.
7. In 2010, 149 Chinese businesses went public on domestic Chinese exchanges, compared with 33 in 2007, the prior boom year, according to Zero2IPO Group, citing data from April 2011 that refers to venture capital and private equity-backed IPOs.
8. CVSource, January 2011, ChinaVenture.com.cn. The Shenzhen SME board offered average returns on investment of 10 percent during 2010.
9. Deloitte Global Chinese Services Group, *Emerging from the Twilight*, October 2010, with Mergermarket. China investment abroad is a growing trend, as Geely's acquisition of Volvo in the first half of 2010 shows.
10. Ranking was based on a 2007 ranking of top 20 countries by ChinaVenture.com.cn and Innovation Works.
11. Of 63 venture-backed Indian tech exits, 14 were from IPOs during 2004 to 2010. From IDG Ventures India research based on Venture Intelligence data.
12. Before Youku, the record holder was ChinaCache, a Beijing-based provider of content for business web sites, which went public on October 1, 2010, and had the biggest first-day rally, at a 95 jump, on a U.S. exchange in three years.

13. On March 30, 2011, Chinese Web browser and security software developer Qihoo 360 listed on NYSE. Its shares soared 134 percent above the IPO price of $14.50 on the initial day of trading.

14. Dangdang was backed by DCM, Youku by Sutter Hill Ventures, and ChinaCache was invested in by Qiming Ventures and Intel Capital. Qihoo took in money from Sequoia Capital as well as Highland Capital Partners, Trustbridge Partners, and Chinese private equity firm CDH Investments.

15. Sohu was trading at 23 times earnings, Netease at 15.5 times earnings, and Sina at 10.5 times earnings.

16. The Chinese video-sharing site reported a 152 percent increase in net revenues to $58.7 million for 2010 and a net loss of $31 million. Youku said the loss was due largely to increased bandwidth costs to keep pace with growth.

17. Youku stock closed May 6, 2011, at 58.84 and hit a low of 26.25 on June 16. The stock closed at $29.14 on June 23, 2011.

18. Dangdang reported a net revenue rise of 57 percent in 2010 to $346 million and slim profits of $4.7 million, after reaching profitability in 2009 for the first time.

19. Dangdang closed at 22.81 on May 6, 2011, hit a low of $10.74 on June 13, 2011, and was at $11.25 on June 23, 2011.

Chapter 12   Go Global from Asia

1. Parks Associates industry report, "Consumer Technical Support Services: Overview" (www.parksassociates.com/industry-reports).

About the Author

Rebecca A. Fannin is the author of *Silicon Dragon* (McGraw-Hill, 2008), a contributor to *Forbes*, and a consultant and public speaker. Her news and events group, Silicon Asia, publishes e-newsletters for venture capitalists and entrepreneurs, provides research, and develops conferences in the world's tech hotspots. Video interviews, photos, articles, and blogs related to her books and programs can be found at www.siliconasiainvest.com.

Ms. Fannin's 20-year journalism career includes posts as international editor at *Red Herring*, the Pulitzer-owned *International Business*, *AdAge*, and Incisive Media's *AVCJ*. She has contributed to *Inc.*, *Worth*, *Fast Company*, *Chief Executive*, *The Deal*, *MediaPost*, and *Harvard Business Review*.

Her consulting work includes a KPMG white paper on China outsourcing, Sony research projects, and Econsultancy editorial content. She has partnered with NASDAQ OMX, Morrison & Foerster, KPMG, SVB Financial Group, O'Melveny & Myers, Sidley Austin, Deloitte, K&L Gates, DLA Piper, InvestHK, SecondMarket, and Wells Fargo on China and India business events. Rebecca has testified as an expert witness on China's Internet before a U.S.-China Commission in Washington, D.C.

Ms. Fannin has appeared as a featured commentator on Fox Business News in the United States, Sky TV in Australia, and CCTV in China. She has lectured at several universities, including Yale, Columbia, Harvard, NUS, Tsinghua, Toronto's Rotman School of Management, Ohio University, and the University of San Francisco, among others. Rebecca has spoken at the Asia Society in San Francisco and Hong Kong, World Affairs Council in San Francisco, Overseas Press Club in New York, the Foreign Correspondents Club in Hong Kong and Tokyo, World Affairs Forum in Greenwich, China Northwest Council in Portland, Vancouver Trade Club in northwest Canada, Washington State China Relations Council in Seattle, and Harvard Club in New York.

Originally from Lancaster, Ohio, Rebecca was raised in an academic household as the daughter of a university professor and a kindergarten teacher. Today, she makes her home in a Manhattan apartment and a colonial house in North Stamford, Connecticut. Her research, writing, and advisory work takes her regularly to the San Francisco area, where she has a base in Burlingame. Rebecca enjoys frequent reporting trips to China, India, and other emerging markets.

Index